The Politics of
Race in New York

The Politics of Race in New York

THE STRUGGLE FOR BLACK SUFFRAGE IN THE CIVIL WAR ERA

BY

Phyllis F. Field

Cornell University Press

ITHACA AND LONDON

CORNELL UNIVERSITY PRESS GRATEFULLY ACKNOWLEDGES
A GRANT FROM THE ANDREW W. MELLON FOUNDATION THAT
AIDED IN BRINGING THIS BOOK TO PUBLICATION.

First published 1982 by Cornell University Press.
Published in the United Kingdom by Cornell University Press Ltd.,
Ely House, 37 Dover Street, London W1X 4HQ.

International Standard Book Number 0-8014-1408-3
Library of Congress Catalog Card Number 81-70717
Printed in the United States of America

*Librarians: Library of Congress cataloging information
appears on the last page of the book.*

*The paper in this book is acid-free, and meets the guidelines
for permanence and durability of the Committee on Production
Guidelines for Book Longevity of the Council on Library Resources.*

PREFACE

The United States is, and always has been, a battleground. Settled by puritans and profligates, African tribesmen and English country gentlemen, it has known the clash of values, classes, and cultures. Today's quarrels over the racial composition of schools, police forces, and the professions, like the debates over slavery more than a century ago, remind us of the persistence of some cleavages. Yet over the years American society has changed, and the boundaries that separate minorities from the dominant culture have continually shifted. Blacks are no longer slaves; Irish-Americans no longer read "No Irish need apply" in the classified ads. Our society, as a whole, has chosen to recognize and respond to some minority concerns while avoiding others. The ways in which our society has done so are most revealing. They tell us both about the character of our society and its potential for future change.

This book is about one minority, black Americans, and the attempt to shift one boundary that separated the races—the right to vote—in nineteenth century New York. The elective franchise, severely restricted or completely denied in most countries of the world, was highly prized in nineteenth century America. The right to vote implied one's acceptance as a responsible citizen of the community with an interest in its future and a right to help shape it. Exclusion from the suffrage was one of the most pervasive legal barriers confronting America's free blacks before the Fifteenth Amendment was adopted in 1870. On the eve of the Civil War only five states, all in New England, in which lived less than ten per cent of the small number of free blacks residing in the North, made no distinction between black and white voters.[1] Black suffrage stirred deep passions. It inspired reformers and outraged conservatives. Sectional controversy, war, and Reconstruction made it a preeminent political issue. For the space of a few years it symbolized the nation's racial dilemmas. The contest to expand the suffrage, central to America's race relations in the nineteenth century, provides an excellent opportunity to study how a minority's position in the larger society may be altered.

Although most people associate struggles over black suffrage with the South, such struggles went on in the North as well. The race problem has never been purely sectional as events in the past two decades have amply illustrated, and it is as proper to examine the basis for racial conflict in the North as in the South. It was the North that provided the leadership that eventually committed the nation to freedom, civil rights, and ultimately political rights for blacks. What racial change there was in the 1860s received its impetus there. The reasons behind the North's commitment, however, have continued to elude historians.[2] Was there really support for changing the racial status quo in the North? If so, where did it come from, and why was it unable to withstand the pressure from conservatives to limit black rights later? If rights for blacks were always unpopular, why did Republicans pursue policies that were potentially self-destructive? What determined whether racial reform was pushed ahead or shelved?

In attempting to answer such questions, historians have examined the personal psychologies and ideologies of many prominent Republicans to determine their philosophies and apparent motivation.[3] They have shown how the president and Congress ap-

1. Leon F. Litwack, *North of Slavery: The Negro in the Free States, 1790–1860* (Chicago: University of Chicago Press, 1961), p. 75.

2. See LaWanda Cox and John H. Cox, "Negro Suffrage and Republican Politics: The Problem of Motivation in Reconstruction Historiography," *Journal of Southern History*, 33 (Aug. 1967), 303–30, and Michael Les Benedict, "Equality and Expediency in the Reconstruction Era: A Review Essay," *Civil War History*, 23 (Dec. 1977), 322–35.

3. See, for example, David Donald, *Charles Sumner and the Rights of Man* (New York: Alfred A. Knopf, 1970).

proached the racial issues of Reconstruction at the national level.[4] But there is another way to study the politics of race in American society at that time, and that is to look at political stands in the context of popular attitudes. Politicians could not afford to ignore their constituents on the race issue; they still cannot, as modern studies also show.[5] America was, and is, a mass society, and politicians can ignore public opinion on sensitive issues only at their peril. But politicians were not simply mirrors reflecting the voters' preferences either. The party organizations to which they belonged played an independent role as well. One of the chief functions of parties in the nineteenth century was to articulate and defend the interests and values of the many diverse groups that made up the party.[6] Yet no large party could fully meet the conflicting demands of all who identified with it. Teetotalers had to cooperate with tipplers at times if party unity and victory were to be achieved. The political party played the vital role of mediator, trying to accommodate as many diverse interests as possible. In the interest of harmony, the party tried to define and shape how an issue such as race was perceived by its constituents. It strove to respond to activist demands but without damaging the fabric of the party itself. To understand how changes in discriminatory laws came about, therefore, we must go beyond the analysis of individual politicians and national-level politics and look at the politics of race as a complex *process* of give and take between mass attitudes, beliefs, and behavior on one hand, and party structures, needs, and strategies on the other.

This type of analysis depends on the systematic identification of popular views on racial questions. It is not enough to know that black rights were generally popular or unpopular. One must be able to show which groups supported or opposed black rights, how strongly they felt about it, and how their opinions changed under different stimuli. To identify public opinion accurately in a pre-poll

4. For example, LaWanda Cox and John H. Cox, *Politics, Principle, and Prejudice, 1865–1866: Dilemma of Reconstruction America* (New York: Free Press of Glencoe, 1963).

5. See, for example, Angus Campbell et al., *Elections and the Political Order* (New York: John Wiley and Sons, 1966), chapter 16; Charles F. Cnudde and Donald J. McCrone, "The Linkage between Constituency Attitudes and Congressional Voting Behavior: A Causal Model," *American Political Science Review*, 60 (Mar. 1966), 66–72.

6. Paul Kleppner, *The Third Electoral System, 1853–1892: Parties, Voters, and Political Cultures* (Chapel Hill: University of North Carolina Press, 1979), pp. 144, 367.

era is no easy task, as Lee Benson has illustrated.[7] In the case of black suffrage, however, the existence of a number of referenda held to modify state constitutional provisions on racial matters are a great benefit. Unlike the traditional sources for the study of past public opinion—such as newspapers, diaries, and letters—referenda offer a much broader and more representative view of public reactions to an issue, since far more people participated in them than ever left written records of their feelings. Referenda provide a valuable standard by which to evaluate impressionistic assessments of the state of popular attitudes. Since referendum voting was distinct from candidate selection, it is also possible to compare the two forms of voter expression to see just how successfully party politicians managed the threats to their popular coalitions posed by the raising of the sensitive race issue. Party platforms and editorial stands, legislative and constitutional convention votes begin to form a pattern as the practical responses to the political environment in which party leaders operated.

The politics of race was most visible at the state and local level in the nineteenth century. The diversity of the country and its federal system of politics made state parties the core of the political system.[8] Local and state governments and political organizations touched the average citizen much more frequently than their national counterparts. They played an active role in the community and often took the lead in matters relating to the status of minority groups. This is not to say that nationally significant issues were distant or irrelevant but rather that when they surfaced, the context was local. It is at the state and local level, therefore, that the study of the politics of race begins. (So that the reader can locate counties discussed later in the book, a map showing county boundaries and names appears on page 16.)

New York is particularly attractive for the analysis of the politics of race. The state held three referenda on black suffrage at key points in the nation's history. The first (1846) took place during the early political agitation over slavery but before the formation of the Republican Party; the second (1860), on the eve of the Civil War itself; and the third (1869), after the upheavals of the war era and just before the Fifteenth Amendment ended the first phase of black

7. Lee Benson, "An Approach to the Scientific Study of Past Public Opinion," *Public Opinion Quarterly*, 31 (Winter 1967), 522–67.
8. See, for example, Michael F. Holt, *The Political Crisis of the 1850s* (New York: John Wiley and Sons, 1978), p. 14.

Americans' struggle to win the franchise. In addition, throughout this period New York was the nation's most populous and wealthiest state. Its political leaders often went on to become the nation's leaders. Party politics in New York was played at a highly sophisticated level, the result of a long, varied, and rich tradition of conflict and competition dating back to the colonial period. Politicians elsewhere paid attention to what went on in New York.

The state also reflected the nation's variety. Almost every ethnic and religious group in the country had representatives in its population. It boasted the largest city in the nation, but within the state's confines were also rural hamlets and villages and smaller cities as well. Its citizens pursued almost every type of economic endeavor undertaken in the North, a variety that resulted in a complex pattern of economic growth and decline, prosperity and poverty. The state even had a slaveholding tradition in its eastern counties. This type of diversity makes it possible to test many hypotheses concerning group support of or opposition to black rights.

The pattern of race relations in New York was a complex one, and the struggle for equal suffrage was long and arduous. Disentangling the many different strands is difficult, but it is necessary if we are to move beyond the stage of broad generalizations concerning black voting rights in the nineteenth century. And the rewards in increased understanding make the effort worthwhile.

My greatest debt as a historian is to Joel H. Silbey, who introduced me to the fascinating world of nineteenth century American politics and who has for many years given me the benefit of his sound criticism and advice. Samuel T. McSeveney and Alan M. Kraut have also helped to shape my understanding of New York politics in the mid-1800s. I am also grateful to Allison Dodge of Cornell University Press for her careful critical reading of the manuscript.

I wish to acknowledge *Civil War History* for permission to use portions of two articles I have written: "Republicans and Black Suffrage in New York State: The Grass Roots Response," *Civil War History*, 21 (June, 1975), 136–47, and (jointly authored with Alan M. Kraut) "Politics versus Principles: The Partisan Response to 'Bible Politics' in New York State," *Civil War History*, 25 (June, 1979), pp. 101–18. For permission to quote from documents I would like to thank the following: the University of Rochester Library, for the William Henry Seward Papers; the George Arents Research Library for Special Collections at Syracuse University, for the Gerrit Smith Collec-

tion; the New York State Library, Albany, for the John V. S. L. Pruyn
Journals; and the Rare Books and Manuscripts Division, New York
Public Library, Astor, Lenox, and Tilden Foundations, for the Hor-
ace Greeley Papers.

And for sharing the practical burdens that writing a book imposes
as well as for giving me the benefit of his own critical insights, I
thank my husband, Douglas C. Baxter.

PHYLLIS F. FIELD

Athens, Ohio

CONTENTS

MAPS AND TABLES

Maps

Tables

13

MAPS AND TABLES

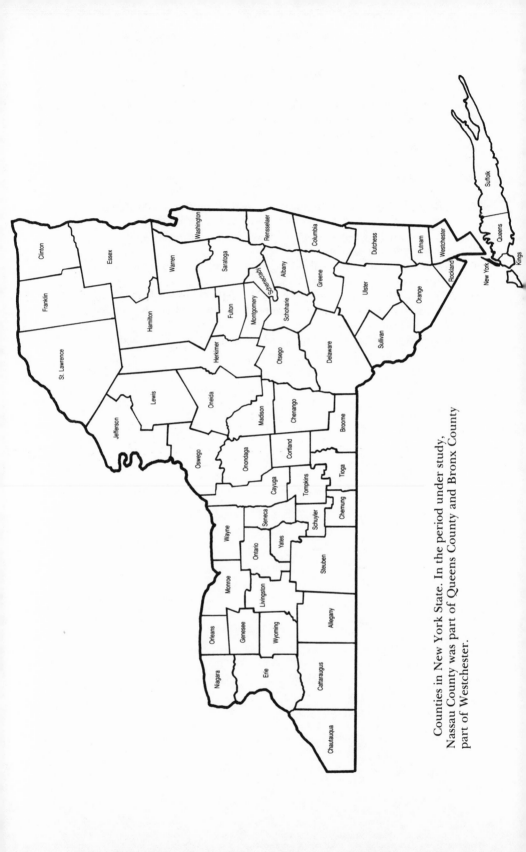

Counties in New York State. In the period under study, Nassau County was part of Queens County and Bronx County part of Westchester.

The Politics of
Race in New York

CHAPTER ONE

The Tradition of Discrimination

The Age of the Common Man, as the early nineteenth century is often called, theoretically began a new era in American politics, one in which all men became political equals, and the requirement that voters own property was abolished forever. Following the trend of the times, New York in its 1821 constitutional convention changed its suffrage provisions. Non-property-holding white males gained new rights, but, at the same time, black males found their right to vote restricted by a freehold qualification. As has happened many times in American history, egalitarian ideals did not cross the color line. Not until almost half a century later, after a long and arduous struggle, did blacks finally win the right to vote on the same basis as whites.[1]

The full meaning of this episode cannot be understood, however, unless it is placed in a larger historical framework. New York's effort to restrict and then expand black rights was not unique, and it must be seen as part of a much larger struggle by American society to cope with cultural diversity. The United States of the nineteenth century had a heritage of racial fears, myths, and stereotypes that helped shape the treatment of minority groups. In addition, specific

1. The general background of this struggle may be traced in James M. McPherson, *The Struggle for Equality: Abolitionists and the Negro in the Civil War and Reconstruction* (Princeton: Princeton University Press, 1964).

historical, social, and cultural conditions in the North in general and in New York in particular influenced the way white New Yorkers reflected this heritage of discrimination in their daily lives. This heritage and these conditions form the background of New York's struggle for equal suffrage.[2]

Sociologists frequently explain discrimination as an outgrowth of conflict between groups who do not share similar values, outlooks, or modes of behavior. When such groups come together, tension results, the exact response depending upon the particular cultures involved and the historical context. Feeling its cultural identity threatened, one group may stereotype the outsiders, emphasizing and exaggerating all the traits that supposedly set them apart. Thus social rejection of the alien through segregation, denial of rights, persecution, etc., becomes that much easier, and fresh attempts to achieve equality of treatment correspondingly harder.[3]

Since people from three continents possessing widely divergent social customs and traditions settled in America, it is hardly surprising that ethnic, racial, and religious conflicts form a major theme in its history. Many Americans have found it difficult to accept the melting pot concept; they have preferred instead to fight to keep their own cultural independence. Michael Zuckerman, for instance, has shown that Massachusetts towns of the eighteenth century drove from their midst not only the non-English, but also those who failed to measure up to the economic, religious, and moral standards set by the community.[4] The towns' citizens considered similarity in beliefs and values more essential for their communities' well-being than the special skills or talents the rejected might possess.

The problem of cultural diversity became especially acute during the early nineteenth century. The transportation and communications revolutions increased people's awareness of the diversity of their country just as the unifying effect of the American Revolution

2. Various aspects of the suffrage struggle are discussed in Dixon Ryan Fox, "The Negro Vote in Old New York," *Political Science Quarterly*, 32 (June 1917), 252–75; Emil Olbrich, *The Development of Sentiment on Negro Suffrage to 1860* (Madison, Wisc., 1912), pp. 26–39, 72–77, 126–27; and John Langley Stanley, "Majority Tyranny in Tocqueville's America: The Failure of Negro Suffrage in New York State in 1846" (Ph.D. diss., Cornell University, 1966).

3. A general sociological analysis of ethnic and racial conflict may be found in James W. Vander Zanden, *American Minority Relations*, 3rd ed. (New York: Ronald Press, 1972).

4. Michael Zuckerman, *Peaceable Kingdoms: New England Towns in the Eighteenth Century* (New York: Alfred A. Knopf, 1970), pp. 107, 110.

began to wear thin. A search for a separate national identity commenced. But, as David Brion Davis has argued, many groups, such as the Anti-Masons, Anti-Mormons, and nativists, sought this identity by labeling the groups they opposed as disloyal, subversive, and morally depraved, thus denying the capacity of such outsiders to be true Americans.[5]

In some respects the black man in America has experienced a rejection similar to that of other ethnic or cultural minorities. There remain important differences, however. No other group has aroused so much anxiety, met such open hostility, or been subjected to second-class citizenship for so long. The origins of this hypersensitivity toward blacks are complex and apparently date back to the first contacts between Englishmen and Africans in the sixteenth century. The English viewed the Africans according to contemporary European cultural standards. Traders rather than anthropologists, they could not appreciate the meaning of African tribal rituals and customs or understand family and social structures unlike their own. To them, scantily clad natives who worshiped strange gods, practiced polygamy, or, as rumor had it, ate one another were simply "heathen," "primitive," and "savage."[6] Most importantly, these perceived cultural differences were a source of anxiety for the English. Not only did Englishmen identify blacks by a color traditionally associated with evil and sin, but their mistaken belief that Africans were sexually promiscuous, unbound by religious scruples, and not answerable to European-style authority figures caused consternation at the thought of such open violations of traditional European standards of behavior. England itself was experiencing social change at this time. Old values were being laid aside as the commercialization of the economy and increased contact with other peoples altered the English way of life. Winthrop Jordan has argued that doubts about their own ability to control criminality, violence, and threats to family stability in a world that was rapidly changing made

5. David Brion Davis, "Some Ideological Functions of Prejudice in Ante-Bellum America," *American Quarterly*, 15 (Summer 1963), 115–25; idem., "Some Themes of Counter-Subversion: An Analysis of Anti-Masonic, Anti-Catholic, and Anti-Mormon Literature," *Mississippi Valley Historical Review*, 47 (Sept. 1960), 205–24.

6. David Brion Davis, *The Problem of Slavery in Western Culture* (Ithaca, N.Y.: Cornell University Press, 1966), chapter 15; Winthrop D. Jordan, *White over Black: American Attitudes toward the Negro, 1550–1812* (Chapel Hill: University of North Carolina Press, 1968), chapter 1; George M. Fredrickson, *The Black Image in the White Mind: The Debate on Afro-American Character and Destiny, 1817–1914* (New York: Harper & Row, 1971). Fredrickson traces the ideology of racism into the nineteenth century.

the English especially susceptible to repressing blacks, who seemed to represent those qualities they most feared in themselves. Thus the groundwork was laid for a stereotype of blacks stressing not only their differentness and inferiority to the European but also their potential threat to society.[7]

The institution of slavery enhanced and perpetuated this stereotype. It provided an economic incentive for the subordination of the black man and necessitated the creation of slave codes to regulate his actions, thereby continuing the notion that the interests of blacks and whites were fundamentally in conflict and that whites could not trust blacks to govern their own lives properly. Slavery also made blackness synonymous with servitude, a status despised by free men who tended to stigmatize the unfree as everything from lazy and shiftless to thieving and murderous. Servitude also placed blacks in such an economically and socially disadvantageous position that even freed slaves could rarely hope to achieve "respectability." But it was the stereotype of the black man rather than slavery itself that served most effectively to condemn him. Alexis de Tocqueville observed in the early nineteenth century: "You may set the Negro free, but you cannot make him otherwise than an alien to the European. Nor is this all; we scarcely acknowledge the common features of humanity in this stranger whom slavery has brought among us. His physiognomy is to our eyes hideous, his understanding weak, his tastes low; and we are almost inclined to look upon him as a being intermediate between man and the brutes."[8] Many Americans showed by their actions that they agreed with Tocqueville. Another observer noted that so many taboos were associated with any sort of racial intermingling that only "the most generous or the most vile" whites would ever violate them. In fact, if the subject of the black arose in public discourse, "the best educated man amongst them [Americans] will utter more nonsense in a given time than the most unlettered clown in the three kingdoms."[9]

The prevalence of racial stereotyping was in part a reflection of the ethnocentricity of American society, but in part also a result of the near absence of evidence to challenge the stereotype. Some sci-

7. Jordan, *White over Black*, passim.
8. Alexis de Tocqueville, *Democracy in America*, trans. Henry Reeve (New York: Vintage Books, 1954), 1:372.
9. E. S. Abdy, *Journal of a Residence and Tour in the United States of North America from April, 1833, to October, 1834* (London: John Murray, 1835), 1:55, 363.

entists in the early nineteenth century espoused a theory of the separate origin of races according to which the races were not only biologically distinct but also rankable in their order of development. Naturally whites believed themselves to be the most advanced race and blacks the least. Even those scientists who argued that environment was responsible for racial differences often concluded that the African environment was inferior to that of Europe and America.[10]

The other and more commonly cited source of authority on race was the Bible. Despite refutation by most biblical scholars of the day, in popular belief Ham, whose son Canaan was cursed by Noah to be "a servant of servants," was considered to be the progenitor of the black race, and the curse was seen as a sign of divine displeasure with all blacks. Thus to some it seemed to be God's will that the black man be treated differently than the white.[11]

There were groups, of course, who refused to accept the notion of innate inferiority based on race. These people, who became the core of the emancipationist and abolitionist movements, drew upon a cultural heritage that rejected the premise of racial inferiority and the morality of discrimination. This heritage derived primarily from certain aspects of the Protestant Reformation and the Enlightenment. The changing cultural milieu is difficult to describe without great oversimplification. Basically, however, in the period prior to these two movements, man was customarily considered essentially corrupt. Evil existed in men, not in the institutions of the world. Men must, therefore, humbly submit to their lot in life knowing that their just rewards would come only after death. By the seventeenth and eighteenth centuries, some religious and philosophical groups began to argue that man was good, his environment corrupting. Perfection (in some views, the millennium) was attainable on earth provided men were free to develop their good qualities. This view had certain implications for race relations. If all men were good, might not black men be inherently good also? And if perfection could be achieved only through individual self-improvement, how could one justify slavery and discrimination, which raised automatic barriers to self-advancement?[12] As William Jay, the abolitionist, pointed out, racial prejudice wrongfully hindered "the virtuous

10. William R. Stanton, *The Leopard's Spots: Scientific Attitudes toward Race in America, 1815–59* (Chicago: University of Chicago Press, 1960).

11. Jordan, *White over Black*, pp. 17–20.

12. Davis, *Problem of Slavery*, chapters 10–15.

struggle of the poor and obscure to improve and elevate themselves."[13]

Even people who drew upon this cultural heritage, however, sometimes had ambiguous feelings about accepting blacks as full members of their communities. Some found acknowledging racial equality extremely difficult when most others treated blacks with contempt. A minister who claimed he was totally unprejudiced declared that he considered eating and sleeping with black men "the severest test of a man's anti-slavery faith."[14] Others rejected the notion of social equality entirely. A member of the executive committee of the American Anti-Slavery Society in 1836 threatened to resign if social intercourse with blacks were required of true abolitionists.[15] Even the most dedicated abolitionists were ethnocentric enough to expect blacks to try to conform to their own cultural standards. Indeed it was this faith in the universal acceptance of their own values which convinced such abolitionists of the credibility of their vision of a racially harmonious American community. Concrete social pressures placed upon abolitionists helped to reinforce this ambivalence about race. In a number of northern cities mobs broke up antislavery meetings and verbally and physically abused those attending.[16] To some abolitionists it seemed wiser to concentrate on the evils of slavery and avoid the divisions inherent in working toward a nonracist America.

Such a powerful and pervasive prejudice against blacks was bound to have practical implications for the way whites and blacks lived together in America. If whites had convinced themselves that the beast predominated in the black—that, as a "primitive," he responded to the world emotionally not rationally, that, as a "heathen," he ignored moral restraints to satiate basic desires, that, as a "slave," he avoided work if he could steal or live off another's charity, and, above all, that if this "outsider" were assimilated into white society, that society would suffer an irretrievable loss—then it was natural to try to protect white society from his presence. From the earliest days of contact with Africans, Americans had seen the black in precisely these terms. Blacks were well aware of it. A group of black leaders

13. William Jay, *Slavery in America* (London: F. Westly & A. H. Davis, 1835), p. 23.
14. *New York Herald,* Oct. 30, 1860.
15. Leon F. Litwack, *North of Slavery: The Negro in the Free States, 1790–1860* (Chicago: University of Chicago Press, 1961), p. 217.
16. Leonard L. Richards, *"Gentlemen of Property and Standing": Anti-Abolition Mobs in Jacksonian America* (New York: Oxford University Press, 1970).

complained in 1853: "Our white fellow-countrymen do not know us. They are strangers to our character, ignorant of our capacity, oblivious of our history and progress, and are misinformed as to the principles and ideas that control and guide us as a people. The great mass of American citizens estimate us as being a characterless and purposeless people; and hence we hold up our heads, if at all, against the withering influence of a nation's scorn and contempt."[17]

The perception of blacks as inferior and unassimilable dictated their treatment as a special class in society. Control over the black man rather than his integration into the community became the goal. Chattel slavery was one such form of control. Although motivated by more than the simple desire for white dominance, it did necessitate for the first time the writing of slave codes, spelling out in law the black man's inferior position. More significantly, whites began to discriminate against free blacks as well. Communities varied in their expectations of free black residents, but they always treated them as a class apart from the rest of society. In most of the southern colonies free Negroes were barred from testifying against whites. In Virginia a black could not strike a white. The purpose was not only to prevent the disruption of the slave system by making freedom look less desirable, but also to establish and maintain a racial distinction regardless of the state of freedom. The royal governor of Virginia explained the exclusion of free blacks from suffrage as an effort "to make the free Negros [*sic*] sensible that a distinction ought to be made between their offspring and the Descendants of an Englishman, with whom they never were to be accounted Equal."[18]

Few blacks ever knew freedom, even in a restricted sense, in the South, but in the North race relations followed a different course. The early demise of slavery inspired new sorts of legal and societal restrictions designed to define the place of the black man in a now free society. North and South had always shared a common stereotype of the black man, but now the North's own unique social conditions and history would determine the treatment he would be accorded.

The reasons for the North's abandonment of slavery were replete

17. Philip S. Foner, *The Life and Writings of Frederick Douglass* (New York: International Publishers, 1950–55), 2:266.

18. Jordan, *White over Black*, pp. 122–27. The quotation is from p. 127. See also Ira Berlin, *Slaves without Masters: The Free Negro in the Antebellum South* (New York: Pantheon Books, 1974).

with ambiguity. Idealism joined with self-interest to spell the institution's doom. Slavery had never dominated the economy of the northern states as it had that of the South. It became, therefore, vulnerable to attacks from those who hated the institution. Although many of these were inspired by ideals of liberty and natural rights stemming from the American Revolution, some saw slavery merely as a threat to white society.[19] With slaves in the community, there was always a danger of insurrection as well as the annoyance of slave crime or even just the presence of the alien Negro. Emancipation might be a first step toward ridding states of their entire black populations either through colonization in Africa or surreptitious sales to slave states farther south.

Not all northern states approached emancipation in the same way. States where slavery had been most firmly established showed the greatest fears of the possible social consequences of emancipation. Pennsylvania, Rhode Island, Connecticut, New York, and New Jersey ended slavery gradually, freeing only the offspring of slaves born after a certain date. Massachusetts, after freeing its slaves, "voted to bar interracial marriages and to expel all Negroes who were not citizens of one of the states."[20] In New York in 1785, a measure providing for immediate emancipation was killed when opponents divided the emancipationist forces by raising the issue of civil and political equality for blacks (in the form of amendments forbidding intermarriage between blacks and whites and denying blacks the right to vote, hold office, or testify against whites in court). Although a modified bill providing for emancipation and denying blacks the right to vote passed in 1785, the Council of Revision vetoed it, and the Assembly refused to override the veto.[21]

In essence, although every northern state had taken steps to end slavery by 1804, blacks were not automatically accepted as equals by northern whites as a result. On the contrary, emancipation merely brought a reformulation of the black man's subordinate status. Whites sought new ways to keep the distance they felt *must* exist between themselves and blacks. Tocqueville observed: "In the North the white no longer distinctly perceives the barrier [slavery] that

19. Litwack, *North of Slavery*, chapter 1; Arthur Zilversmit, *The First Emancipation: The Abolition of Slavery in the North* (Chicago: University of Chicago Press, 1967), pp. 226–29. Zilversmit sees the "intellectual ferment of the Revolutionary era" as the most important cause of emancipation.

20. Litwack, *North of Slavery*, pp. 3, 16. The quotation is from p. 16.

21. Zilversmit, *First Emancipation*, pp. 147–50. Cf. Edgar J. McManus, *A History of Negro Slavery in New York* (Syracuse: Syracuse University Press, 1966), pp. 163–65.

separates him from the degraded race, and he shuns the Negro with the more pertinacity since he fears lest they should some day be confounded together. . . . Thus, the prejudice which repels the negroes seems to increase in proportion as they are emancipated, and inequality is sanctioned by the manners while it is effaced from thè laws of the country."[22]

By dwelling upon the black's shortcomings, whites reassured themselves of their own dominance and justified continued discrimination against the blacks. Discriminatory laws were particularly important in this process. They treated blacks as a distinct class whose loyalty and capabilities were automatically suspect, thereby reinforcing whites' perceptions of the black man's differentness and danger to society. Such laws too involved *all* law-abiding citizens in the recognition of white supremacist practices. It is hardly surprising that the removal of such laws became the chief goal of those who abhorred prejudice.

Discriminatory laws in the North (called "black laws") varied from efforts to exclude blacks from the population altogether to attempts to secure special prerogatives for whites in such areas as the educational, judicial, and governmental systems. Historians have linked several factors to the types of laws passed: the size of the black population, the cultural and socioeconomic background of the white community, the proximity to slave territory, and white perceptions of new threats to the racial status quo.

Exclusion laws were perhaps the severest form of discrimination and reflected the belief that whites and blacks could never form a harmonious community. Illinois, Indiana, Iowa, Oregon, and Ohio (until Ohio repealed such laws in 1849) all had laws denying blacks the right of permanent residence.[23] With the exception of Oregon all bordered on slave territory with a more numerous black population, which may partially explain their reaction. An abortive attempt to settle 518 freed slaves from Virginia in a town in southern Ohio led to threats of armed resistance from the inhabitants. Whenever Negro exclusion was submitted to the voters for approval, it won enthusiastic endorsement, in Illinois by a margin of more than two to one and in Oregon by more than eight to one.[24]

22. Tocqueville, *Democracy*, 1:274.
23. There is a convenient compendium of statutes and constitutional provisions concerning the black in the various states in Henry W. Farnam, *Chapters in the History of Social Legislation in the United States to 1860* (Washington: Carnegie Institution, 1938), pp. 416–74.
24. Litwack, *North of Slavery*, pp. 69, 71.

Blacks who already resided in northern states found they were far from equal citizens in the eyes of the law. Fearing that blacks could not be trusted to give unbiased testimony concerning whites, the states of Illinois, Indiana, Iowa, Ohio (until 1849), Oregon, California, and the territory of Nebraska refused to let blacks be witnesses against whites. The middle western and western states once again took the lead.[25] Since the performance of civic duties might bring blacks and whites into "social" contact, Illinois and Indiana excluded blacks from their militias. Most other states did so by custom, a means also used to keep blacks off juries. Concerning the more sensitive issue of interracial marriage, at least ten northern states and territories at one time officially banned it.[26]

By far the most common legal distinction made between whites and blacks concerned the right to vote. Voting was a sensitive issue because it implied not only the wielding of power but also the acceptance of the voter as a responsible member of the community. As late as the early nineteenth century it had been common to limit suffrage to freeholders because only a property owner was considered to have a real vested interest in the well-being of the community.[27] Most blacks in this early period being neither free nor freeholders were seldom eligible to vote. But a few did meet the qualifications, and when they voted, the losing candidates often protested vociferously that the black votes should not have been counted.[28] When the adoption of manhood suffrage in many states threatened to increase dramatically the number of black voters, the response in most states was to limit the vote to whites. Unrestricted suffrage might encourage the migration of "black outcasts and worthless vagrants" or lead blacks to suppose "they are entitled to equal rights and equal privileges with the white man, when, by our laws of society, they are not, and cannot be permitted to exercise

25. For a further discussion of midwestern and western racial attitudes see V. Jacque Voegeli, *Free But Not Equal: The Midwest and the Negro during the Civil War* (Chicago: University of Chicago Press, 1967) and Eugene H. Berwanger, *The Frontier against Slavery: Western Anti-Negro Prejudice and the Slavery Extension Controversy* (Urbana, Ill.: University of Illinois Press, 1967).

26. Litwack, *North of Slavery*, pp. 93–94; Farnam, *Chapters*, pp. 416–74.

27. Chilton Williamson, *American Suffrage from Property to Democracy, 1760–1860* (Princeton: Princeton University Press, 1960), p. 5.

28. Edward Raymond Turner, *The Negro in Pennsylvania: Slavery-Servitude-Freedom, 1639–1861* (Washington: The American Historical Association, 1912), pp. 179, 184–85; Fox, "Negro Vote," pp. 256–57.

them." New Jersey, Pennsylvania, Connecticut, and Rhode Island (from 1822 to 1842) moved to insert "white" in their suffrage provisions. After the change in the state's suffrage provisions in 1821, New York allowed most whites, but only blacks with $250 freeholds, to vote. Every other state, with the exception of the New England states of Maine, Massachusetts, Vermont, and New Hampshire, where few blacks lived, excluded them from suffrage. In 1860 only six per cent of northern blacks lived in states that granted them equal suffrage.[29]

Some states allowed local communities to decide on the desirability of segregation, for example, in education. The black population of the North tended to be highly concentrated in urban centers, parts of the eastern seaboard, and some rural areas such as the lower Midwest.[30] In such areas segregation was the rule. In rural areas with relatively few blacks a dual system was sometimes impractical, although some communities may have dealt with this situation by discouraging blacks from attending the local schools altogether. A few states also adopted this practice. Ohio in 1829 excluded blacks from the public schools and returned their school tax. In 1849 the state relented slightly, making segregated schools mandatory. Illinois restricted its schools to whites, although some communities where few blacks lived permitted blacks to attend. Indiana had a similar statute, opponents of black education openly declaring that the "privilege" of equal education "might . . . induce the vain belief that the prejudice of the dominant race could ever be so mollified as to break down the rugged barriers that must forever exist between their social relations."[31]

Integration, of course, implied to many whites association of the races as equals, the corruption of white youth, and "amalgamation." In only one state before the Civil War (Massachusetts in 1855) did integration of schools become mandatory. Even there the fight was long and bitter and the political maneuvering required to accomplish it extraordinary. Boston school officials predicted violence and the withdrawal of white students should integration occur. Their fears proved unwarranted, however.[32]

29. Litwack, *North of Slavery*, p. 74–91. The quotation is from p. 76.
30. For some excellent maps showing the distribution of the free black population see Wilbur Zelinsky, "The Population Geography of the Free Negro in Ante-Bellum America," *Population Studies*, 3 (March 1950), 391, 395.
31. Litwack, *North of Slavery*, chapter 4; Carter G. Woodson, *The Education of the Negro Prior to 1861* (Washington: Associated Publishers, 1919), pp. 332–33.
32. Litwack, *North of Slavery*, pp. 143–49.

The absence of discriminatory laws did not necessarily imply an absence of discrimination. The social mores of the white citizens often resulted in de facto segregation where the law itself was silent. In general, wherever there was a sizable black population, hotels, restaurants, theaters, assembly halls, trains, omnibuses, hospitals, and even cemeteries were segregated. Churches, whose pews customarily were assigned according to social rank, often relegated blacks to the back rows or gallery. In a number of northern cities (New York, Philadelphia, and Cincinnati in particular) whites indicated more brutally their determination to maintain white preeminence—by periodic mob attacks on the black population.[33]

No laws required blacks to hold menial jobs in the North, but evidence of job discrimination abounds, and many whites with low-status jobs feared black competition for employment. Because blacks holding responsible positions contradicted racial stereotypes, blacks obtained few except the lowest paid, unskilled jobs—usually as servants or laborers. The few blacks who endured the proscriptive environment of white colleges found little to justify the effort. John Rock, a Massachusetts black, noted: "Their [blacks'] education aggravates their suffering. . . . The educated colored man meets, on the one hand, the embittered prejudices of the whites and on the other the jealousies of his own race. . . . You can hardly imagine the humiliation and contempt a colored lad must feel by graduating the first in his class, and then being rejected everyplace else because of his color."[34] It was equally difficult for those who sought to enter the skilled trades. "No one will employ me; white boys won't work with me," complained one youth. Even common laborers had a hard time. Many white workers (especially Irish immigrants according to several observers) feared the loss of their low-paying jobs to blacks who would work for even less. Violent clashes between the races on the docks or in the streets were a common occurrence.[35]

Thus the North in the period after it abolished slavery had substituted a variety of other means, both formal and informal, to assure white dominance. The specific actions taken varied according

33. Ibid., pp. 97–100, 106–11, chapter 6. Prior to the Civil War segregation was successfully challenged only in Massachusetts, where state legislators pressured the railroads into desegregating their cars despite the owners' contention that separation was an established custom and public opinion demanded it.

34. James M. McPherson, *The Negro's Civil War* (New York: Pantheon Books, 1965), pp. 248–49.

35. Litwack, *North of Slavery*, pp. 154, 159.

to time, place, and circumstance, but certainly the North, considered as a whole, had not rejected its cultural attitudes concerning the black man. Indeed through political, judicial, economic, educational, and social discrimination the North had forced blacks to become what their detractors indicated they were naturally—impoverished, uneducated, and unskilled. This circumstance merely confirmed what whites already wanted to believe—that blacks were inferior and that to treat them as equals would be foolish and unnatural.

The state of New York participated in this general pattern of discrimination against blacks in ways that were a function of circumstances peculiar to New York. The state had one of the most firmly established slave systems of the northern states. The Dutch West India Company imported the first blacks to the colony in the early 1600s, and the slave system evolved gradually. Although the law code of 1665, issued after the takeover of the colony by the English in 1664, recognized slavery as an institution, servitude embraced some whites as well as blacks. As slavery became exclusively racial, relations between the races became a matter less of contractual obligation of servant to master than of social control of one race by another. By 1746 New York had a larger proportion of slaves in its population (fifteen per cent) than any other northern colony.[36]

Slavery in New York differed in several important ways from the plantation slavery of the South. The majority of slaves belonged to individuals who owned only a few slaves: a man with as many as ten slaves was a rarity. Slave occupations in New York were diverse. Although some slaves performed farm labor, many were personal servants or skilled artisans. The owner of skilled slaves often hired them out to people in need of their special talents. All these factors tended to diminish the effectiveness of the state's control over slavery. Slave artisans had to be free to journey to and from employment, and their skills gave them more bargaining power with their owners. Servants needed to be able to run errands. Strict enforcement of laws about slave movement and assembly might upset the actual workings of the slave system. The small number of slaves per owner also made discipline primarily a personal, not a state, matter.[37]

36. Jordan, *White over Black*, pp. 83–84; McManus, *Slavery*, pp. 4, 24, 42, 80; Carl Nordstrom, "The New York Slave Code," *Afro-Americans in New York Life and History*, 4 (Jan. 1980), 10–11.
37. McManus, *Slavery*, pp. 41–42, 45–51.

Periodically, however, the government intervened to place new controls on the black population. The fear of slave revolts (especially after two conspiracy scares in New York City in 1712 and 1741) prompted occasional flurries of restrictive legislation designed to curb both the rights of slaves and free blacks. Slaves could not assemble in groups of three or more or own weapons. They faced death if convicted of arson, rape, or the murder of a freeman. They could be tried only in slave courts, where black testimony against whites was inadmissible. As a deterrent to theft, blacks were not allowed to sell goods. Legally they had no right to marry or hold property, although some blacks apparently did so anyway. Indeed lax enforcement characterized all the laws.[38]

With the end of the foreign slave trade in 1808 and a large influx of white immigrants, the proportion of slaves in the population declined. Meanwhile humanitarian attacks on slavery continued, and soon the whole system of controls began to weaken. Slave labor was no longer as important to the economy, and the growing white population seemed less fearful of the black presence. In 1785, as noted, the legislature by a close vote attempted to abolish slavery altogether, but the Council of Revision vetoed the action. The voting alignments were closely related to the delegates' own property interests in slaves. Those upholding slavery were more likely to be wealthy, from commercial farming areas, Dutch Reformed, educated, cosmopolitan, and non-Clintonians.[39] The legislature was able to ameliorate the condition of the slaves, though. For example they removed the barriers to private manumission and ended the special judicial standing of the slave. In 1799 New York finally agreed to free all children of slaves born after July 4 of that year, but, to pay their masters for their upbringing, required them to work for their former owners until they reached a specified age. Slave marriages were now retroactively legitimized, the right of blacks to hold property formally admitted, and masters required to ready their slaves for freedom by teaching them to read. In 1817 a final act was passed which would free in 1827 all slaves born before 1799.[40]

Although New York did away with many of the laws that had

---

38. Ibid., chapter 5; Edwin Olson, "The Slave Code in Colonial New York," *Journal of Negro History*, 24 (Apr. 1944), 147–65.

39. Jackson Turner Main, *Political Parties before the Constitution* (Chapel Hill: University of North Carolina Press, 1973), p. 142.

40. McManus, *Slavery*, pp. 166–67; Olson, "Slave Code," pp. 147–48, 151, 164.

placed blacks and whites on a separate and unequal footing, white New Yorkers still did not accept racial equality. As had occurred even under the slave system, custom rather than law governed race relations. Those who violated accepted racial norms found out quickly that they had erred. Passengers on a steamboat warned a French traveler that he had behaved badly by accepting a light for his cigar from a black man. Another foreigner who spoke courteously to a black woman was pelted with brickbats.[41] A well-to-do mulatto from Haiti found himself abruptly turned away when he sought to register at one of New York's better hotels.[42] In 1848 Frederick Douglass, New York's foremost black abolitionist, complained:

> Slaves to *individuals* at the South, we are but little better than slaves to *community* at the North. The community sport with our rights with as much impunity, as if we formed no part of the family of man. They tax us, deny us the right to suffrage, take our money to build schoolhouses, and spurn our children from their doors. Prejudice pursues us in every lane of life. Even our courts of law are against us. We are tried by our enemies. The judge, jury and counsellors are all under the influence of a bitter prejudice against us. In such a state, justice is but a name.[43]

Community norms, however, varied throughout the state. Slavery was on the wane in New York before the western part of the state had been completely settled. Consequently, throughout the early nineteenth century the black population remained concentrated in the New York City-Hudson Valley region.[44] The people of Dutch, Palatine, and early British origin who primarily inhabited this area and whose way of life was characterized by "ingrained resistance to change, stubborn preservation of old modes of thought and old ways of doing things, and the operation of powerful sanctions to maintain group solidarity and adherence to group norms" showed particular hostility to any change in the status of blacks.[45] They put up the strongest opposition to emancipation and later almost unanimously rejected the antislavery Liberty Party. In western New York there seemed to be a greater degree of uncertainty on racial matters. There were fewer blacks and most of the whites had migrated

41. Abdy, *Journal,* 1:301–302.
42. Thomas Hamilton, *Men and Manners in America,* 2nd ed. (Philadelphia: Carey, Lea & Blanchard, 1833), 1:59.
43. Foner, *Douglass,* 1:302.
44. McManus, *Slavery,* p. 43.
45. Lee Benson, *The Concept of Jacksonian Democracy: New York as a Test Case* (Princeton: Princeton University Press, 1961), pp. 298, 303–304.

from New England, where racial proscription, while sometimes present, was not as firmly embedded in the laws. Some parts of western New York supported abolition, and treatment of blacks varied according to the particular community. In 1818, for example, a black man attempting to marry a white woman was turned away by a justice of the peace in Rochester but had his request granted, albeit reluctantly, in a nearby rural town.[46]

As in the rest of the North the elimination of slavery led to more distinct patterns of racial separation. In New York City blacks began to found their own churches rather than accept second-class treatment in white ones.[47] As the concept of public education emerged, so also did that of segregated schools. In 1823 New York began to organize all-black schools, and in 1841 the legislature authorized any school district that so desired to establish separate schools for black children. By 1847 fifteen (out of fifty-nine) counties had done so, and the number of such counties actually increased over the next few decades. (In 1868 twenty-two counties containing 75.9 per cent of the state's black population had separate schools.) But in areas where prejudice was not as great, blacks attended the common schools.[48] Many public facilities were also segregated. Most streetcar lines in New York City had separate cars for blacks or forced them to ride on the outside platform. Most places of public amusement also distinguished between black and white patrons.[49] No one knows the geographic extent of segregation practices in New York because no one kept records. Complaints about segregation, however, surfaced most often in the New York City area.

White New Yorkers perhaps best clarified their feelings toward the black presence in the state by their legislation on the right of blacks to vote. As in most northern states, the reluctance to share power and to incorporate blacks as part of the community soon appeared. According to the state constitution of 1777, any man could vote for assemblyman (and hence congressman) if he possessed a £20 ($50) freehold, rented a 40 shilling ($5) tenement, or had been

46. Howard W. Coles, *The Cradle of Freedom: A History of the Negro in Rochester, Western New York and Canada* (Rochester: Oxford Press, 1941), pp. 30–31.

47. Roy Ottley and William J. Weatherby, eds., *The Negro in New York* (Dobbs Ferry, N.Y.: Oceana Publications, 1967), pp. 50, 53.

48. Woodson, *Education of the Negro*, pp. 311–12; Ena Lunette Farley, "The Issue of Black Equality in New York State, 1865–1873" (Ph.D. diss., University of Wisconsin, 1973), pp. 180–83.

49. Rhoda Golden Freeman, "The Free Negro in New York City in the Era before the Civil War" (Ph.D. diss., Columbia University, 1966), pp. 98–103.

a freeman of Albany in 1777 or of New York City in 1775; to vote for state senator or governor required a £100 ($250) freehold.[50] In practice it appears that public officials routinely allowed their friends and neighbors of reputable character to vote regardless of their property holdings.[51] Although the qualifications were not overtly racial, they bore more heavily upon blacks, many of whom were not free men, much less owners of property or the respected friends of local officials. Any liberalization of the suffrage laws, therefore, would tend to enfranchise proportionately more blacks than whites. In the early nineteenth century agitation to remove the property qualification for voters rocked New York. Voting, the argument went, was a natural right, inherent in citizenship, not something to be granted only to those with a property stake in the community. Reform leaders immediately faced the problem of whether blacks possessed natural rights too.

In 1821 New York held a constitutional convention primarily for the purpose of expanding the suffrage.[52] That the revised constitution did not totally disfranchise blacks, as happened in most states, was probably due to the relatively stable race relations at the time and the unwillingness of the convention to reject completely the stake-in-society theory of voting. The percentage of blacks in New York's population had begun a steady decline that was to continue for much of the century. (See Table 1.1.) In 1820 the population was only 2.9 percent black compared to 7.6 per cent thirty years earlier. Only one-quarter of these blacks were slaves, but many of the free blacks were children freed under the gradual emancipation act of 1799.[53] Emancipation was proceeding smoothly and without public protest. Delegates could, therefore, approach black balloting as one aspect of the larger struggle over suffrage, not in the context of sectional or racial controversy.

Federalists at the convention, such as Chancellor James Kent and Rufus King, regarded voting as a privilege that should be extended

50. Charles Z. Lincoln, *The Constitutional History of New York* (Rochester: Lawyers Co-Operative, 1906), 1:171–72, 175.
51. Richard P. McCormick, "Suffrage Classes and Party Alignments: A Study in Voter Behavior," *Mississippi Valley Historical Review,* 46 (Dec. 1959), 409.
52. The most important recent study of the convention is John Anthony Casais, "The New York State Constitutional Convention of 1821 and its Aftermath" (Ph.D. diss., Columbia University, 1967). On the general movement away from property qualifications see Williamson, *American Suffrage.*
53. Leo H. Hirsch, Jr., "The Negro and New York, 1783–1865," *Journal of Negro History,* 16 (Oct. 1931), pp. 391n., 415n.

TABLE 1.1.

Black population of New York,
1814-1870

Year	Number	Per cent of state population
1814	30,094	3.7
1820	39,367	2.9
1825	39,701	2.5
1830	44,945	2.3
1835	43,770	2.0
1840	50,031	2.1
1845	44,256	1.7
1850	49,069	1.6
1855	45,286	1.3
1860	49,145	1.3
1865	44,708	1.2
1870	52,549	1.2

SOURCE: *Census of the State of New York for 1875* (Albany, 1877), p. xiv.

to neither poor blacks nor poor whites; they insisted that the races be restricted in the same way. At the other end of the suffrage spectrum a few men like James Tallmadge followed the natural rights philosophy to its natural limits—the right to vote for *all* men, black and white alike. Most of the delegates, however, accepted neither the stake-in-society nor the natural rights extremes.[54] Although cautiously sympathetic to the expansion of the electorate, they saw blacks, as one put it, as a "peculiar people" who were "incapable of exercising that privilege [voting] with any sort of discretion, prudence, or independence."[55] It was the age-old story once again: blacks were not a true part of the community. By a vote of 63–59 the convention did agree to strike the word *white* from the suffrage provisions. Most support for this change came from the Clintonians and Bucktail Federalists, but few were satisfied with this result.[56] In

54. Benson, *Concept*, pp. 7–9. Fox, "Negro Vote," p. 260, argues that the discriminatory property qualification was adopted because of Democratic fears that blacks would support the Federalists. Although blacks for a variety of reasons did favor the Federalist Party, and some evidence exists that in New York City their voting strength was occasionally of concern to some, John L. Stanley, who has studied the convention, has concluded that a party interpretation of the suffrage voting is oversimplified. John Langley Stanley, "Majority Tyranny" (Ph.D. diss.), p. 34.

55. *Reports of the Proceedings and Debates of the Convention of 1821* (Albany: E. and E. Hosford, 1821), p. 180.

56. Casais, "Convention of 1821," p. 185. The political designations are those used by Casais. The Clintonians were followers of DeWitt Clinton and generally believed

the end the convention compromised. Most white males gained the vote, but in order to vote they still were required to prove their interest in the community by paying taxes or performing militia or highway service.[57] Blacks were not excluded from the suffrage but had to meet a high property qualification, the constitutional provision stating:

> No man of colour, unless he shall have been for three years a citizen of this state, and for one year next preceding any election, shall be seized and possessed of a freehold estate of the value of two hundred and fifty dollars, over and above all debts and incumbrances charged thereon; and shall have been actually rated, and paid a tax thereon, shall be entitled to vote at any such election. And no person of colour shall be subject to direct taxation unless he shall be seized and possessed of such real estate as aforesaid.[58]

The black man, more than any white, had to prove his capacity to vote. In committee of the whole, 72 of 102 delegates favored the property qualification. Most of the opposition came from the Clintonians.[59]

As a consequence of this new suffrage provision some blacks who had previously been able to meet the lower qualification required to vote for assemblymen lost their franchise. The property qualification easily barred the polls to most blacks. In 1825 only 298 blacks in a total population of 29,701 possessed the mandatory freehold.[60]

"No one of the negro's champions pretended to regard him as a desirable citizen," notes one student of the convention.[61] Yet white New Yorkers often denied the illiberality of their actions. Most blacks could not vote, they admitted, but they were not taxed either. And the property qualification was not an onerous burden but rather, they argued, a positive incentive to work harder to acquire property.

The public readily ratified the new constitution with its discriminatory property qualification for blacks. The provision stirred little popular reaction either for or against it. Yet within two decades the black suffrage question would bitterly divide New Yorkers and become the center of a struggle that would last for thirty years. Race

---

that suffrage restrictions should be equally applicable to all voters. Bucktail Federalists were members of a Republican faction who had formerly been Federalists.

57. These requirements were removed for white voters in 1826.
58. Lincoln, *Constitutional History*, 1:199.
59. Casais, "Convention of 1821," p. 186.
60. New York State Assembly, *Journal*, 49th Sess., 1826, Appendix C, Table X.
61. Olbrich, *Sentiment on Suffrage*, p. 34.

became an increasingly sensitive issue and one with definite political overtones.

A number of factors made race more relevant to New Yorkers and helped determine initial group reactions to the race issue as it was politicized. First, greater black activism prompted some whites to feel a loss of control over the black minority in their communities. Following the completion of gradual emancipation in 1827, blacks began to form their own institutions and assert their independence from the white community. New York blacks founded their first newspaper, *Freedom's Journal*, in 1827 to promote African colonization as a means to escape persecution; *The Rights of All*, another journal founded in 1829, warred against racial prejudice. In 1833 the Phoenix Society of New York devoted itself to the struggle to gain equal political and civil rights, and in 1834 a convention of blacks began to petition the legislature for an end to second-class citizenship. The unequal suffrage provision, the absence of trial by jury for fugitive slaves, and a legislative loophole that allowed travelers to bring slaves into New York for up to nine months were the objects of attack.[62] Some black leaders also deliberately defied white community norms by refusing to accept passively segregation and the restriction of their rights. Frederick Douglass deliberately walked down Broadway arm-in-arm with two English ladies of his acquaintance. He found the reaction of the "refined" to be "a distortion of the countenance, a red and furious look about the cheek, a singular turn up of the nose, and a 'lower me!' expression of the eyes" while the "vulgar" responded with "head shaking, teeth grating, hysteric yells and horrid imprecation."[63] Abolitionist newspapers of the period record many similar instances of public commotions greeting attempts by blacks to stay in respectable hotels, eat at public houses, obtain cabin space on steamboats, etc.

Whites had expected gradual emancipation to result in only minor changes in the relations between the races. They saw challenges to white supremacy as distinctly threatening and distasteful. As Frederick Douglass noted, whites had no objections to servile blacks, but "to aspire to anything above them [slavery and servitude], is to

62. Herman D. Bloch, "The New York Negro's Battle for Political Rights, 1777–1865," *International Review of Social History*, 9 (1964), 70–71; see also Charles H. Wesley, "The Negroes of New York in the Emancipation Movement," *Journal of Negro History*, 24 (Jan. 1939), 65–103.
63. Foner, *Douglass*, 1:385.

contradict the established views of the community—to get out of our sphere and commit the provoking sin of *impudence*."[64]

White attention was further focused on blacks because of the growth and expansion of the abolition movement within the state. Beginning in the mid-1820s a major evangelical revival swept the nation and New York and led to heightened concern among many over moral issues including slavery. Convinced of the innate goodness of all men and the sinfulness of laws or institutions that stood in the path of individual self-improvement and realization, abolitionists felt a moral imperative to denounce both slavery and discrimination. Slavery could no longer be considered a legitimate social institution that could be reformed or removed at society's discretion. It was a *sin* that all men must renounce if America were to be saved. Equally repugnant to many abolitionists, of course, was New York's property qualification for black voters.

Most New Yorkers were not moved, however. Abolition and the religious ferment from which it derived touched the hearts of many in the Yankee-settled, socially maturing western region of the state but were rejected in most other areas.[65] As whites joined blacks to fight discrimination, tensions mounted. Many white New Yorkers came to despise the abolitionists. Nonevangelicals disliked the ultraist rhetoric of the reformers and their appeals to individual conscience (often directed at traditionally subordinate groups such as women and children). To the antiabolitionists the antislavery men seemed to be irresponsible disrupters of the traditional social order. In many communities men gathered to break up abolitionist meetings and scare away the troublemakers. The violence was climaxed by a full-scale riot causing many injuries in New York City in 1834.[66]

Great social changes in the state also focused attention on blacks. Between 1820 and 1860 the population of New York more than

64. Ibid., 2:129.
65. David Brion Davis, "The Emergence of Immediatism in British and American Antislavery Thought," *Mississippi Valley Historical Review*, 49 (Sept. 1962), 209–30; John L. Thomas, "Romantic Reform in America, 1815–1865," *American Quarterly*, 17 (Winter 1965), 656–57; Whitney R. Cross, *The Burned-Over District: The Social and Intellectual History of Enthusiastic Religion in Western New York, 1800–1850* (Ithaca, N.Y.: Cornell University Press, 1950), p. 226; John L. Hammond, *The Politics of Benevolence: Revival Religion and American Voting Behavior* (Norwood, N.J.: Ablex, 1979).
66. Richards, *"Gentlemen,"* pp. 145–50; Linda K. Kerber, "Abolitionists and Amalgamators: The New York City Race Riots of 1834," *New York History*, 48 (Jan. 1967), 28–39. See also Lorman Ratner, *Powder Keg: Northern Opposition to the Anti-Slavery Movement, 1831–1840* (New York: Basic Books, 1968).

doubled. No simple change in the birthrate accounted for the growth. Families were indeed multiplying, but thousands of new-comers were also crowding into the state. New York lost three citizens through westward migration for every one who came to it from New England, Pennsylvania, and New Jersey. Most new arrivals were from Europe. From 1845 (the first year in which the state census recorded place of birth) to 1860 the proportion of foreign-born persons in the population nearly doubled, from thirteen to twenty-five per cent. Although there were significant numbers of Welsh, Scotch, English, and Canadian immigrants, the overwhelming majority of the newcomers were from either Ireland or Germany. The Catholic church grew accordingly. In 1855 it was the largest single denomination in the state and claimed thirty-five per cent of all church members. Even though Protestants retained a healthy majority of all church members and most of the unchurched continued to come from Protestant backgrounds, many native-born Protestants considered Catholics a threat, and nativism flourished.[67]

The new groups entering the state brought with them their own distinctive cultural baggage which affected how they reacted towards blacks. The Irish Catholics, victims of persecution themselves because of their religion, seemed particularly hostile to blacks. "Observers remarked that the Irish detested the Negro more than they did the Englishman or the native whites, that they considered them a 'soulless race,' and that they 'would shoot a black man with as little regard to moral consequences as they would a wild hog.'"[68] They had scant sympathy for the moral reformers and abolitionists who often saw the Catholic church as a barrier to human progress as great as slavery. In contrast to the Irish stood the newly arrived Yankees, who were much involved in the evangelical revivals. Some groups, such as those from Pennsylvania and New Jersey, came to New York from states with long heritages of racial discrimination.

Economic change and dislocation also accompanied the social ferment and had implications for the level of racial conflict in New York. Blacks and unskilled immigrants, for instance, often competed for the same jobs. Blacks sometimes served as strikebreakers as well. In 1855, for instance, violence erupted during a strike in which blacks replaced white longshoremen on the New York City

67. *Census of the State of New York for 1865* (Albany: Charles Van Benthuysen & Son, 1867), pp. lxxi-lxxii; David M. Ellis et al., *A History of New York State* (Ithaca: Cornell University Press, 1967), pp. 280–82, 302.
68. Litwack, *North of Slavery*, p. 163.

docks.[69] This incident was by no means unique. On the whole, however, it was the Irish who usually displaced black workers. "Every hour sees us elbowed out of some employment to make room perhaps for some newly arrived immigrants, whose hunger and color are thought to give them a title to especial favor," observed Frederick Douglass.[70] Nevertheless, the fear was still widespread among whites that emancipation would send thousands of blacks streaming northward to take their jobs.[71]

Other forms of economic change clearly upset traditional patterns of living but were not overtly associated with attacks on blacks. As the transportation network of canals and railroads expanded, western New York turned from subsistence to commercial farming. And farmers on the worn-out lands of eastern New York began to switch from raising wheat to dairying and vegetable production. Those who could not adapt to the changing agricultural conditions were often drawn to the cities, which by 1855 claimed over thirty per cent of the state's population. Whatever the economic transition, adjustment to new ways was frequently difficult and often associated with fears and frustrations that could easily be released on black scapegoats.[72]

Thus in the period after 1821 a variety of social, economic, and ethnocultural tensions existed within New York State, some of which resulted in greater attention being paid to black rights. On the one hand stood the abolitionists, who wished to change in some way the racial status quo and, on the other, their opponents, who felt threatened by black advancement. By 1846 a delegate to the state constitutional convention could rightly comment that there "existed much diversity of opinion and great sensitiveness on the question of general suffrage as applied to the colored people."[73]

Equal suffrage for blacks became the focal point of discussion be-

69. Ibid., p. 160; Freeman, "Free Negro," pp. 301–302. The *New York Times*, March 2, 1869, and Williston Lofton, "Northern Labor and the Negro during the Civil War," *Journal of Negro History*, 34 (July 1949), 256, imply some immigrant groups were more hostile to blacks than others. Robert Ernst, *Immigrant Life in New York City, 1825–1863* (New York: King's Crown Press, 1949), p. 67, and Litwack, *North of Slavery*, p. 166, imply any differences were the result of the different economic positions of the groups.

70. Foner, *Douglass*, 2:249–50; see also Freeman, "Free Negro," pp. 301–302.

71. See, for example, *New York Herald*, Nov. 6, 1860.

72. Ellis et al., *New York*, p. 281, chapters 20–22.

73. William G. Bishop and William H. Attree, *Report of the Debates and Proceedings of the Convention for the Revision of the Constitution of the State of New York, 1846* (Albany: Evening Atlas, 1846), p. 1035.

cause the property qualification was the most clear-cut example in New York of legalized, socially approved discrimination. More generalized anxieties about blacks quickly became involved in the struggle over it. Because the issue was also a legal one, it had to be approached primarily through the political system, and so the political parties became involved in the struggle.

By the 1830s parties had clearly emerged as important and powerful institutions. Ordinary citizens looked to them as spokesmen for their basic needs and concerns. Parties also acted to explain and interpret the sometimes strange and perplexing political world to their constituents. Apparently they filled an important need, for they won from the public almost incredible loyalty and devotion. One scholar has observed of this period, "Men proudly carried party labels and loyalties to the edge of the grave. Party regularity was a virtue, straight ticket voting was the political duty of every good man, and switching from party to party was condemned as a vice."[74]

Parties, therefore, faced almost immediately the problem of responding to the suffrage question. In doing so, however, they had to take into account their own institutional needs as well as the state of public opinion. Party strength in New York throughout this period was closely balanced, and winning elections depended on maintaining the solidarity of party coalitions. Issues had to be viewed in this light, and so the resolution of the black suffrage question was further complicated.

Thus New York in the mid-nineteenth century partook of the tradition of discrimination against blacks which dated back to the nation's founding. But it also had its share of those who wished to break tradition, to push back the barriers to black advancement. New York's property qualification for black voters became the focal point of this conflict. The ensuing struggle would test the effects of social, cultural, and economic differences on the community's ability to modify its racial patterns. It would also provide a direct challenge to the era's politicians to control the emerging conflict without being overwhelmed by it.

74. William Nisbet Chambers and Walter Dean Burnham, eds., *The American Party Systems* (New York: Oxford University Press, 1967), pp. 11–14, 90–116. The quotation is from p. 13.

CHAPTER TWO

Equal Rights and
the Second Party System

Scarcely a generation passed between New York's restriction of black voting rights and the first attempts to reverse that decision. Those years were important ones, however, for reshaping the political arena in which the new struggle for equal rights would be fought. Disciplined, well-developed political parties replaced the loose-knit factions of 1821. Interest in politics reached phenomenal levels as the suffrage was broadened, communications improved, and the state's rapid economic expansion and population growth aroused new concern about governmental policies at all levels. Whig and Democratic parties dominated the political landscape of this "second party system," drawing about them loyal and enthusiastic supporters who saw in them an answer to their new needs.[1]

The issue of black rights threatened this new partisan arrangement. It polarized the electorate, but not along already established party lines. The blacks rights issue was, like slavery nationally, a dangerous challenge. To make a mistake on it could cost a party political control of the state. But to use the issue shrewdly might well weaken a party's opponents without endangering its own position. Thus political concerns were destined to shape the struggle for equal suffrage in the 1840s.

1. Lee Benson, *The Concept of Jacksonian Democracy: New York as a Test Case* (Princeton: Princeton University Press, 1961) gives an excellent account of the rise of the second party system in the state.

The opportunity to revise the property qualification came with the calling of a new constitutional convention in 1846. The 1821 document was now sadly dated, and a variety of groups wished its overhaul. Many Whigs wanted to decrease the number of state officers appointed by the governor. Although support for the political parties was fairly evenly divided, the Whigs had elected a governor only twice in their history. They also felt they would be more competitive in legislative races if members could be elected from single-member districts rather than multiple-member districts, which could be easily gerrymandered by the Democrats.

Others were also dissatisfied with the constitution. The radical Democrats, or "Barnburners," who opposed heavy state spending for internal improvements, were eager to place a limit on the state debt. Tenant farmers on the ancient manorial estates of eastern New York, who had already resorted to violence to prevent the collection of long overdue back rents, wanted a review of the entire land lease-hold system. Some felt too that a new constitution would be better able to handle the problems of canals, banks, and corporations so important for the economic development of the state.[2]

The cumbersomeness of the amendment procedure under the old constitution made a new convention practically a prerequisite for significant changes to occur. Yet there was no constitutional provision for calling a new convention. In addition, many conservative Democrats (the "Hunkers") who were cool to many of the proposed reforms opposed tinkering with the constitution except by the arduous amendment route and used their strength in the legislature to prevent action on convention bills. In 1845, however, the Whigs in the Assembly under the astute leadership of John Young took advantage of the temporary absence of a number of the conservative Democrats to force a convention bill to be reported out of committee. With the help of radical Democrats the bill passed. The conservatives tried hard to tack on crippling amendments requiring a majority vote of the people (based upon the high turnout in the presidential election in 1844) to approve the holding of the convention. They also demanded separate submission to the people of all

2. For a contemporary account of the events surrounding the calling of the convention see Jabez D. Hammond, *Political History of the State of New York* (Syracuse: L. W. Hall, 1848) 3:chapter 18. See also Lloyd Ray Gunn, "The Decline of Authority: Public Policy in New York, 1837–1860" (Ph.D. diss., Rutgers University, 1975), a sophisticated analysis relating the convention to the modernization process in New York.

amendments that the new convention might propose.[3] Although failing in this, they provided their party with a rationale for proposing separate submission whenever members faced a controversial issue in the subsequent delegate election and convention.

Pressure to include black suffrage as one of the convention's reforms came primarily from black and abolitionist organizations. Coincident with the decision of a Pennsylvania constitutional convention in 1837 to disfranchise all black citizens, New York blacks stepped up their efforts to assure their own rights. In August 1837, Henry Highland Garnet, Charles Reason, and George Downing, all noted black leaders, launched a petition drive in support of full black suffrage. In the following year a New York City suffrage association was formed, and two years later a state convention attended by as many as 140 delegates was held in Troy.[4] The strategy was to organize all blacks throughout the state, coordinate a systematic petitioning campaign to show the intense interest of blacks in the suffrage, provide information to political leaders through lobbying efforts in Albany, and similarly educate the public through published appeals. Between 1837 and 1842 the legislature received equal suffrage petitions from blacks in New York, Albany, Oneida, Dutchess, Erie, Onondaga, Schenectady, Orange, Queens, and Rensselaer counties among others.[5] Garnet appeared as a lobbyist before the Assembly's Judiciary Committee in 1841.[6]

Abolitionist organizations were also active. With the decline of colonization and the rise of immediatism in the antislavery movement, abolitionists began to use activist tactics. They deluged Congress with petitions for immediate abolition and overwhelmed the state legislature with demands that it grant fugitive slaves a trial, revoke the law permitting slaves to be brought into the state for

3. Hammond, *Political History*, chapter 18; Herbert D. A. Donovan, *The Barnburners: A Study of the Internal Movements in the Political History of New York State and the Resulting Changes in Political Affiliation, 1830–1852* (New York: New York University Press, 1925), pp. 68–69.

4. Jane H. Pease and William H. Pease, *They Who Would Be Free: Blacks' Search for Freedom, 1830–1861* (New York: Atheneum, 1974), pp. 174–76, 182; Philip S. Foner and George E. Walker, eds., *Proceedings of the Black State Conventions, 1840–1865* (Philadelphia: Temple University Press, 1979-), 1:2.

5. New York Assembly, *Journal*, 60th Sess., 1837, p. 416; 64th Sess., 1841, pp. 195, 208, 234, 307, 446; 65th Sess., 1842, p. 648; Rhoda Golden Freeman, "The Free Negro in New York City in the Era before the Civil War" (Ph.D. diss., Columbia University, 1966), pp. 128, 134–36.

6. George Walker, "The Afro-American in New York City, 1827–1860" (Ph.D. diss., Columbia University, 1975), p. 175.

ninety days, and remove the property qualification for black voters. In 1838, probably not the peak year for petitions, the Judiciary Committee reported that it had received petitions for equal suffrage signed by 9,300 persons and three years later concluded, "public sentiment in all quarters, is strongly indicated in its [a suffrage amendment's] favor."[7] In 1838 abolitionists took another step, querying candidates for state office on their views on equal suffrage and threatening to boycott those who were opposed to it. When this tactic proved unsatisfactory, some abolitionists moved on in 1840 to form their own political party, the Liberty Party, which also backed equal suffrage. Thus at the time of the convention there were insistent pressure groups supporting suffrage reform.

Suffrage activists posed a dilemma for major-party politicians. Politically, blacks had little to offer. Only a thousand were eligible to vote, and these were divided between those who preferred the principles of the Liberty Party and those pragmatists who believed only major-party candidates could win.[8] In addition prejudiced voters would presumably oppose attempts to advance blacks. The Liberty men, however, were a somewhat different story. They too were few in number. Their party reached its highest total vote at 16,097 in 1843, its highest percentage of the total at 4.7 per cent in 1845.[9] But those few votes could act as a balance of power in a closely divided state like New York. Rightly or wrongly, some politicians believed that the Liberty Party's presidential candidate in 1844 had cost Henry Clay the election by permitting James K. Polk to carry New York.[10] The dedication of Liberty men to their cause and their ability to appeal to a concerned minority in a closely divided state meant that both the Liberty Party and the issues it held dear could never be ignored.

Liberty men differed on how to take advantage of their unusual position. Their dilemma became more acute as the prospect of actually changing the constitution's suffrage provisions loomed nearer. Some liked the idea of being a swing faction compelling major-party politicians to accede to their demands. Since their party was obviously too weak to elect its own delegates to the convention, it made

---

7. New York State Assembly, *Journal*, 61st Sess., 1838, p. 1101; New York State Assembly, *Documents*, 64th Sess., 1841, No. 183, p. 4.

8. *Census of the State of New York for 1845* (Albany: Carroll and Cook, 1846); Foner and Walker, *Proceedings*, 1:7, 32, 39.

9. Benson, *Concept*, p. 135.

10. *New York Tribune*, Dec. 24, 1844; *Albany Argus*, Nov. 23, 1844.

sense to endorse major-party candidates who were willing to support equal suffrage.[11]

Other Liberty men, however, saw themselves as first and foremost moral reformers. Believing absolutely that slavery and discrimination were immoral, they refused to admit the legitimacy of the two major "slaveholding" parties or to cooperate with them in any way. Gerrit Smith, philanthropist, wealthy landowner, and founding father of the Liberty Party, led the forces opposed to cooperation.[12] At a party convention in Winfield in Herkimer County (which officially approved his position) and in several public statements, he argued that for abolitionist goals to be achieved, the principles on which they were based had to be accepted unconditionally. To vote for a member of a party that accepted slavery just because he favored equal suffrage was to act out of expediency, not principle. Indeed, even if blacks should obtain the right to vote, he cynically observed, most would enroll in "proslavery" (that is, nonabolitionist) parties "ready, in the selfishness of their hearts, and in the ignorance of the character and duties of Civil Government, to vote for slavery." Thus the antislavery ideal would be no nearer fruition.[13] A good end could not be achieved through improper means.

The indecision within the Liberty Party provided an opening for its opponents. Through the use of the suffrage issue Liberty voters might be weaned away from their party and that party's spoiler role eliminated once and for all. Such considerations shaped the strategies of the major parties on the suffrage question before the selection of convention delegates on April 28, 1846.

Caution was required since within each party neither the leadership nor the constituents were entirely united on the propriety of equal suffrage. A group of New York blacks who surveyed the situation in 1845 admitted that the reform was definitely not "popular with all parties." It was "clear" that "no very considerable portion" of the Democrats supported it and a "certainty" that some Whigs opposed it.[14] Still, of the two parties, the Whigs had the closest ties

11. George W. Allen to Gerrit Smith, Sept. 8, 1845; Silas Hawley, Jr. to Smith, Dec. 17, 1845; Edward Chase to Smith, Jan. 13, 1846, Gerrit Smith Collection, George Arents Research Library for Special Collections at Syracuse University, Syracuse, N.Y.

12. Lawrence J. Friedman, "The Gerrit Smith Circle: Abolitionism in the Burned-Over District," *Civil War History,* 26 (Mar. 1980), 18–38, describes the distinctive position of the Smith group in the antislavery movement.

13. Hammond, *Political History,* 3:688; Gerrit Smith, "Reply to the Colored Citizens of Albany," printed letter, Mar. 13, 1846.

14. Ransom F. Wake et al., to Gerrit Smith, June 13, 1845, Smith Papers.

to Liberty voters. Many Liberty men in New York had formerly been Whigs and that party's tendency to favor positive state action to correct society's ills had long appealed to some reformers. Liberty men themselves seemed to have a greater trust in the prosuffrage protestations of the Whigs.[15]

Indeed some Whigs had already given proof of their interest in equal suffrage. In 1837 an overwhelmingly Democratic Assembly had rejected two petitions in favor of equal suffrage by votes of 74–23 and 71–23 and upheld a Judiciary Committee decision 109–11 to deny the equal suffrage requests in another set of petitions.[16] Over eighty per cent (84.8%) of the Whigs voted at least once in favor of the petitioners compared to only 2.1 per cent of the Democrats. Over half (53.6 per cent) of the prosuffrage Whigs reversed themselves on one or more votes, however. In 1838 when the abolitionists interrogated political candidates, Luther Bradish, the Whig choice for lieutenant governor, supported the abolitionists wholeheartedly, while William H. Seward, a Whig running for governor, though equivocating and ultimately opposing equal suffrage, had at least not openly insulted the reformers as William Marcy, his Democratic counterpart, had done.[17] Later, as governor, Seward in his annual message to the legislature in 1841 referred to the property qualification as "arbitrary" and "incongruous with all our institutions." Whigs controlled the legislature, and the Assembly Judiciary Committee actually reported out a resolution to amend the constitution to permit equal suffrage. Despite their partisan majority, however, the Whigs never voted to consider this report.[18] Some Whig politicians also observed the black state convention in 1840, and William Seward wrote in a letter to another such assemblage in 1845, "I look impatiently for the restoration of your right of suffrage."[19]

Many of the prosuffrage Whig leaders apparently believed along with the abolitionists that blacks ought to be given the same oppor-

15. Benson, *Concept,* pp. 134, 198–208; George W. Allen to Smith, Sept. 8, 1843, Smith Papers.

16. New York State Assembly, *Journal,* 60th Sess., 1837, pp. 210, 417, 1232.

17. Franklin [pseud.], *An Examination of Mr. Bradish's Answer to the Interrogations Presented to Him by a Committee of the State Anti-Slavery Society, October 1, 1838* (Albany: Hoffman & White, 1838); George E. Baker, ed., *The Works of William H. Seward* (Boston: Houghton, Mifflin and Co., 1884), 3:428–29; Dwight Lowell Dumond, *Antislavery: The Crusade for Freedom in America* (New York: W. W. Norton, 1961), p. 292.

18. New York State Assembly, *Journal,* 64th Sess., 1841, pp. 118, 541, 859, 863, 877, 1051.

19. Foner and Walker, *Proceedings,* 1:6, 38.

tunity as other men to participate in politics, and they saw the property qualification as both immoral and a violation of natural rights. Yet it also appears that they were sensitive to the political implications of the suffrage question. According to his foremost biographer, Seward hoped to bring antislavery and perhaps black voters to the Whig Party.[20] A number of Whig papers, led by Horace Greeley's *New York Tribune* and Thurlow Weed's *Albany Evening Journal*, campaigned for equal suffrage throughout the delegate election. They primarily stressed the need for Liberty men to support Whig candidates, however. Gerrit Smith's opponents in the Liberty Party were widely quoted to demonstrate that Liberty leaders themselves saw the need to vote Whig.[21] Liberty men were reminded that if they wasted their votes on their own candidates, blacks would not be enfranchised, but if they voted for Whig delegates, the opposite would be true.[22] Basic to this argument was the proposition that Democrats would not or could not support black suffrage. To prove the point, Whig editors reprinted antisuffrage editorials appearing in Democratic newspapers. A delegate to the 1821 convention was called on to remind readers that Democrats had opposed suffrage at that time while the Clintonians (future Whigs) had supported it.[23] In a letter to a fellow Whig, Greeley predicted, "The Birneyites [Liberty men] will mostly vote with us unless the Locos [Democrats] make them believe that *they* too are for Black Suffrage which they threaten to do. . . . We are full of hope, however."[24] Yet only in private did he mention that even if Whigs triumphed, equal suffrage was "pretty sure to lose" at the convention.[25]

The Liberty Party strategy was also a source of danger to the Whigs. To woo members of a party who were responsible for the defeat of Whig hero Henry Clay in 1844 seemed outrageous to many loyal Whigs. In Oneida County party supporters from several towns met to declare their opposition to equal suffrage and express their disapproval of Whig journals that ignored the "true feelings" of Whigs and courted abolitionists with promises of black suffrage.[26]

---

20. Glyndon G. Van Deusen, *William Henry Seward* (New York: Oxford University Press, 1967), pp. 51, 94.

21. *Albany Evening Journal*, Feb. 16, 1846.

22. *Jamestown Journal*, Apr. 17, 1846; *New York Tribune*, Feb. 17, 1846.

23. *Yates County Whig*, Mar. 17, 1846; *Utica Daily Gazette*, Mar. 27, 1846.

24. Horace Greeley to Schuyler Colfax, Jan. 22, 1846, Horace Greeley Papers, New York Public Library, New York City.

25. Greeley to Colfax, Apr. 22, 1846, Greeley Papers.

26. *Utica Daily Gazette*, Apr. 11, 1846.

New York City Whigs in 1845 rebuffed Greeley's efforts to insert a prosuffrage plank in the local Whig platform.[27] Other Whig county conventions also pointedly ignored equal suffrage. This indifference or opposition to equal suffrage was largely centered in counties where the Liberty Party was weak or nonexistent and blacks unpopular. Significantly, when a Whig paper in conservative Dutchess County did endorse equal suffrage, it did so without mentioning race. It merely called for "equal rights and equal privileges to all classes of citizens, and the abolition of all property qualifications for office holding or electors."[28] In Liberty Party areas Whigs ignored this discontent. "No Whig County Convention has been held without an emphatic and unconditional declaration against the property qualification," claimed one paper.[29]

The success of the Whig strategy was mixed. Although the Liberty Party vote was reduced in the delegate election, even Greeley had to admit that "Whigs lost several delegates because of the Nigger yell."[30] However, since the Whigs had won only fifty of one hundred twenty-eight delegates anyway, he argued that the issue had not been decisive. As planned, the Whig strategy identified the party with black rights, but it had also demonstrated that such a course was potentially dangerous.

That there was genuinely less sentiment in favor of black suffrage among Democratic leaders did not prevent some of them from attempting to counteract the Whig efforts to gain Liberty votes. In areas where antislavery feeling was common, the party often took a stand in favor of equal suffrage. For example, in Clinton County in the Adirondacks bordering Vermont, a "True Democrat" wrote, "As to abolishing the property qualification, of negroes, to entitle them to vote—that is the first lesson in democracy, and we, in this section, *all* go for it" (emphasis added).[31] In this way the Liberty vote could at least be split. Lemuel Stetson, the Democratic candidate for convention delegate in Clinton County, openly espoused black voting

27. *New York Tribune*, Oct. 30, 1845.
28. *Poughkeepsie Journal and Eagle*, Apr. 11, 1846.
29. *Rochester Daily American*, Apr. 1, 1846.
30. *New York Tribune*, June 2, 1846. In five of the fourteen counties in which Greeley thought the Liberty Party held the balance of power, Liberty men did not offer a separate slate. Still, Whigs won only one-third of the delegates in these counties. (The Anti-Rent agitation over the land leasehold system also affected voting.) The Liberty Party was wounded, however. Even in Madison County, Gerrit Smith's home, their vote declined to one-quarter of its level six months before. (Returns are from newspaper reports.)
31. *Plattsburgh Republican*, Feb. 21, 1846.

rights, which greatly angered the local Whigs.[32] In Cortland County not only did the Democratic convention pass a resolution supporting the abolition of the property qualification, but the local Democratic paper stressed that Democratic principles were the "only ones" that could be relied upon in carrying out suffrage reform. It even suggested that Whigs were "secretly hostile to giving the right of suffrage to the colored population of this state."[33] At least some of the Democratic candidates in four other counties were thought to be pledged to equal suffrage.[34]

In many other counties, however, the Democrats were silent or (unlike the Whigs) vociferously opposed to equal suffrage or indeed *any* black voting. They assumed, correctly it appears, that more voters could be won through racism than through appeals to humanitarian sentiments. The Democrats of Suffolk County were willing to let blacks who already voted continue but "unqualifiedly opposed" any extension. New York City Democrats declared that they disapproved of blacks voting with or without a property qualification. Brooklyn Democrats took much the same view.[35] The greater agreement among Democrats probably reflects their traditional strength among groups hostile to both blacks and reform.[36]

Although the taking of contradictory stands in different geographical areas seems to have been a characteristic of parties during the second party system, it was always a dangerous tactic.[37] Democrats helped resolve their dilemma by supporting the idea of separate submission for each part of the new constitution first suggested by the Hunker faction. Thus suffrage would be left to the "will of the people" and politicians would be absolved from blame for either its victory or defeat. The editor of the Democratic *Rochester Daily Advertiser* first pointed out the appropriateness of separate submis-

32. Ibid., Apr. 18, 25, 1846.
33. *Cortland Democrat*, Feb. 25, Apr. 22, 1846.
34. *Auburn Journal* cited in *Utica Daily Gazette*, Apr. 28, 1846. The other counties were Madison, Onondaga, Chautauqua, and Tompkins. The paper probably was in error concerning the Tompkins delegate.

35. *Long Islander* (Huntington), Mar. 20, 1846; *New York Herald*, Apr. 25, 1846; *Brooklyn Eagle*, Apr. 17, 1846.

36. Benson, *Concept*, pp. 301–304. For a history of the Democrats' opposition to black suffrage see Dixon Ryan Fox, "The Negro Vote in Old New York," *Political Science Quarterly*, 32 (June 1917), 252–75. This article does contain errors and should be read in conjunction with John L. Stanley, "Majority Tyranny in Tocqueville's America: The Failure of Negro Suffrage in 1846," *Political Science Quarterly*, 84 (Sept. 1969), 412–35.

37. Michael F. Holt, *The Political Crisis of the 1850s* (New York: John Wiley & Sons, 1978), p. 38.

sion of the suffrage issue, and a number of Democratic newspapers in counties where differences existed on the suffrage question readily endorsed the idea. Tompkins County Democrats specifically declared their desire to see black suffrage submitted separately.[38] Greeley cynically observed:

> Wherever in our state there is no pervading anti-slavery sentiment, there the loco-focos are red-mouthed and vociferous against black suffrage at all hazards. Hostility to "niggers" is their greeting card, by which they hope to carry the delegates in the city and all close river counties. But west of Albany, where there are a good many thorough anti-slavery men, enough to hold the balance of power in several important counties, they endeavor to blank the suffrage question by going for "separate submission." . . . [In] one case as in the other . . . They mean to deprive those colored men who are now entitled to vote of the right of suffrage. But they say, "if we come out for what we mean in Oneida, Jefferson, Oswego, Onondaga, Cortland, Tompkins, &c &c, the men of Liberty voting will cut loose from their reckless leaders and support the Whig candidates, who are known to be advocates of Equal Suffrage and we shall lose the convention."[39]

Yet in Oneida County, where Whigs had protested the suffrage stand of some of their leaders, the local Whig papers also favored separate submission, and indeed research in numerous local papers reveals only one Whig meeting—a citizens' committee in Oswego—that specifically opposed separate submission.[40]

The behavior of the convention delegates sheds further light on partisan assessments of the race issue. The convention, which met on June 1, 1846, was easily organized by the Democrats, who held a 78 to 53 advantage in seats.[41] On July 15, the committee on the elective franchise reported an article limiting the suffrage to white male citizens. One of the Democratic members later explained that the majority had felt that a property qualification was an anomaly in a democratic age, but since blacks could not be fit voters, they ought to be excluded entirely. The committee was willing to submit black suffrage to a vote of the people, however.[42] One of the strongest

38. *Rochester Daily Advertiser,* Feb. 23, 1846; *Ithaca Journal,* Apr. 8, 1846.
39. *New York Weekly Tribune,* Apr. 8, 1846.
40. *Utica Daily Gazette,* Apr. 11, 1846; *Albany Evening Journal,* Apr. 16, 1846.
41. James Powers of Greene and William Maxwell of Chemung, although Democrats, were elected with the help of Whigs. Eleven men (three Democrats and eight Whigs) were chosen on Anti-Rent tickets.
42. S. Croswell and R. Sutton, *Debates and Proceedings in the New York State Convention for the Revision of the Constitution* (Albany: Albany Argus, 1846), pp. 246, 783.

arguments of the prosuffrage forces before the convention had been the undemocratic nature of the property qualification. (Voters had overwhelmingly defeated a property qualification for office-holding in 1845 by a thirty-to-one margin.) Now, ironically, the removal of a property qualification threatened to disfranchise all blacks.

Debate on the controversial suffrage article was delayed until October, barely a month before the document was due for submission to the electorate. The proposal of the suffrage committee that whites alone should vote prompted four major votes on the topic of black voting rights on the convention floor. In the first, a motion to strike the word "white" from the proposed suffrage article (thus removing any distinction between black and white voters) was soundly defeated 37–63. Next some delegates suggested restoring the old property qualification so that some blacks, at least, might continue to vote. Before this could be voted on, an amendment to lower the qualification to $100, thus permitting a larger number of blacks to vote, was narrowly defeated 42–50. In the third vote, the old qualification was adopted 62–32. Finally, near the end of the convention, a Democrat who had been absent the day of the earlier votes brought on a fourth vote by proposing that the property qualification be removed so that no distinction would be made between white and black voters. This motion was defeated, 29–75.[43] The final result was that there was no change. Blacks, unlike their white neighbors, would still have to meet a property qualification in order to vote.

When arranged, not chronologically but according to the amount of support they received, these four votes reveal the spectrum of views on black suffrage within the convention. The motion that won the least support was the last. Relatively little sentiment in favor of unrestricted black suffrage existed, and once the convention had declared itself for the property qualification, even some original supporters of equal suffrage saw no reason to challenge the consensus. Starting with this vote one can order the other votes according to their relative popularity with the delegates. This arrangement of votes is called a Guttman scale and may be used to identify blocs of delegates who consistently voted on the side in each vote that would have enlarged the black electorate, who consistently voted on the

43. Croswell and Sutton, *Debates and Proceedings*, pp. 783, 790, 791, 820. The third vote was recorded as 63–32, but only 62 names were listed in favor. Similarly, the last vote was given as 28–75, but 29 names were listed as favoring the resolution.

side restricting black voting, or who fell somewhere in between. Five groups of delegates (whose votes are said to form a "scale type") emerge from the four suffrage votes. Scale type 0 is made up of those who always voted on the side that would have permitted more blacks to vote. Next (scale type 1) come those who voted on the blacks' side up until a consensus against suffrage had been achieved in the convention; they opposed the motion to reject the property qualifcation made at the end of the convention. Scale type 2 includes those who opposed voting equality between the races but would go so far as to permit blacks with a property qualification of either $100 or $250 to vote, while those in scale type 3 would not budge beyond the current $250 qualification. Those in scale type 4 voted against enlarging the black electorate whenever the opportunity arose.[44] Thus those in scale types 0 to 2 showed at least some interest in permitting more blacks to vote; those in the final scale types (3 and 4) did not. The identification of these voting blocs enables one to examine their composition and observe the possible effects of party affiliation and constituency opinion on the willingness of politicians to support black voting rights.

Table 2.1 reveals that there were dramatic differences between the parties in the voting on the suffrage proposals. (Thirty-six delegates absent on two or more roll calls are not scaled; they are listed in Appendix A.) Eighty per cent of the Democrats who were placed in the scale wanted either no change in the property qualification or a complete disfranchisement of blacks (scale types 3 and 4); ninety per cent of the Whigs who were scaled fell into scale types 0, 1, and 2, indicating a preference for some sort of liberalization, whether a lower property qualification (ten per cent) or equal suffrage (eighty per cent). Still, only slightly more than half the Whigs went so far as to support the problack position on every vote. (That is, they continued to support equal suffrage even after the majority in the convention had chosen to retain the property qualification.) The franchise committee had accurately expressed the views of the convention in calling the property qualification an anomaly. A majority in each party opposed it. Yet since their solutions were diametrically opposed (total exclusion versus total inclusion), the stage was set for compromise on the old suffrage provision for blacks.

Were apparent partisan differences really a function of greater

44. On Guttman scaling see Lee F. Anderson et al., *Legislative Roll-Call Analysis* (Evanston, Ill.: Northwestern University Press, 1966), chapter 6. Details of the suffrage scale are given in Appendix A.

TABLE 2.1.

Party division of delegate votes on black suffrage in
the 1846 convention

Scale type[a]	Whigs		Democrats	
	Number	Per cent	Number	Per cent
0	21	52	3	5
1	11	28	1	2
2	4	10	7	13
3	4	10	14	26
4	0	0	29	54
Total	40	100	54	100

$\chi^2 = 57.5$ for 4. d.f. Significant at .001.
[a]Scale type 0 is most favorable, 4 least favorable to
black voting. (See page 54.)

sympathy toward black suffrage among the constituents of Whigs
than among those of Democrats?[45] Very few delegates came from
counties where equal suffrage triumphed in the November referendum authorized by the convention. But if one reclassifies the
delegates into those who represented counties in which in the fall
thirty-five per cent or more voted prosuffrage and those in which
less than thirty-five per cent voted prosuffrage, it appears that
ninety-one per cent of the men representing relative "prosuffrage"
counties on the four votes favored some increase in the number of
black voters, while seventy-two per cent of the "antisuffrage" representatives wanted to keep their numbers constant or decrease
them.[46] (See Table 2.2.) If one looks at such prosuffrage and antisuffrage areas separately, however, as in Table 2.3, a partisan effect
is still visible although less pronounced. Thus while neither measure
alone is entirely adequate, party and area taken together do seem to
"explain" a large number of votes.[47] Of the individuals in scale types
zero and one, for instance, only two were neither Whigs nor from

45. John Langley Stanley, "Majority Tyranny in Tocqueville's America: The Failure
of Negro Suffrage in New York State in 1846" (Ph.D. diss., Cornell University, 1966),
pp. 132ff.
46. Thirty-five per cent is, of course, an arbitrary figure, and its lowness may cause
the case for a constituency effect to be overstated. Nevertheless, a minority of thirty-
five per cent, if disproportionately in one party, might make a delegate feel that a
majority of *his* supporters wanted equal suffrage.
47. If one looks at the parties separately, a prosuffrage/antisuffrage variation is still
visible. It is not as pronounced as the party variation in Table 2.3.

TABLE 2.2.

Constituency division of delegate votes on black
suffrage in the 1846 convention

Scale type[a]	Prosuffrage[b]		Antisuffrage[c]	
	Number	Per cent	Number	Per cent
0	16	49	8	13
1	11	33	1	2
2	3	9	8	13
3	2	6	16	26
4	1	3	28	46
Total	33	100	61	100

$\chi^2 = 47$ for 4 d.f. Significant at .001.

[a]Scale type 0 is most favorable, 4 least favorable to black voting. (See page 54.)

[b]"Prosuffrage" here means more than 35 per cent favoring black voting.

[c]"Antisuffrage" here means less than 35 per cent favoring black suffrage.

TABLE 2.3.

Party division of delegate votes from prosuffrage and antisuffrage areas in the 1846 convention

Scale type[a]	Prosuffrage[b]				Antisuffrage[c]			
	Whigs		Democrats		Whigs		Democrats	
	Number	Per cent	Number	Per cent	Number	Per cent	Number	Per cent
0	15	58	1	14	6	43	2	4
1	10	38	1	14	1	7	0	0
2	1	4	2	29	3	21	5	11
3	0	0	2	29	4	29	12	25
4	0	0	1	14	0	0	28	60
Total	26	100	7	100	14	100	47	100

For prosuffrage areas, $\chi^2 = 16.2$ for 4 d.f. Significant at .01. For antisuffrage areas, $\chi^2 = 25.2$ for 4 d.f. Significant at .001.

[a]Scale type 0 is most favorable, 4 least favorable to black voting. (See page 54.)

[b]"Prosuffrage" here means more than 35 per cent favoring black voting.

[c]"Antisuffrage" here means less than 35 per cent favoring black voting.

"prosuffrage" counties; of those in scale types three and four, *all* were either Democrats or from "antisuffrage" areas.

When partisan and constituency interests conflicted, absenting oneself was one way to resolve the dilemma.[48] Although undoubtedly some of the men who missed half or more of the suffrage roll calls were not intentionally absent, eight of ten Whig and six of twenty-four Democratic absentees did come from areas where popular views on equal suffrage were different from those held by a majority of the delegate's party at the convention. Thus while most Whig delegates favored increased black voting and most Democratic ones did not, some took note of apparent public opinion and either abstained or voted with the majority of the opposing party. Only a few were as courageous as the Whig Isaac Burr of Delaware County, who forthrightly defended equal suffrage although he knew his constituents opposed it.[49] Relatively more Whigs than Democrats seem to have felt conflicting partisan and constituency pressures, however.

How can one explain the actions of the Whig and Democratic leaders? Certainly many were very pragmatic in their behavior. As the analysis of the delegate election has shown, the amount of stress the suffrage issue received and even the position taken on it were often related to practical political considerations. Thus both parties in counties with Liberty Party voters had vied for the support of the abolitionists while qualifying their suffrage stands elsewhere. At the convention, too, delegates were sensitive to both party and constituency needs. Both parties seemed troubled by their lack of unity on black suffrage and, as a precaution, agreed by a bipartisan vote at the convention's close to submit the property qualification directly to the state's voters in a referendum, thus relieving themselves of final responsibility for its fate.[50] Politicians simply put politics first; they treated the race issue cautiously as befitted its explosive nature. Pragmatism, of course, did not preclude complete sincerity on the suffrage question. It was possible to support the concept of equal rights without placing it in the foremost position in one's hierarchy of values. The well-being of the party was simply most important to many politicians, and no action could be taken without regard to it.

48. See also Stanley, "Majority Tyranny" (Ph.D. diss.), p. 131.
49. William G. Bishop and William H. Attree, *Report of the Debates and Proceedings of the Convention for the Revision of the Constitution of the State of New York 1846* (Albany: Evening Atlas, 1846), p. 1014.
50. Croswell and Sutton, *Debates and Proceedings*, p. 836.

Arguments advanced in debate and in the press reveal individual perceptions of the race problem as well as how opinion on it might be most easily swayed. Equal rights enthusiasts normally chose a humanitarian stance stressing the innate justice and morality of their position. The property qualification was antirepublican and a contradiction of the principles in the Declaration of Independence. It did not harmonize "with the genius of our institutions, or with the spirit of the age."[51] The people's sense of "justice and magnanimity" was invoked to "say whether the bar which, without any fault of their own, rests upon and depresses a portion of their fellow beings shall be removed."[52] It was white oppression that was responsible for the blacks' apparent degraded state.[53] Horace Greeley summed it up: "On the one side stand Equality, Reason, Justice, Democracy, Humanity; on the other are a base, slavery engendered prejudice and a blackguard clamor against 'Niggers.'"[54]

At times, however, concern for "principle" seemed to outweigh concern for the black man himself. One Whig declared, "The interest . . . of the colored people themselves, is comparatively of minor consequence. It is all important that we [whites] should do right. . . ."[55] Greeley himself disclaimed any "peculiar friendship" for blacks and informed his readers:

> Reared in utter ignorance of that Race, we were measurably imbued with the common prejudices against or aversion to them, which experience and reflection have but slowly removed. So far as we have any partialities, they are of course against the African blood and hue. But reared in and devoted to Republican principles, how *can* we say that they should not enjoy the sacred right of Self Government the same as other men?[56]

Such statements indicate how difficult it was for even those whites sympathetic to equal rights to shed their ethnocentrism. They had constantly to reassure themselves and their white followers that they were merely righting a past wrong and nothing more. While such an approach probably helped to minimize antagonism toward them,

51. Bishop and Attree, *Report of Debates*, pp. 1014–15; *Rochester Daily Democrat*, Oct. 14, 1846. Quote is from *Jamestown Journal*, Apr. 3, 1846.
52. *Utica Daily Gazette*, Nov. 3, 1846.
53. Croswell and Sutton, *Debates and Proceedings*, p. 785.
54. *New York Tribune*, Apr. 21, 1846.
55. *Fredonia Censor*, Oct. 27, 1846.
56. *New York Tribune*, July 21, 1846.

it offered few positive attractions except to voters similarly imbued with a sense of *noblesse oblige* toward blacks.

Equal rights advocates did try some tactics designed to win over prejudiced voters. They sometimes equated opponents of equal suffrage with groups likely to be unpopular with the white majority: southerners, slaveholders, and immigrants, for instance. Antisuffrage men were the friends of slavery, the argument went, and they acted at the South's behest.[57] Comparing native blacks to foreign whites, one editor asked, " . . . is it just, is it democratic, to admit the *drunken* white *bondman,* fresh from every foreign *lordling* on the globe, to the right of ruling us, through the ballot box, if we at the same time deny that right to those born free among us and reared in the same cradle of liberty with ourselves?"[58] Thus divisions among the white community served to help the blacks.

Although Whig leaders most commonly supported equal suffrage, party divisions normally prevented them from presenting the issue in a strictly partisan fashion. Many Whig leaders unsympathetic to the cause ignored it completely. Indeed when Greeley criticized some Whigs for not backing equal suffrage in the referendum, a Whig editor sharply rebuked him with the admonition that many "upright, conservative men had opposed the reform."[59]

The most dedicated group supporting equal suffrage proved to be New York's black community. Not only did they actively lobby the convention itself, but they also issued public addresses and letters throughout the referendum campaign to explain why they wanted and needed the franchise.[60] Their arguments closely paralleled those of the white equal suffrage advocates. They were mild in tone, steeped in the rhetoric of the American Revolution, and clearly intended to assuage rather than accentuate white fears. A typical effort published in a western New York newspaper appealed to the generosity of the voters and stressed that blacks had "striven to merit" the franchise, faithfully abiding by the law despite their "oppression by it."[61] Thus the prosuffrage forces, both black and

57. Bishop and Attree, *Report of Debates,* p. 1035; *Jamestown Journal,* Oct. 20, 1846.
58. *Albany Herald* cited in *Newburgh Telegraph,* Oct. 29, 1846. See also *Jamestown Journal,* Oct. 20, 1846.
59. *Jamestown Journal,* Dec. 5, 1846.
60. Croswell and Sutton, *Debates and Proceedings,* p. 783; Freeman, "Free Negro," p. 140.
61. *Fredonia Censor,* Mar. 24, 1846. See also *Rochester Daily Democrat,* Oct. 29, 1846; *Rochester Daily Advertiser,* Mar. 28, 1846; *New York Tribune,* Apr. 28, 1846.

white, were guarded in their attacks on discrimination, relying primarily upon "reason" to persuade people to change their racial views.

By contrast, the antisuffrage forces showed little caution in their tactics and simply employed the common stereotype of the black to condemn equal suffrage. Blacks were inherently different from and inferior to whites, they argued, and therefore did not merit "equal" treatment. One editor put it bluntly: "Negroes are among, but not of us."[62] Where antisuffrage advocates differed was simply in their reasons for believing blacks inferior (the biblical curse, the teachings of science, the statistics of crime and poverty) and their predictions of what would happen should equal suffrage come about (an influx of fugitive slaves and free blacks from the South, black acquisition of the balance of political power in the state, competition between black and white workers, jury and militia service by blacks, and social equality and amalgamation).[63]

Unlike the suffrage advocates, who mainly admonished the voters to do right, the Democrats first created the specter of black power and then offered to protect their constituents from this menace. Workers learned that blacks in other states were only waiting to secure rights in New York to flock to that state where their presence would lower the wage rate and possibly force white laborers to leave.[64] While some Whig leaders had played on their constituents' antiforeign sentiments to win white votes for "native" blacks, the Democrats, who often benefited from Irish and German support, employed the opposite tactic. One Democrat noted that white foreigners "of our own race and kindred" had to wait five years to vote. How foolish it was then, he argued, to give the franchise to blacks who had never been able to sustain democratic political institutions in four thousand years.[65] An Orange County paper told its readers that some young Whigs wanted the "truckling, ignorant and subservient Negro" to vote as an offset to the Irish because they could not "brook" the latter's "manly and honest independence."[66] Democrats also tapped the hatred for the moralistic, evangelical reformers,

62. *Eastern State Register* (White Plains) cited in *Newburgh Telegraph*, Apr. 16, 1846.
63. Bishop and Attree, *Report of Debates*, pp. 1027–29, 1043; *Newburgh Telegraph*, Apr. 9, 1846; *Cayuga Patriot* cited in *Elmira Gazette*, May 19, 1846; *Brooklyn Eagle*, Apr. 17, 1846; *New York Tribune*, Nov. 1, 1845; *New York Herald*, Oct. 17, 1846.
64. Bishop and Attree, *Report of Debates*, p. 1019; *New York Tribune*, Nov. 1, 1845.
65. Bishop and Attree, *Report of Debates*, p. 1018.
66. *Newburgh Telegraph*, May 14, 1846.

whom they characterized as "fanatics" who "would take to their bed and board, the extreme link of humanity, simply because it is the extreme link of humanity." [67]

Thus Democrats, by playing upon basic white fears of blacks, used the race issue to strengthen their hold on foreign born, working class, and antievangelical voters. Although Democrats in prosuffrage areas remained silent, the party as a whole used race in a partisan fashion, openly portraying Whigs as dangerous, fanatical "nigger lovers." Whigs countered this strategy by simply ignoring equal suffrage in areas where it was unpopular, thus making the Democrats' charges that Whigs were rabidly prosuffrage appear ridiculous. The continued factionalism and disorganization within the Liberty ranks even meant that Whig journals that had played hard for Liberty support in the spring could afford to drop the subject in the fall.[68] The late completion of the constitution (less than a month before the election) and the great interest in the gubernatorial race helped the Whigs to divert attention from the race issue.

The voters, recipients of all these arguments concerning the suffrage, had a chance to make their own views known in November when the discriminatory property qualification (along with the constitution) was submitted to the electorate for its approval. The ballot's wording—"Equal Suffrage to Colored Persons?"—to be answered yes or no made it clear that the question involved race. Defeat of the proposition would mean that the property qualification would remain in effect. Although separate submission had been superficially a victory for the prosuffrage forces (it reopened the possibility of full black voting rights), a massive defeat would certainly discredit the equal suffrage movement and, above all, the pesky Liberty Party.[69]

Equal suffrage was overwhelmingly defeated in the election by a vote of 224,336 to 85,406 or a margin of 2.6 to 1. Voter interest was strong. There were only five thousand more votes on the constitu-

---

67. Bishop and Attree, *Report of Debates,* p. 1028. See also *New York Herald,* Mar. 17, 1846.

68. See, for example, the *Rochester Daily American.*

69. Because of the interdependence of its sections, the constitution (with the exception of suffrage) was presented as a unit instead of as separate amendments as some Democrats had originally suggested. The wording of the suffrage ballot was chosen by the select committee arranging the submission and agreed to without comment by the convention. Opposition to the idea of separate submission of black suffrage came from those most opposed to *any* black voting. See Croswell and Sutton, *Debates and Proceedings,* p. 836.

tion (which was adopted) than on the suffrage proposition. Over three-quarters (76.3 per cent) of the people voting for governor participated in the suffrage referendum. The turnout was quite respectable, especially considering that the average participation by those at the polls in nine statewide referenda since 1826 had been only 47.4 per cent.[70] Still, a quarter of those at the polls expressed opinions on neither the constitution nor suffrage, a reminder that some at least apparently were indifferent or unsure about the proposed changes. There was little pattern to the abstentions. Participation, overall, did tend to be slightly higher in strongly antisuffrage areas.[71] This may indicate that a few Democrats in prosuffrage areas, members of a party whose position on suffrage was fairly clear, may have felt conflicting pressures and abstained.

As Figure 2.1 illustrates, support for equal suffrage varied tremendously. In eleven counties, headed by Queens at 97.9 per cent, over nine-tenths of the electorate opposed any increase in the number of black voters; in another ten counties, led by Clinton at 72.8 per cent, a majority of electors favored equal voting privileges. (The actual percentages for each county may be found in Appendix B.) The large majority of the state's population, however, lived in counties that were heavily against equal suffrage. (See Table 2.4.) Indeed 76.3 per cent of the prosuffrage voters were residents of counties where a majority had opposed the reform. A sectional cast to the vote is also apparent. Southeastern New York was more uniformly hostile to black voting than either the northern or western portions of the state.

Voting behavior on the referendum, however, can be more usefully analyzed by looking at units smaller than the rather populous, heterogeneous counties. Returns by township and ward are available for almost sixty per cent of the state's counties (marked on the map) and are used below to give some insight into popular responses to black suffrage.[72]

70. Edgar A. Werner, *Civil List and Constitutional History of the Colony and State of New York* (Albany: Weed, Parsons & Co., 1891), pp. 128–30.

71. The correlation between turnout and per cent prosuffrage was −.32. Of twenty-three towns with more than ninety-five per cent participation in the referendum, all but four voted against equal suffrage, most quite decisively.

72. These counties are listed and compared to the state as a whole on a number of variables in Appendix C. See Appendix D for the sources of these returns and Appendix E for a discussion of methods of analysis. The demographic data for this study came from the *Census of the State of New York for 1845* (Albany: Carroll and Cook, 1846) except as noted.

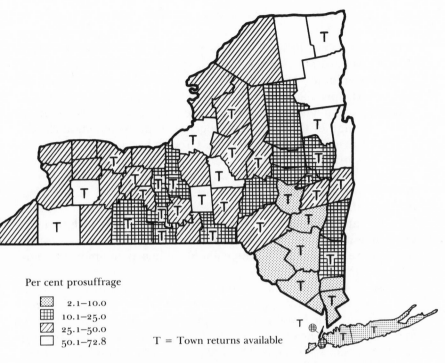

Per cent prosuffrage

▦ 2.1–10.0
⊞ 10.1–25.0
▨ 25.1–50.0
☐ 50.1–72.8   T = Town returns available

FIGURE 2.1. Distribution of the prosuffrage vote, 1846 referendum.

TABLE 2.4.
Prosuffrage voting by counties, 1846 referendum

Per cent prosuffrage	Counties[a]		Per cent of state population
	Number	Per cent	
2.1-10.0	11	18.6	13.0
10.1-20.0	8	13.6	23.9
20.1-30.0	14	23.7	22.4
30.1-40.0	12	20.3	22.7
40.1-50.0	4	6.8	6.4
50.1-60.0	8	13.6	9.4
60.1-70.0	0	0.0	0.0
70.1-72.8	2	3.4	2.2
Total	59	100.0	100.0

[a]Fulton and Hamilton are treated as one county. Townships composing Schuyler (not yet formed) are combined and treated as a county. (See Appendix E.)

Political analysts in 1846 thought primarily in terms of the voters reacting as partisans to black suffrage. Jabez Hammond, the author of a three-volume political history of New York which encompassed this period, speculated in a letter to Gerrit Smith, "If the Whigs as a party, that is if a majority of them vote for it [equal suffrage], there will be enough of the Democrats together with the abolition classes to carry the amendment."[73] Horace Greeley had less confidence in Whig support; he predicted: "We fear the great mass of the swindling pretenders to Democracy will vote to deprive Colored Men of all voice in framing the Laws they are required to obey and levying the taxes they are compelled to pay, and that enough short-sighted, hollow-hearted, expediency-governed Whigs will unite with them to give them a triumph."[74] Still, both Hammond and Greeley anticipated more support for suffrage among Whigs than among Democrats.

If we examine the correlations between the prosuffrage voting and party voting in 1844 (an election that showed normal voting patterns and little factionalism), 1846 (the year of the referendum), and 1848 (the year of the Free Soil revolt), an interesting pattern emerges. (See Table 2.5.) The highest correlations (about .6) occurred between Liberty Party voting in the 1840s and prosuffrage voting. The Free Soil Party, which in 1848 tried to broaden its anti-slavery base by decreasing its emphases upon immediate abolition and racial egalitarianism, also showed a positive association with support for equal suffrage but at a much lower level (.34) than the Liberty Party.[75] The Whigs showed almost no correlation except when combined with the Liberty or Free Soil Parties, while the Democrats correlated negatively (about −.4). A nativist party (strong only in the New York City area) also ran candidates in the 1846 election. It drew its support primarily from former Whigs but was opposed to equal suffrage. When its vote is combined with that of the Democrats, the negative correlation with equal suffrage is greater than for the Democratic Party alone. Stressing the plight of the "native born" blacks had not paid off for the Whigs.

Thus only areas of Liberty Party strength seemed to give relatively consistent support for equal rights. That party appears to have fulfilled its pledge to support the legal equality of the black

73. Jabez D. Hammond to Smith, Oct. 30, 1846, Smith Papers.
74. *New York Tribune*, May 4, 1846.
75. Eric Foner, "Racial Attitudes of the New York Free Soilers," *New York History*, 46 (Oct. 1965), 311–29.

TABLE 2.5.

Correlation between prosuffrage and party voting, 1846
referendum[a]

Year and party	Correlation	Coefficient of variability
1844 Democratic	−.37	4.53
1846 Democratic	−.38	3.62
1846 Democratic/Nativist	−.41	3.57
1848 Democratic	−.40	1.70
1848 Democratic/Free Soil	.03	4.73
1844 Whig	.07	4.11
1844 Whig/Liberty	.36	4.50
1846 Whig	.18	3.80
1846 Whig/Liberty/National Reform[b]	.41	4.02
1848 Whig	−.07	3.91
1848 Whig/Free Soil	.37	5.32
1844 Liberty	.62	.75
1846 Liberty/National Reform	.60	.67
1848 Free Soil	.34	1.72
1848 Free Soil/Liberty	.37	1.72

N = 520.

[a]Town-level data.

[b]Liberty and National Reform Parties supported the same candidate in 1846.

man. Towns where many men were willing to forsake old party ties and vote for a hopelessly small third party advocating reforms that would benefit an outcast group in society were precisely those most likely to support the principle of equal suffrage as well. At best, however, the Liberty vote was only an approximate index of antidiscrimination sentiment. Not all egalitarians were mobilized in the Liberty Party by any means, and the proportion who were varied greatly according to local political circumstances.

Much of the rest of the support for equal suffrage apparently did come from Whigs, although that party was clearly seriously divided on the issue. Indeed the contrast between Whig leaders in the convention and the voters is striking. The Whigs won the gubernatorial race in 1846. Yet even making the assumptions that three-fourths of the Liberty men voted in the referendum (about the normal rate of participation by all voters) and only ninety per cent favored equal suffrage, no more than 38.6 per cent of the Whigs who voted for governor could possibly have favored equal suffrage. Indeed, if one calculates the number of towns in the sample in which the antisuffrage votes were more than fifty per cent higher than the Democratic total (meaning a sizable number of Whigs must have opposed equal suffrage—especially when one considers that not all Democrats probably voted in the referendum), one quarter of all the towns fell into this category. Most were in the Hudson Valley counties that were so heavily opposed to black voting. Still, only six of the thirty-five counties sampled had *no* such towns.[76] Clearly, Whig opposition to equal suffrage was not limited to a single region.

In contrast, in only two per cent of the towns in the sample did the prosuffrage vote exceed the combined Whig and Liberty votes by *any* amount, thereby indicating definite Democratic crossovers. There were four other Democratic towns where prosuffrage obtained a majority (and participation in the referendum was too low to establish certain Democratic support). Nearly all these towns (eighty per cent) were in prosuffrage counties. Half were in Oswego, where abolitionists had mounted an active campaign against the property qualification.[77] Democratic defections may easily have been even greater since not all Whigs and Liberty men participated in the referendum or supported equal suffrage. For instance, William Brown, a black antislavery agent, held a meeting in Warsaw, Wyoming County (a prosuffrage town where Democratic support cannot be definitely established), at which a Democrat seconded a motion for equal suffrage and another Democrat chaired a second prosuffrage gathering shortly thereafter.[78] Still, prosuffrage Democrats were an oddity, and the contrast between the behavior of the Whig and of the Democratic rank and file is notable. Certainly most Democratic voters, like their leaders, seem to have been satisfied with the suffrage status quo.

If voters did not respond entirely to party cues, what other factors affected them? As noted earlier, some whites had reacted strongly to displays of black independence and assertiveness. In contemporary America, too, the presence of a large black population is often associated with white hostility toward moves for equality. Some observers in the 1840s thought they perceived a similar phenomenon. The *Newburgh Telegraph* explained it from the racist viewpoint: "In

76. They were Chemung, Clinton, Cortland, Madison, Oswego, and Yates. Four of these were prosuffrage counties.

77. Charles M. Snyder, "The Antislavery Movement in the Oswego Area," *Oswego County Historical Society Publication*, No. 18 (1955), pp. 5–6.

78. Carter G. Woodson, *The Mind of the Negro as Reflected in Letters Written during the Crisis, 1800–1860* (1926; reprint ed., New York: Russell & Russell, 1969), p. 352.

this region, where we all understand the broad line of demarcation between the African and the white race—where we witness daily the imbecility, vice and degradation of those of 'sable hue'—we think there can be but few who will say that the Negro should be invested with the privileges and the rights of the white man."[79] Others, however, insisted that whites did not need to see blacks physically to recognize their inferiority. At the constitutional convention a delegate declared: "St. Lawrence County has no blacks, and never had a slave. Her citizens abhor slavery, and are in no wise responsible for its existence elsewhere. But they consider it a mock philanthropy, which requires them to share their own dear-bought political privileges with any class of men, who are not intellectually and morally competent to appreciate our institutions, and faithfully sustain them."[80]

Blacks made up only 1.7 per cent of the population of New York State in 1845.[81] That population was largely concentrated, however, in eastern New York, where slavery had once flourished. The highest percentage of blacks in any town was just under twenty per cent (18.7). While the townships with many blacks were solidly opposed to equal suffrage, so were many others with almost none. Thus the correlation between black population and prosuffrage voting is negative but rather low ($-.36$). At the county level the correlation is much higher ($-.6$) reflecting the regional concentration of blacks in an area that opposed suffrage for a variety of reasons.[82] Of the six per cent of the sample towns with black populations of more than six per cent, all were antisuffrage, and all but two gave less than eighteen per cent of their support to suffrage reform. Not one prosuffrage town had a black population of more than four per cent. Yet one-third of all towns with few blacks (two per cent or less) still cast three quarters of their ballots against equal suffrage. Such towns were by no means exclusively in eastern New York. They were in all but four counties with town returns available, including three

79. *Newburgh Telegraph*, Oct. 22, 1846.
80. Bishop and Attree, *Report of Debates*, p. 1019.
81. *Census of 1845*.
82. The area most hostile to blacks appears to have been that which was settled well before the massive migrations from New England after the American Revolution. To test for the independent effect of this region, a dummy variable scoring towns one or zero depending on whether or not they were settled in 1790 was created for the regression analysis. Counties considered settled in 1790 were Albany, Chemung, Columbia, Dutchess, Fulton, Greene, Herkimer, Kings, Montgomery, New York, Orange, Otsego, Putnam, Queens, Rensselaer, Richmond, Rockland, Saratoga, Schenectady, Schoharie, Suffolk, Ulster, Warren, Washington, and Westchester.

of the seven prosuffrage counties surveyed. Thus while the presence of blacks was associated with a willingness to discriminate against them, their absence did not assure liberality. The stereotype of the black pervaded even areas where blacks were virtually unknown.

Factors other than party affiliation and size of black population have also been hypothesized to affect people's reactions towards changes in the black man's status. Ethnic loyalties and cultural orientations are known to have been extremely important during this era, and Ronald P. Formisano has found that in Michigan "racial politics were inseparable from the ethnic and religious politics that so profoundly shaped . . . partisan loyalties."[83] Indeed, race was a natural ethnocultural issue because it dealt with community values (the morality of discrimination) and also with possible threats to the ways of life of various groups. For example, Irishmen might fear the triumph of moralistic do-gooders who would then attack the "evil" Catholic church, while evangelical Protestants might anticipate the wrath of God should they fail to help the oppressed blacks.

It is difficult to isolate groups who shared similar values in the past (especially after years of intermingling), but crude generalizations are possible, and we may note differences in reactions to black suffrage among native New Yorkers and those from other states and nations.

The Dutch, for instance, were among the first white settlers of New York. They were the first slaveholders, and they lived in a society that was hierarchical in most of its social, political, and religious relationships. The Dutch were never known for their egalitarian ethic. Yet William Goodell, traveling through Columbia, Greene, and Westchester counties as an abolitionist organizer in 1834, was pleased to see men of Dutch descent working side by side with blacks in the fields with no visible signs of prejudice.[84] The Dutch population was centered in the eastern part of New York, but since the censuses of this time list place of birth rather than nation of origin, one cannot analyze the prosuffrage vote in terms of the proportion of "Dutch" living in an area. It is possible, though, to get an approximation of Dutch *influence* by looking at towns with Dutch Reformed churches. About twenty-three per cent of the towns avail-

83. Ronald P. Formisano, "The Edge of Caste: Colored Suffrage in Michigan, 1827–1836," *Michigan History*, 56 (Spring 1972), 20.
84. John L. Myers, "The Beginning of Anti-Slavery Agencies in New York State, 1833–1836," *New York History*, 43 (Apr. 1962), 159.

able for study contained such churches, and *all but one* of these towns cast a majority of its votes against equal suffrage.[85] Of the six towns which contained only Dutch Reformed churches, none was more than twelve per cent prosuffrage. All the towns Goodell had visited were over ninety per cent opposed to removing the property qualification. The Dutch may have lived on friendly terms with blacks, but they did not consider blacks political equals.

In stark contrast to the Dutch stood the Yankees. Although some New Englanders had reached the state as early as the seventeenth century, many of New York's Yankees had settled in the state fairly recently. Beginning after the American Revolution, they poured into the western and northern portions of the state. Their frequent quarrels with the native Dutch suggest that the two groups did not see eye to eye on many matters.[86] In New England, in contrast to New Amsterdam, economic, political, and religious institutions had been structured so as to place primary responsibility on the individual for his personal conduct and economic and political well-being. This emphasis on individualism helped foster an egalitarian ethic, for "rank" and "privilege" were the antitheses of individual endeavor. New England had been the first area in the United States to free its slaves, and in 1846 only one New England state (Connecticut) denied blacks the right to vote. Thus a discriminatory property qualification, if portrayed as an unjust imposition on the rights of some individuals and a threat to egalitarian institutions, was peculiarly suited to arouse the ire of this segment of the population. Indeed, the correlation between the percentage born in New England and the percentage voting prosuffrage was .60, one of the highest in the analysis. Almost ninety per cent of the prosuffrage towns had more Yankees than the sample as a whole.

Of course, the criterion of New England *birth* isolates primarily areas of *recent* Yankee settlement. If Lee Benson is correct that almost two-thirds of New York's population was of New England ori-

85. The correlation between per cent prosuffrage and per cent of all churches that were Dutch Reformed is $-.31$ ($r^2 = .10$). The Dutch Reformed church had been the official church of the early Dutch. The church did not actively seek new members among the general population, and although many of Dutch descent probably were no longer associated with it, the churches themselves did draw upon the Dutch segment of the population.

86. See David Maldwyn Ellis, "The Yankee Invasion of New York, 1783–1850," *New York History*, 32 (Jan. 1951), 1–17. The cultural outlooks of Yankees and the non-Yankee population of early New York are discussed in Dixon Ryan Fox, *Yankees and Yorkers* (New York: New York University Press, 1940).

gin in 1844, it is clear that many people of New England descent must have opposed equal suffrage.[87] Long Island, for instance, which was first settled by Connecticut Yankees in the 1640s, was strongly antisuffrage. Thus prosuffrage sentiment was more common in areas where Yankee culture was a relatively fresh import. Significantly, the major area of "new Yankee" settlement, western New York, had recently undergone a series of powerful religious revivals well calculated to reinforce old values and arouse interest in all manner of reforms.[88]

While the Yankees and the Dutch were the principal native groups in New York there were a few others—the descendants of early French, British, and German settlers and more recent migrants from the neighboring states of Pennsylvania and New Jersey. All were minorities in most areas, and impressionistic evidence is necessary both to locate them and evaluate their behavior. Still, the evidence we do have suggests these groups were far closer in their behavior to the Dutch than to the Yankees and again indicates the importance of the western Yankee settlements for the prosuffrage cause. All of the most heavily Palatine (early German) towns (according to Lee Benson's categorization) were more than eighty-five per cent opposed to equal suffrage. The same was true of early British and Huguenot (early French Protestant) towns.[89] Neither Pennsylvania nor New Jersey granted blacks the right to vote, and the settlers from these states seemed not to favor black suffrage. Jersey settlers were most numerous in southeastern New York, the most uniformly antisuffrage area in the state. Pennsylvania settlement was greatest in the Southern Tier, especially in a roughly triangular area extending northward to Seneca and including Yates, Tompkins, Steuben, and Chemung Counties. Figure 2.1 shows a very similar enclave of high antisuffrage voting.[90]

Like the native born, the foreign born were divided on the ques-

---

87. Benson, *Concept*, p. 342. Paul Kleppner, *The Third Electoral System, 1853–1892: Parties, Voters, and Political Cultures* (Chapel Hill: University of North Carolina Press, 1979), pp. 61–2, suggests that Yankees held most firmly to their group loyalties and behavior when they felt they were in conflict with other neighboring groups.

88. See John L. Hammond, *The Politics of Benevolence: Revival Religion and American Voting Behavior* (Norwood, N.J.: Ablex, 1979).

89. Benson, *Concept*, pp. 180–83.

90. See the map in Whitney R. Cross, *The Burned-Over District: The Social and Intellectual History of Enthusiastic Religion in Western New York, 1800–1850* (Ithaca, N.Y.: Cornell University Press, 1950), p. 68. The simple correlation between "Penn-Jersey-ites" and prosuffrage was −.19.

tion of equal suffrage. Their own experiences as minorities in America as well as their culturally determined values helped shape their reactions to the race issue. Thus English-speaking Protestants (especially those who were from nonconformist sects in Britain), who were readily accepted in America, often behaved similarly to native New Englanders, many of whose values they shared. But Catholic Irish and Germans, who daily faced hostility because of their religion and ever growing numbers, were slow to endorse a reform so dear to some of their oppressors.

It will be recalled that some Whigs thought blacks were as well qualified as "foreigners" to vote, the implication being that blacks and foreigners were similar in their inferiority to "native" whites. Such attitudes were common. Democrats, realizing the vulnerability that the Irish in particular felt, routinely played upon their racial fears and encouraged them to resist more equitable policies toward blacks. Even in 1845, Greeley, commenting on whether to call a constitutional convention, complained that in New York City "nearly all the Adopted Citizens were induced to vote against the convention by the cry of 'Niggers Voting' kept up by the Democrats."[91] Similarly, he lamented after the delegate election in April:

> The polls were given up almost wholly to the Adopted Citizens of German or Irish birth, who are always on hand . . . but who on this occasion were called out by skillful appeals to their hatred of the unfortunate African Race. It was mournful to see hundreds who have not been six years in the country earnestly and abusively clamorone [*sic*] for the disfranchisement of men whose fathers' fathers were born here, and many of them shed their blood for our liberties in the war of the Revolution. To see a man who enjoys Political Rights among us by Naturalization voting to disfranchise those who have for forty years been voters, is indeed a melancholy spectacle.[92]

Specifying the voting patterns of immigrant groups is complicated both by the presence of varying numbers of nonvoting aliens in many communities and also by the 1845 state census's failure to distinguish the country of origin of those from "Great Britain and its Possessions."[93] Still, certain patterns do emerge which suggest that Irish and German towns and wards were predominantly antisuffrage and other "British" areas prosuffrage. Of five towns with

91. *New York Tribune*, Nov. 5, 1845.
92. Ibid., Apr. 29, 1846.
93. The correlation between proportion of males eligible to vote and proportion foreign born is $-.48$. The fraction of aliens in the population has been taken into account in analyzing the behavior of the foreign-born areas.

more than ten per cent of the population German-born, all were antisuffrage and three overwhelmingly so.[94] Table 2.6 shows the preferences of towns that were over sixteen per cent British reclassified according to whether the Irish, or the Welsh, Scots, English, and Canadians predominated in them. (This classification is based upon the federal manuscript census of 1850 which did list the place of birth of all inhabitants.[95]) Clearly Irish areas were much more likely to be antisuffrage, and heavily so, than non-Irish communities. Impressionistic evidence confirms the distinctive reactions of these groups. The Welsh, an important component of the population in Oneida County, had often participated in antislavery causes, and the Scotch and English, while less active in such movements, had acquired a similar reputation.[96] Thus towns dominated by the more assimilable, largely Protestant groups seem to have had fewer objections to changing the political status of blacks than areas of Irish and German concentration, the latter affected as they were by a sense of competition with blacks to stay off the bottom rung of American society.

Another way to examine the importance of cultural outlook on suffrage voting is to compare suffrage voting with voting on another reform. In May of 1846 New York voters (except those in New York City) decided whether to license the sale of alcohol in the towns in which they lived.[97] Temperance was a reform of very wide appeal, and the result was an overwhelming victory for that cause throughout the state. The temperance and suffrage referenda correlated at .29. This relatively weak association was due to the widespread endorsement of this particular reform even in areas which had little history of support for other reforms. Still, prosuffrage towns *were* somewhat more likely than antisuffrage ones to vote "dry." (Indeed, 92.3 per cent of the prosuffrage towns opposed licensing.) And "wet" towns, few though they were, rarely supported equal suffrage

94. The correlation between German voting and prosuffrage voting was a mere $-.09$ ($r^2 = .01$), primarily because so few towns had significant German populations.

95. The 1850 figures, of course, pose some problems. The number of Irish immigrants in these towns had undoubtedly increased between 1846 and 1850, but the relatively most Irish towns and wards in comparison to others in the state was less likely to have changed dramatically.

96. Leonard L. Richards, *"Gentlemen of Property and Standing": Anti-Abolition Mobs in Jacksonian America* (New York: Oxford University Press, 1970), p. 142; Benson, *Concept*, p. 169.

97. The official returns for this referendum may be found in the New York State Assembly, *Documents*, 70th Sess., 1847, Doc. 40.

TABLE 2.6.

Prosuffrage voting of Irish and non-Irish "British" towns and wards,
1846 referendum[a]

Per cent prosuffrage	Irish towns		Non-Irish towns		Evenly balanced towns	
	Number	Per cent	Number	Per cent	Number	Per cent
0.0–25.0	21	51.2	0	0.0	0	0.0
25.1–50.0	12	29.3	5	31.2	1	50.0
Over 50.1	8	19.5	11	68.8	1	50.0
Total	41	100.0	16	100.0	2	100.2

[a]The towns and wards are assigned according to which group, the Irish or other British, formed a majority of the the British-born population. Other factors—the percentage of aliens, the rate of participation in the referendum, the composition of the rest of the population—may also have affected the suffrage voting patterns.

(90.1 per cent, in fact, opposing it). Despite the greater popularity of temperance than suffrage, areas that definitely liked or hated moral reform in general did exist.

Closely paralleling ethnic and cultural backgrounds in shaping people's outlooks on many issues in this period was religion. As Ronald P. Formisano, among others, has pointed out, religion defined and articulated values and gave people a common outlook and strategy for coping with events.[98] Unfortunately, the religious data for the towns of New York in this period are very sketchy. We know only which churches (broadly classified by denomination) were in which towns and cities. The matter is further complicated by the fact that a number of Protestant denominations were divided on the issues of slavery and black rights. In the referendum the two denominations whose behavior was most clear-cut were the Congregational and Dutch Reformed. There was a positive but weak correlation between the percentage of churches that were Congregational (mostly in areas settled by Yankees) and the percentage voting for equal suffrage. The corresponding correlation for Dutch Reformed churches, as previously noted, was weak but negative.[99] The behavior of other denominations, some of which were splintering along evangelical/nonevangelical lines or which drew upon relatively more heterogeneous groups, was impossible to evaluate.

98. Ronald P. Formisano, *The Birth of Mass Political Parties: Michigan, 1827–1861* (Princeton: Princeton University Press, 1971), pp. 137–38.
99. The correlations were .28 (r^2 = .08) and −.31 (r^2 = .10) respectively. See Appendix E for a discussion of the difficulties in measuring religious preference.

Despite the economic tensions of this period, clear-cut class voting on black rights did not emerge. If anything, less prosperous areas (defined in terms of average value of dwelling per capita) were more favorable to equal suffrage, but the tendency was slight ($-.13$).[100] Nor from the evidence available can one detect differences among agricultural, manufacturing, or commercial areas in their suffrage vote.[101]

Since Democratic politicians particularly emphasized the dangers of job competition, the voting behavior of one economic group, the urban working class, is most relevant.[102] Many lower-class wards were indeed antisuffrage, but so closely correlated were the Irish with common worker status that it is virtually impossible to determine statistically whether non-Irish workers in the city responded more to ethnic or economic cues.[103] The overall support for equal suffrage, however, was higher in such cities as Rochester and Troy, where the native population was mostly Yankee, than in New York, Albany, or Brooklyn. The factors of ethnic origin and economic class may have reinforced one another; rejection by native-born Americans may have heightened the economic insecurity of the Irish and their hostility toward the black.

The presence of several variables all correlated in some degree with voting patterns on equal suffrage raises questions about the independent importance of each. For instance, was the high support for black voting in Yankee areas really significant, or was it simply a function of the concentration of the Liberty Party in the same region? One way to answer this question is by multiple regression analysis.[104] Through such an analysis it is possible to estimate a

100. The variable, based on data from the 1855 state census, was calculated by dividing the total value of all dwellings by the number of people, adjusting proportionately if the value of only a portion of the total dwellings was recorded. If values for at least seventy per cent of all dwellings was unavailable, the town was dropped from this analysis. The data are taken from the 1855 census, nine years after the referendum, because no such data for towns were available in earlier censuses. The relative position of towns probably did not vary greatly over the period. On the utility of housing data as a measure of class see Richard K. Lieberman, "A Measure for the Quality of Life: Housing," *Historical Methods Newsletter*, 11 (Summer 1978), 129–34.

101. Such areas were identified using the U.S. Census for 1840.

102. Leon F. Litwack, *North of Slavery: The Negro in the Free States, 1790–1860* (Chicago: University of Chicago Press, 1961), pp. 162–68.

103. Stanley, "Majority Tyranny" (Ph.D. diss.), pp. 207–28, provides a convenient compilation of the ethnic, political, and economic statuses of the wards of the largest cities.

104. On regression see Mordecai Ezekiel and Karl A. Fox, *Methods of Correlation and Regression Analysis*, 3rd ed. (New York: John Wiley & Sons, 1959). On the importance

dependent variable (in this case, the percentage of the vote in favor of equal suffrage) from a combination of independent variables, taking into account the complex interrelationships among them. By comparing how towns *actually* voted on equal suffrage with the *estimates* resulting from a combination of independent variables in a multiple regression equation, one can obtain a measure (expressed frationally by R^2, the square of the multiple correlation coefficient) of the overall explanatory power of the variables. One can also generate standardized partial regression coefficients, which indicate the relative importance of each independent variable in "explaining" the dependent variables while taking into account the effects of all other independent variables.

Table 2.7 shows the results of a stepwise multiple regression (which identifies how much additional explanatory power a particular variable contributes when it is added to other independent variables in the regression equation).[105] The five variables listed added one per cent or more to the total explained variance in the prosuffrage vote. It appears that a community's willingness to back the reformist Liberty Party was most important in determining the amount of support the community gave to equal suffrage. Only slightly less significant was the New England-born population of the area. (Thus support for equal suffrage in Yankee areas was *not* solely a function of the strength of the Liberty Party there.) Interest in temperance reform also had an independent and measurable impact on opposition to racial discrimination in voting. But wherever the Democratic Party was strong—even in 1848 when Free Soil defections weakened it in many places—there one would find little sentiment to extend the rights of blacks.

This does not necessarily mean that the other variables were totally insignificant. Measuring the strength of some native and foreign groups presented many problems. Also, only a few towns had large numbers of blacks, Germans, or certain other ethnic groups, and one cannot expect them to influence the prosuffrage vote statewide, although in particular towns they might be crucial.

---

of standardized coefficients for the type of data being used here see John L. Hammond, "New Approaches to Aggregate Electoral Data," *Journal of Interdisciplinary History,* 9 (Winter 1979), 473–92.

105. The variables entered in the regression equation were per cent Liberty vote 1844, per cent black, per cent born in New England, per cent churches Dutch Reformed, per cent Democrat/Nativist 1846, per cent Democrat 1848, per cent for temperance, early settlement area (see note 82), and value of dwelling per capita. On the criteria for entry see Appendix E.

TABLE 2.7.
Variables explaining votes for equal
suffrage, 1846 (partial regression
coefficients)

Variable	Beta
Per cent Liberty 1844	.36
Per cent born New England	.34
Per cent Democrat/Nativist 1846	−.21
Per cent Democrat 1848	−.15
Per cent for temperance 1846	.11

Fraction of explained variance, 60.2%.

One way to examine the voting behavior on suffrage of groups that made up a small share of the population is to examine those towns where the percentage support for equal suffrage was markedly different from what regression estimates suggested it should be. The term "residual" refers to the difference between the actual and predicted value of a dependent variable; the standard error of the estimate of a regression is the typical size of a residual. Towns with residuals greater than this figure are the most atypical.

A few tentative generalizations may be made from an examination of the residuals larger than one standard error in the 1846 regression. Their analysis sheds new light on an observation by John L. Stanley, an earlier student of the 1846 referendum, that there was an apparent difference in suffrage voting between cities over twenty thousand in population and their "proximate rural surroundings" (i.e., rural towns in the same county as the city or, in the case of New York City, the twelve nearest counties). Urban areas appeared to be somewhat more favorable to equal rights.[106] Cities, however, often differed from rural towns in many ways other than their degree of urbanization. When the impact of other independent variables is taken into account, urban-rural differences in pro-suffrage voting appear far less dramatic. Among the towns that gave more support for equal suffrage than predicted were some large cities, but by no means all. Rochester, Troy, and about half the wards of Albany did give an unanticipated number of votes for equal suffrage, but New York and the rest of Albany's wards did not.[107] Considering somewhat smaller cities, between ten thousand and twenty

106. Stanley, "Majority Tyranny," *Political Science Quarterly*, p. 429.
107. Brooklyn and Buffalo, which Stanley used, are omitted from the analysis because the only available returns were unofficial and appear to be incomplete.

thousand population in 1850, Poughkeepsie and Utica did not have large residuals, and although Oswego did, so did almost every other township in that prosuffrage county. Thus an urban environment alone did not noticeably increase support for black voting in every instance. Also appearing among the residual cases were a number of Canadian-English-Scotch towns. This suggests that the latter's preference for equal suffrage was not simply a characteristic of other political or social factors in these towns. Still, the behavior of most of the residual cases cannot be accounted for.

Of the towns that had a considerably lower prosuffrage vote than predicted, very few had a large black population.[108] Thus it seeems that the mere presence of blacks in a town did not heighten significantly the degree of white antagonism toward them. Similarly, Irish and German areas were not more antisuffrage than other Democratic, antireform locales. More typical of the areas that were unusually opposed to black voting were towns with a relatively large number of Yankees, but where the rest of the population tended to be from antisuffrage groups. For example, Dover in Dutchess County was dominated by the Dutch, although ten per cent of its population came from New England. Olean in Cattaraugus County was about thirteen per cent New England-born, but almost as many people had come to the area from Pennsylvania and Ireland. Neither apparently was Yankee in culture, and both were heavily antisuffrage.[109]

The results of the 1846 referendum reveal a number of features of the early struggle over black rights. The greatest polarization of the population on black suffrage was along cultural lines, but the prosuffrage and antisuffrage sides were unevenly balanced. Support for equal suffrage was limited to a few rather distinctive groups. In areas where reform in general was accepted and approved—such as Liberty Party (and to a lesser extent temperance) strongholds—the majority of voters were willing to let blacks vote. New Englanders with their traditionally high regard for equal opportunity and individual effort were the only significant ethnic group to countenance black voting. The rhetoric of the prosuffrage forces simply did not appeal to other groups. Their speeches and editorials stressed abstract right and adherence to principle but

108. Two towns were six per cent black.
109. Local factors and idiosyncrasies in the measures used may account for much of the unexplained variation in the prosuffrage vote. Thus the sensational murder of four prominent Cayuga County residents by a deranged black may have contributed to five of its towns being unusually antisuffrage.

failed to take into account or effectively counteract the practical reality of racial stereotyping and prejudice in New York. As a result, black suffrage was a reform of markedly low appeal.

Thus the typical prosuffrage township in 1846 was likely to have been recently settled by Yankees, have given support to the Liberty Party, and have voted not to permit liquor licensing. It was also more likely to have a Whig/Liberty than a Democratic majority. Such towns were unusual in New York; most towns were hostile to black voting.

The structure of the prosuffrage vote had important implications for the politics of race. The overthrow of legalized discrimination was impossible without organized political support. Yet only one party, the Liberty Party, was in any sense dedicated to that goal. That party had been in the field for seven years and still had been able to organize no more than fifteen per cent of those who had supported equal suffrage in the referendum. In addition, the party's disruptive role in electoral politics made it a natural target of the major parties. For them to adopt the Liberty program was clearly impossible. As the suffrage campaign illustrated, such a tactic would alienate as many votes as it would win.[110] Instead, Whigs, and to a lesser extent Democrats, turned to demonstrating the futility of the Liberty effort. The drubbing of equal suffrage in the referendum showed even the most optimistic that black suffrage was strongly opposed by most New Yorkers. Blacks and abolitionists, despite their Herculean efforts, had not converted public opinion, as they had earlier hoped. The Liberty Party was forced into a steady retreat. Its only vote gains after 1845 came through extraneous, unsolicited endorsements from other political malcontents (land reformers, Anti-Renters, etc.). By 1848, with the birth of the Free Soil Party in the ashes of the Liberty Party, the whole concept of a party that put considerations of morality before those of political prudence, was laid to rest. The Free Soilers' endorsement of Martin Van Buren, who had helped insert the property qualification into New York's constitution in 1821, was the final proof that times had indeed changed.

Thus as 1846 came to a close, the outlook for equal suffrage was grim. The decisiveness of its defeat had warned Whigs away from its indiscriminate advocacy, and without some partisan backing

110. There are many examples of Whig reluctance to accept the issue as partisan. See, for instance, *Ithaca Daily Chronicle*, Oct. 23, 1846; *Jamestown Journal*, Dec. 5, 1846.

there was little hope for changing the new constitution. Only if the nature of partisan divisions in New York changed, as some Whig leaders such as Seward hoped would happen, could the issue possibly become politically viable.[111] The pursuit of equal rights had proved illusory. Agitation of the issue had simply resulted in the deliberate discrediting of its few political friends. Equal suffrage was dead—for the moment.

111. Van Deusen, *Seward,* p. 94.

CHAPTER THREE

Partisan Realignment and the Revival of Equal Suffrage

For a decade following the defeat of black suffrage in 1846, the prospects for overturning the property qualification seemed hopeless. The mere mention of the issue brought warnings by politicians of its dangers. Greeley, still claiming to be the friend of equal suffrage, declared in 1855 that it would be "many weary years" before the property qualification could be removed, and he insisted that efforts to abolish it would "not hasten the enfranchisement of the Blacks, but . . . strongly tend to the practical disfranchisement of the Whites who favor their claim. We did what we could for Equal Suffrage in 1846," he lamented, "with feeble hopes of success, but with a perfect consciousness that we incurred general obloquy and injured our political associates by so doing."[1]

Yet from 1855 to 1860 proposals to change the constitution's black suffrage provision were introduced in every legislature—and actually passed both houses in three different sessions. By 1860 a proposal to amend the state constitution was on the ballot. Only a sustained, dedicated effort could have achieved such a result. To amend the constitution was extremely difficult, requiring approval by a majority of elected members of both houses of the legislature, publication of the proposed change three months before the next general election of state senators (chosen biennially), the consent of

---

1. *New York Tribune*, Sept. 22, 1855.

a majority of the legislators chosen in *that* election, and finally ratification by at least half of the eligible electorate. Of dozens of amendments proposed in the 1846–1860 period, only one other made it to the balloting stage.[2]

This startling reversal in the political fortunes of the black suffrage movement may be attributed to three phenomena of the 1850s. First, there was a realignment of the popular bases of support for the major political parties which made equal suffrage a more viable political issue. Second, and related to the first, the suffrage question in New York gradually became caught up in the heated debate between North and South and also in the controversy stemming from the growing power of immigrant groups in New York. It thus acquired a "relevance" that gave it great symbolic value in partisan struggles. Third, blacks launched a major new drive to convince politicians that they would never rest until they had obtained equal suffrage.

Factionalism had always been a feature of the second party system, but in the 1850s partisan coalitions of a generation's standing were literally torn apart. The successive shocks of nativism, the slavery-extension controversy, and serious economic dislocations—all issues the existing parties found divisive—proved too much for partisan leaders to handle.[3] By 1854 the Whig Party had disappeared in New York, a new nativist party (the American Party) had been founded, and the Democratic Party had been splintered and shaken to its very roots. Until 1860 fragmentation of the electorate remained the rule. No party won an election by a majority vote until 1859, and even then the nativist American Party determined the outcome by throwing its weight behind selected candidates on the Democratic and Republican slates.

The correlation matrix in Table 3.1 shows the electoral support for the Democratic Party for over a decade and a half. (Rival party factions in 1848 and between 1853 and 1855 are combined to facilitate comparison.) From 1844 to 1853 the relatively high interelection correlations indicate that the Democrats drew support from

2. Charles Z. Lincoln, *The Constitutional History of New York* (Rochester: Lawyers Co-operative, 1906), 2:chapter 7.

3. For a broad overview of these changes see Joel H. Silbey, *The Transformation of American Politics, 1840–1860* (Englewood Cliffs, N.J.: Prentice-Hall, 1967) and Michael F. Holt, *The Political Crisis of the 1850s* (New York: John Wiley & Sons, 1978). On New York politics see Mark L. Berger, *The Revolution in the New York Party Systems, 1840–1860* (Port Washington, N.Y.: Kennikat Press, 1973), which, despite its title, deals mainly with the mid–1850s.

TABLE 3.1.

Correlation matrix of the per cent Democratic vote, 1844-1860[a]

	1844	1845	1846	1847	1848	1849	1850	1851	1852	1853	1854	1855	1856	1857	1858	1859[b]	1859[c]
1845	.76																
1846	.65	.69															
1847	.57	.59	.57														
1848	.53	.40	.26	.23													
1849	.82	.74	.65	.60	.65												
1850	.87	.75	.70	.58	.60	.91											
1851	.86	.62	.58	.49	.56	.79	.82										
1852	.89	.71	.62	.61	.23	.70	.79	.81									
1853	.84	.65	.56	.52	.45	.76	.85	.84	.86								
1854	.46	.14	.28	.24	.26	.29	.39	.48	.48	.50							
1855	.51	.40	.44	.46	.06	.38	.51	.46	.68	.63	.59						
1856	.44	.41	.41	.46	-.15	.26	.37	.36	.64	.53	.45	.83					
1857	.55	.45	.50	.52	-.04	.39	.50	.49	.72	.65	.53	.87	.93				
1858	.58	.48	.51	.57	-.04	.39	.48	.48	.72	.61	.53	.81	.93	.95			
1859[b]	.43	.39	.36	.46	-.31	.21	.28	.32	.65	.46	.35	.61	.79	.76	.79		
1859[c]	.57	.51	.51	.62	-.13	.35	.46	.45	.73	.58	.48	.72	.85	.87	.89	.90	
1860	.48	.40	.41	.49	-.26	.26	.34	.36	.69	.51	.43	.67	.87	.82	.86	.94	.92

[a]County-level data. For details concerning the construction of the table see Appendix E.
[b]Secretary of state (supported by American Party also).
[c]Comptroller.

roughly the same areas. (Factionalism between 1846 and 1848 did lower some correlations, but the decline was temporary not permanent.) In the 1854 election, however, correlations sank dramatically. While areas of Democratic support had correlated at .86 between 1852 and 1853, between 1853 and 1854 the association was only .50. Elections after 1855 were more highly correlated among themselves but bore markedly less resemblance to those of the 1840s. New political coalitions were emerging, although a fair amount of instability continued too.

This realignment of voters had implications for the suffrage struggle. Prior to 1854 the political environment in which black suffrage had gone down to defeat in 1846 remained relatively unchanged. Factional disputes—between Barnburners and Hunkers, Silver Grays and Seward Whigs, and Hard and Soft Democrats—which often had at least a nominal basis in the controversy over slavery, did affect the outcome of elections. But as Tables 3.2 and 3.3 indicate, they did not change the fundamental relationship between the two major parties and the sources of support and opposition for equal suffrage. Partisan alignments did not correspond to those on equal suffrage. In 1852 the defection of some Democrats to a smaller, but less racist Free Soil Party did increase the negative association between the remaining Democrats and equal suffrage, but only temporarily. In 1853 backing for the "Soft Shell" Democrats violated Democratic tradition and correlated positively with support for equal suffrage, though at a very low level. (The "Softs" were the ideological descendants of the Barnburners and likely to be hostile to the "Slave Power," as they termed the South. Their conservative rivals were called "Hards.") With the exception of 1848, Whig voting strength showed a consistently low but positive association with prosuffrage voting. Overall the vote of *neither* major party correlated *consistently* with the suffrage vote.

Only the tiny Liberty Party (Table 3.4) continued to be comparatively strong in prosuffrage areas, but it also remained politically impotent, never winning a single elective office.[4] The much larger Free Soil Party of 1848, which actually outpolled the Democratic Party in that year, was only moderately associated (.38) with the 1846 prosuffrage vote. As Eric Foner has pointed out, it attempted to broaden its political appeal by dropping the Liberty Party's com-

---

4. The lower correlation in 1847 is explained by the coalescence of Anti-Rent supporters with the Liberty Party in that year.

TABLE 3.2.

Correlation between Democratic voting, 1844-1853, and prosuffrage voting in 1846 and 1860[a]

Referendum	1844	1845	1846	1847	1848	1849	1850	1851	1852	1853[b]	1853[c]
1846	-.53	-.45	-.43	-.35	-.37	-.34	-.34	-.31	-.59	-.28	.08
1860	-.52	-.47	-.43	-.52	-.55	-.31	-.35	-.34	-.69	-.46	.21

[a] County-level data.
[b] "Hard."
[c] "Soft."

TABLE 3.3.

Correlation between Whig voting, 1844–1853, and prosuffrage voting in 1846 and 1860[a]

Referendum	1844	1845	1846	1847	1848	1849	1850	1851	1852	1853
1846	.18	.13	.18	.21	-.16	.30	.24	.31	.25	.37
1860	.17	.16	.17	.32	-.27	.26	.26	.34	.25	.46

[a] County-level data.

TABLE 3.4.

Correlation between Liberty/Free Soil voting and prosuffrage voting in 1846 and 1860[a]

Referendum	Liberty 1844	Liberty 1845	Liberty 1846	Liberty[b] 1847	Free Soil 1848	Free Soil 1852
1846	.74	.64	.71	.16	.38	.59
1860	.73	.64	.74	.22	.59	.74

[a]County-level data.
[b]Also supported by Anti-Renters.

mitment to racial equality. Thus it tried to unite all those opposed to slavery extension including those who wished to preserve the territories for free *white* men. Since the Free Soilers who had been Democrats largely returned to their former party the next year, about all the Free Soil movement accomplished, in an immediate sense, was to weaken the Liberty Party, which was a shadow of its former self after 1848.[5] Although the Free Soil Party again fielded candidates in 1852, it obtained fewer than a quarter of the votes it had had in 1848 and indeed was much more a momentary revival of the Liberty Party than the original Free Soil Party.[6]

No major party, then, in the period before 1854 really had a strong incentive to revive the issue of black suffrage. Only the Liberty Party possessed a leadership and following attuned to the issue of equal rights, and it was totally without power and almost nonexistent after 1847.

As long as this situation continued, most politicians did not take the suffrage issue seriously. It came before the legislature rarely, and when it did, was quickly disposed of. With the demise of the Liberty Party, Whig leaders seemed inclined to avoid the issue. In 1849 the Assembly received petitions from citizens of Cortland and Montgomery Counties requesting a constitutional amendment to extend the suffrage rights of blacks. The Whigs had a five-to-one majority but failed to act. A resolution rejecting the petitioners' prayer was

5. Eric Foner, "Racial Attitudes of the New York Free Soilers," *New York History*, 46 (Oct. 1965), 311–29. The correlation between the Free Soil percentage and the prosuffrage percentage in the 1860 referendum is fairly high (.59), which suggests that Free Soil areas did eventually move toward support of equal suffrage.

6. The 1852 Free Soil vote correlated more highly with the Liberty Party vote in 1846 (.83) than the Free Soil vote in 1848 (.63). But although the Free Soil Party's platform called explicitly for the abolition of slavery in 1852, equal rights were still not openly advocated. Kirk H. Porter and Donald B. Johnson, *National Party Platforms, 1840–1964* (Urbana, Ill.: University of Illinois Press, 1966), pp. 18–20.

agreed to without a formal vote. Again in 1850 blacks living in New York City petitioned for a constitutional amendment to remove the property qualification, but their petition was never acted upon by the Committee on Privileges and Elections to which it was referred. In 1854 blacks once more petitioned a Whig-controlled State Senate for the vote. When the Judiciary Committee, to which the petition was referred, offered a resolution that the petitioners' request be denied, the Senate agreed by a vote of 13–12 (seven were absent). Although all those opposed to the resolution were Whigs, a third of the Whigs present and voting sided with the Democrats in opposition to the petitioners.[7] In general, the antisuffrage Whigs came from districts where black suffrage had proved unpopular in 1846. Seven of the ten counties they represented gave less support for equal voting rights than *any* of the twenty-four counties in the districts of Whigs who endorsed suffrage reform. Thus the absence of enough interested Whigs, the same basic problem which had plagued the equal rights cause since 1846, prevented any action from being taken.

Inertia on black voting ended only with the collapse of the second party system. The realignment was spurred by issues only tangentially related to equal rights—primarily reactions to the extension of slavery into the territories, the political influence of the South, and the growing power of the foreign born in America. But it dissolved the strong sense of voter identification with the Whig and Democratic Parties which had accounted for much of the stability of the old party system. New political groupings were formed and competed for followers. The American or Know Nothing Party emerged in 1854 to express the growing hostility of "native Americans" to the immigrant. In the same year a fusion ticket endorsed by an anti-Nebraska state convention (called to protest the Kansas-Nebraska Act), a state temperance convention, and the Free Democrats replaced the Whig Party on the ballot. In 1855 the Republican Party appeared for the first time and provided a more permanent organizational structure for many of the fusion groups of the previous year. These new parties attracted some former Democrats but also repelled many ex-Whigs, thereby changing the nature of the Demo-

7. New York State Assembly, *Journal,* 72nd Sess., 1849, pp. 133, 492, 792; New York State Senate, *Journal,* 73rd Sess., 1850, p. 281; ibid., 77th Sess., 1854, pp. 507, 564.

cratic coalition, already hopelessly split between the Soft and Hard factions.[8]

The new electoral combinations and the struggle for majority status among them had implications for equal suffrage. The new parties were more polarized on black suffrage than the major parties of the past decade had been. (See Tables 3.5, 3.6, 3.7.) Increasingly, Democrats tended to come from those areas (southeastern New York) which objected least to racial discrimination and Republicans from areas (the west and north) more willing to vote for equal rights. The correlations of Republican voting and prosuffrage voting were generally higher (.8 to .9) for the 1860 referendum than the 1846 one (.5 to .6), which suggests that areas becoming Republican increased their support for equal suffrage, but even for the 1846 referendum, the relationships were stronger than for any major party in the prealignment period. To illustrate the change in another way, the top fifteen prosuffrage counties in 1846 *all* voted Republican in 1860 and had a median Republican strength of 63.5 per cent; of the fifteen least prosuffrage counties in 1846, nine voted Democratic and six Republican (only thirteen counties went Democratic in 1860), and their median Republican percentage was 48.3. By contrast, in 1844 six of the fifteen counties that were most prosuffrage in 1846 and three of the fifteen least prosuffrage had a Whig majority, and the median Whig percentages of the two groups were almost identical, 46.8 and 46.6.

Thus as the result of the realignment, the intraparty divisions over the suffrage issue were greatly reduced. The Republicans had a different sort of constituency than the Whigs had had. They were not nearly as dependent as the latter on support from the southeastern section of the state (now mostly Democratic) and were, therefore, freer to act on the subject of equal rights. Still, the correlation between the Republican Party vote and support for black suffrage was hardly perfect, and the Know Nothings, who tended to come from antisuffrage areas, continued to hold the balance of power in the state.[9] The Know Nothings were thought to be op-

8. On New York politics in this era see Willis Fletcher Johnson and Ray B. Smith, *Political and Governmental History of the State of New York* (Syracuse: Syracuse Press, 1922), 2:400–436, and De Alva Stanwood Alexander, *A Political History of the State of New York* (New York: Henry Holt and Company, 1906–1909), 2:190–255.

9. The correlation between the percentage voting for the American Party and the percentage favoring prosuffrage was negative but low except in 1856 when the "North" Americans, who had broken with the rest of their party on slavery in

TABLE 3.5.

Correlation between Democratic voting, 1854-1860, and prosuffrage voting in 1846 and 1860[a]

Referendum	1854			1855			1856	1857	1858	1859[b]	1859[c]	1860
	Soft	Hard	Total	Soft	Hard	Total						
1846	-.11	-.22	-.24	.09	-.45	-.39	-.47	-.48	-.52	-.66	-.60	-.65
1860	-.19	-.31	-.37	.02	-.57	-.57	-.72	-.72	-.76	-.88	-.85	-.90

[a]County-level data.
[b]Secretary of state (supported by American Party).
[c]Comptroller.

TABLE 3.6.

Correlation between Republican voting, 1854-1860, and prosuffrage voting in 1846 and 1860[a]

Referendum	1854[b]	1855	1856	1857	1858	1859[c]	1859[d]	1860
1846	.48	.35	.57	.54	.56	.66	.60	.65
1860	.53	.67	.84	.83	.84	.88	.85	.90

[a]County-level data.
[b]Fusion ticket.
[c]Secretary of state.
[d]Comptroller (supported by American Party).

TABLE 3.7.

Correlation between American Party voting, 1854-1858, and
prosuffrage voting in 1846 and 1860[a]

Referendum	1854	1855	1856	1857	1858
1846	−.16	.00	−.47	−.29	−.22
1860	−.11	−.17	−.67	−.47	−.36

[a]County-level data.

posed to black suffrage. Horace Greeley estimated in 1857, "Of their [the American Party's] one hundred and thirty thousand voters, we doubt that so many as ten thousand could be induced to vote to enfranchise the blacks."[10] But the Republicans needed the support of some members of such groups that traditionally had been opposed to equal suffrage to achieve a statewide majority. The party had, in other words, a much stronger *potential* than the Whigs to act favorably on black suffrage, but for black suffrage to be realized cooperation would still be required from those who had formerly opposed black voting.

In contrast to the pre-1854 period, proposals to abolish the property qualification were introduced in every legislature from 1855 to 1860 and received serious consideration in four of the six sessions. The impetus to reconsider equal voting rights for blacks came at first from the desire of new parties to experiment with the issue in the wake of the collapse of the second party system and later from an organized lobbying effort.

With the collapse of the Whig Party any discipline that it could exert simply disappeared. That the emerging Republican coalition explored the black suffrage issue, despite its sensitivity, is not strange. New parties are built by those who have been disappointed in the past, a category into which equal rights advocates clearly fell. They longed to see progress on the issues they cared about, and for a young party to survive and grow it had to convince enthusiasts on issues like black suffrage that the party could respond to some of their concerns.

The 1855 legislature, the first to act on an equal suffrage resolution, may be seen as a transitional body. The Senate had been elected in 1853 before the breakup of the Whigs, while the Assem-

the territories, endorsed a separate candidate who withdrew in favor of the Republican, Fremont.

10. *New York Tribune*, Sept. 26, 1857.

bly had been chosen in 1854, the most chaotic election of the decade.[11] The majority still used the designation "Whig" but many in both chambers had Know Nothing proclivities.[12] Confusion and controversy reigned during the legislative session. Unrestrained by any sense of obligation to their former political associates, members let out their pent up frustrations concerning a number of issues. Black suffrage, Demon Rum, secret societies, and the Kansas-Nebraska bill were alternately praised and damned.[13]

In January the Assembly received a petition from blacks on Long Island making the usual plea for an end to the property qualification. When a month later the Judiciary Committee to which the petition had been referred still had not reported, Levi Blakeslee, a first-term Whig assemblyman from Oneida County, introduced his own resolution to amend the suffrage article by removing its discriminatory section. In the Senate in late March, Ben Field, a Vermont-born Whig from Orleans County, proposed a similar resolution. Field moved the third reading of his resolution late in the session at a strategic moment right after the chamber had adopted resolutions opposing the Kansas-Nebraska bill in Congress. If legislators were going to thumb their noses at the Slave Power, they could do so equally well by showing their unwillingness to uphold racial discrimination in their own state.

As so typically occurred in this session, however, the resolution quickly became entangled with equally controversial amendments restricting officeholding to native-born citizens and nonministers. Eager to finish other business before adjournment, the Senate voted 14–9 to refer the resolution back to committee, thus killing it. The division was similar to that in the previous year on the suffrage question.[14] All but one Democrat voted for referral while the Whigs divided seven in favor and eight opposed. The only three Whigs to oppose the anti-Nebraska resolves earlier were in the group of seven as were all five Whigs who had favored the proposal to limit officeholding to the native born. Thus National Whigs and budding nativists, those most hostile or indifferent to the slavery issue and

11. Senators were elected every two years in odd-numbered years. Assemblymen were chosen annually.
12. So many political groupings were endorsing candidates in this year that party designations in the legislature must be considered approximate.
13. Johnson and Smith, *Political and Governmental History*, 2:406–10.
14. Seven Whigs and three Democrats failed to vote. Of the seven Whigs who sided with the Democrats, five had voted the same way the previous year, one had been absent, and the other had changed his position.

sectionalism and least likely to be attracted in the future to the Republican Party, were the prime component of the anti-black Whigs in the Senate.[15]

Two days later Blakeslee's resolution came up in the Assembly. Apparently the imminent close of the session made debate unwelcome; Blakeslee was allowed to print his speech but not deliver it. The speaker quashed an attempt by opponents to delay a vote by introducing the question of women's suffrage. The resolution then passed by a vote of 66–34. For the first time a branch of the New York legislature had endorsed the principle of equal suffrage for all males.

The Assembly Whigs were more unified than those in the Senate. Over eighty per cent of the Whigs who voted (sixteen per cent did not) approved equal suffrage, while over eighty per cent of the Democrats who voted opposed it. (See Table 3.8.) Party lines would be drawn even tighter in future years, but the new trend was apparent. Equal suffrage was becoming a partisan issue. Once again there was some connection with attitudes on Kansas. The Assembly passed anti-Nebraska resolutions the day after the suffrage vote. A Democrat, angered by the absence of an opportunity to debate the resolutions, urged opponents to abstain from voting. As Table 3.9 shows, three-quarters of the prosuffrage Whigs condemned the Kansas-Nebraska Act while only one-quarter of the antisuffrage Whigs did so. The five prosuffrage Democrats, however, reacted very similarly to the rest of the Democrats on the resolutions, suggesting that they perceived black suffrage in terms distinct from national politics.[16]

Immediately after the Assembly's equal suffrage resolution was passed, it was sent to the Senate. Since that body had already disposed of the suffrage question once, the resolution was laid on the table and not taken up before the session ended the next day.[17] Black suffrage thus had been defeated. But there had been interest

15. New York State Assembly, *Journal*, 78th Sess., 1855, pp. 170, 435, 528, 659; New York State Senate, *Journal*, 78th Sess., 1855, pp. 489, 703–704.

16. New York State Assembly, *Journal*, 78th Sess., 1855, pp. 1255–56; *Albany Argus*, Apr. 13–15, 1855. (The precise title of this newspaper changed several times during this period. Herein it will be referred to by its common designation, the *Albany Argus*.) Several of the dissenting Democrats, three of whom were Softs, represented districts in counties (Allegany, Chautauqua) that markedly increased their support for equal suffrage between 1846 and 1860. The dissenting Whigs also tended to come from districts in New York City and environs and the Hudson Valley, which remained solidly hostile to rights for blacks through 1860.

17. New York State Senate, *Journal*, 78th Sess., 1855, p. 784.

TABLE 3.8.

Votes on equal suffrage resolution, Assembly, 1855, by party

Position	Whig		Democrat		Other[a]	
	Number	Per cent[b]	Number	Per cent[b]	Number	Per cent[b]
For	58	71 (84)	5	12 (18)	3	75 (100)
Against	11	13 (16)	23	55 (82)	0	0
Absent	13	16	14	33	1	25
Total	82	100 (100)	42	100 (100)	4	100 (100)

χ^2 = 37.2 for 2 d.f. Significant at .001.
[a]Two independent and two Maine Law (temperance) men.
[b]Figures in parentheses are percentages excluding absentees.

TABLE 3.9.

Crosstabulation of votes on anti-Nebraska and equal suffrage resolutions, Assembly, 1855

Position on equal suffrage resolution	Votes on anti-Nebraska resolution							
	For		Against		Absent		Total	
	Number	Per cent	Number	Per cent	Number	Per cent	Number	Per cent
Whigs for	44	74	1	1	15	25	60	100
Whigs against	3	27	1	9	7	63	11	99
Democrats for	0	0	1	20	4	80	5	100
Democrats against	0	0	7	30	16	70	23	100

in it and significant support for it (at least in the Assembly) for the first time since its rejection in 1846. Two new trends were apparent. The vote in the Assembly (chosen in one of the most chaotic elections of the realignment) was largely partisan. There were also parallels between divisions on the suffrage question and on emerging issues of national concern, such as the Kansas-Nebraska bill. The interest in suffrage did not extend far beyond the legislature at this moment, however. The press took little note of the Assembly's action.[18]

Still, the success of the Assembly resolution did regalvanize lobbying efforts by the group most likely to be affected by the proposed constitutional change, New York's black community. In fact, James McCune Smith, a prominent black leader, believed that the Assembly triumph in 1855 had been immeasurably aided by the "eloquent advocacy" of Frederick Douglass, who had delivered a speech on equal suffrage in the Assembly chamber during the session.[19] To expect one man to bear the burden of agitation, however, was too much. Drawing upon their previous experience with collective action and encouraged by the Assembly triumph in 1855, blacks now moved rapidly to establish an effective organization to back equal suffrage. It was this campaign that kept the suffrage question continually before the legislature and prevented the shelving of the issue after its initial defeats.

In September, 1855, five months after the Assembly's favorable vote, a state convention of blacks met in Troy to form the New York State Suffrage Association. This body continued to meet annually until the 1860 referendum. Frederick Douglass, named head of the new organization, gave the keynote address. Besides making a strong appeal for equal suffrage on rational and moral grounds, he attempted to relate the measure to current political concerns—not only slavery but also the role of the immigrant in American life. Aware that the growing number of foreign-born voters and the changing character of many urban areas were alarming many Americans, he declared that it was unfair to deny native-born blacks the vote when the foreign born could vote without restrictions within a few years of their arrival.[20]

18. *New York Tribune*, Apr. 14, 1855; *Albany Argus*, Apr. 16, 1855.
19. *New York Tribune*, Sept. 12, 1855. *Frederick Douglass' Paper* (Rochester), Mar. 16, 1855.
20. Howard Holman Bell, *A Survey of the Negro Convention Movement, 1830–1861* (New York: Arno Press and The New York Times, 1969), pp. 185–90; *New York Trib-*

Compared with their earlier suffrage campaigns, blacks relied less on speeches and public statements in their suffrage efforts than on concrete measures to pressure the state's lawmakers. Stephen Myers, a resident of Albany and veteran of the suffrage struggle, was appointed to lobby the legislature. For a time he even published a newspaper, *The Voice of Freedom*. Other blacks helped in this effort. In 1859, for instance, William J. Watkins, a general agent of the association, gave a public address on behalf of equal suffrage in the Assembly chamber which was attended by many legislators. Blacks renewed efforts at local organization, too, urging the clergy to use their influence to get blacks politically involved. Petitions needed to be circulated, and blacks eligible to vote had to be registered and made aware of the power of their ballots. In all these activities the black press played a role of active encouragement.[21]

The petition campaign began with enthusiasm. At least nineteen petitions bearing sixteen hundred names were presented to the 1856 legislature.[22] The number fell off thereafter—five petitions in 1857, one in 1858, five in 1859, and three in 1860. At least seventeen (of sixty) counties were eventually represented in the petitions, mostly in the immediate New York City area where many blacks lived and in western New York. The suffrage associations in the larger cities (New York, Brooklyn, Buffalo, and Syracuse) seemed to maintain the greatest momentum, sending petitions to more than one legislature during the period.[23] These petitions served as the formal justification for the legislature's continued involvement with the suffrage question.

Black leaders, encouraged by the belief that inflation and the gradual increase in real wealth had made the property qualification easier for blacks to meet, started organizing politically at the grass-

---

une, Sept. 6, 1855; Rhoda Golden Freeman, "The Free Negro in New York City in the Era before the Civil War" (Ph.D. diss., Columbia University, 1966), p. 144.

21. Philip S. Foner and George E. Walker, eds., *Proceedings of the Black State Conventions, 1840–1865* (Philadelphia: Temple University Press, 1979-), 1:76, 89–92.

22. Poor indexing of the Senate and Assembly journals is responsible for some imprecision as to the exact number of petitions in a session. Some petitions were sent by whites as well.

23. *New York Tribune,* Sept. 12, 1855; Stephen Myers to Gerrit Smith, Mar. 22, 1856, Gerrit Smith Collection, George Arents Research Library for Special Collections at Syracuse University, Syracuse, N.Y.; *Albany Evening Journal,* Jan. 15, 1859; New York State Assembly, *Journal,* 79th Sess., 1856, pp. 205, 248, 306–307, 587, 657; 80th Sess., 1857, pp. 226–27, 433, 636, 656, 757; 81st Sess., 1858, p. 176; 82nd Sess., 1859, pp. 64, 203, 312; 83rd Sess., 1860, pp. 108, 222, 425; New York State Senate, *Journal,* 79th Sess., 1856, pp. 235, 269, 321; 82nd Sess., 1859, p. 440.

roots level. A New York City convention of blacks appointed a committee of seven to mobilize all blacks eligible to vote. They intended to enlist five hundred to seven hundred new voters who were expected to stand aloof from party and support candidates on the basis of their suffrage stands. The threat of their bloc vote, it was anticipated, would be sufficient to overcome any prejudice a legislator or his other constituents might possess.[24]

Later, some blacks were to reject this balance-of-power strategy in favor of direct support for the Republican Party. In 1856, for instance, a black state convention endorsed the Republican ticket. Henry Highland Garnet, the main speaker, admitted that the party was far from perfect, but it did come closest to positions on suffrage and slavery favored by blacks and should be supported "regardless of the unkind things uttered by some of the Republican leaders." Certainly the Republicans had contributed support for equal suffrage in the legislature, but Garnet was also drawn to them by the increasing number of antiblack immigrants in the Democratic ranks: "The oppressed Irismen [sic], once naturalized, are the loudest shouters for Buch[anan] and Breck[enridge] and Slavery extension, and the bitterest foes of the negro."[25] Blacks also found an implied threat in the Dred Scott decision and the prospect that slavery might become national, which again drew them toward support of a major party like the Republicans. Democrats and aliens were now the negative referents for supporters of equal suffrage.

As time went on, the blacks became even more convinced that the Republicans were the key to success on equal rights. A suffrage convention meeting in Troy in 1858 resolved, "We can accomplish nothing in this direction [securing the franchise] save over the defeat and ruin of the so-called Democratic party, our most inveterate enemy." Stephen Myers stated the case more bluntly: "If we should vote against the Republican ticket, we should commit suicide, so far as the right of franchise is concerned."[26]

Yet important obstacles stood in the path of the black suffrage lobby. The blacks of New York were not a wealthy group, and the suffrage association lacked adequate funding for its projects. Stephen Myers was complaining as early as 1856 that he had not been

24. *New York Tribune*, Sept. 12, 1855. There were local suffrage associations also in such places as Rochester and Poughkeepsie. *Frederick Douglass' Paper*, Sept. 21, Oct. 5, 1855.
25. *New York Tribune*, Sept. 24, 1856.
26. *National Anti-Slavery Standard* (New York), Oct. 9, 1858.

sent any funds and that he was living on personal contributions from Frederick Douglass.[27]

Also the petition campaign never reached the dimensions of that in the 1837 to 1841 period. Many whites had lost faith in this tactic and no longer added their energies to those of the blacks. The attention of most of them was riveted on the national stage, where the drama of making Kansas free or slave was being acted out. Gerrit Smith, the former Liberty Party leader, did address the legislature in 1856, urging it to deliver the people from the devilish spirit of prejudice (represented by the property qualification) and to show the slaveholders that blacks could live successfully in freedom.[28] But even he soon became "completely absorbed" by the popular sovereignty controversy.[29] Smith's new political party, the Radical Abolitionists, was too weak (it was little more than Smith's personal following) to provide a possible vehicle for organized white support of the blacks' equal suffrage campaign.

Blacks also found it difficult to organize impressive numbers of new black voters. A group of blacks addressing the people of New York in 1852 claimed that four-fifths of the adult male blacks were already eligible to vote under the property qualification, but this claim appears to have been an exaggeration.[30] According to the state census of 1855, there were 45,286 blacks in New York, 35,956 of whom were not taxed and therefore ineligible to vote.[31] Of the 9,330 who remained, many must have been women or men who did not meet the three-year residency requirement for black voters. (White voters had to meet only a one-year residency requirement. Surprisingly, little comment had ever been made on the injustice of this distinction between the races.) Although the 1855 census did not distinguish between black voters and taxpayers (i.e., those who owned at least $250 real property), in 1845 the ratio between these

27. Myers to Smith, Mar. 22, 1856, Smith Papers.

28. *Gerrit Smith on Suffrage. His Speech in the Capitol, Albany, February 28th 1856* (n.p., [1856]).

29. Ralph V. Harlow, *Gerrit Smith, Philanthropist and Reformer* (New York: Henry Holt and Co., 1939), p. 343.

30. *New York Herald*, Jan. 29, 1852. The group was arguing against colonization on the grounds that blacks were doing well in America. H. H. Garnet stated in 1856 that 5,000 to 6,000 blacks were eligible to vote. Joel Schor, *Henry Highland Garnet: A Voice of Black Radicalism in the Nineteenth Century* (Westport, Conn.: Greenwood Press, 1977), p. 142. A suffrage convention in 1858 put the number at 11,000. Foner and Walker, *Proceedings*, 1:100.

31. *Census of the State of New York for 1855* (Albany: C. Van Benthuysen, 1857).

two categories had been one to two.[32] Assuming this ratio remained the same in 1855, one may estimate a maximum potential black electorate then of only 4,600.[33] In New York City, where the suffrage association had hoped to register up to seven hundred voters, five hundred at most were available according to estimates based on the census, and, of course, no one could expect the campaign to be one hundred per cent effective. Black voters suffered another handicap as well. They tended to live in districts that were predominantly Democratic. Even registered and organized, blacks had little hope of affecting most electoral outcomes.

The assumption that whites would respectfully listen to black demands for equal rights proved questionable. Horace Greeley in an editorial in the *New York Tribune* bluntly warned blacks that their "conspicuous advocacy" would only hurt their cause and that whites would be less moved by logical arguments for black rights than by the belief that blacks would be desirable electors (which he felt they could demonstrate by rejecting servile occupations in the cities in favor of independent farming). This deliberately insulting editorial which closed with the thought that the political, social, and moral elevation of the blacks was desirable mainly because it would benefit the white community, was a great blow since it came from a man who was the editor of the most influential newspaper in the state and who had historically backed the black suffrage cause. Replying to it, Douglass insisted that blacks had the right and duty to agitate for their rights regardless of the attitude of the white community.[34]

It was not crucial for suffrage advocates at this time, however, that the black suffrage lobby be well financed or universally popular. The lobbying effort needed only to continue to serve a useful purpose. The legislators it approached were more receptive to the suffrage cause than ever before, not only because of the changing popular bases of the parties, but also because of their emerging ideological differences. In 1846 and even 1821 some people had seen racial prejudice as peculiarly linked to two groups, southerners and foreigners (especially the Irish). But by the late 1850s southerners and immigrants had themselves become subjects of important

32. This ratio is probably slightly inaccurate because of the obvious confusion of some census takers over the definitions of the different categories.

33. A press estimate in 1860 was even lower, 1,500. *Albany Evening Journal*, Feb. 13, 1860.

34. *New York Tribune*, Sept. 22, 1855; Philip S. Foner, *The Life and Writings of Frederick Douglass* (New York: International Publishers, 1950–1955), 2:370.

political controversies—ones that had helped to define the new political coalitions. The Republicans, a party with significant strength only in the North, used antisouthern rhetoric to bind together its disparate elements. As Michael Holt has pointed out, the southern-dominated Democratic Party symbolized for Republicans "a receptacle of aristocracy, slavery, tyranny, and corruption—antirepublicanism incarnate."[35] And what better example than the property qualification could be found of a Democratic effort to subvert basic political liberties by tyrannizing over a weak and helpless minority? "Priest-ridden" Catholic immigrants could also be seen as a threat to the republic. While less ostentatiously anti-immigrant than the Know Nothing Party, the Republican Party lost few opportunities to demonstrate its suspicions of some of the foreign born who so often ended up in the ranks of the despised Democrats. Equal suffrage thus could be portrayed both as an indication to the South of northern independence from the South's racial prejudices and as a sign to the Irish that they did not merit preferential treatment compared to blacks.

The Democrats, on the other hand, increasingly dependent on the votes of northern immigrants and southerners, catered to some immigrants' fears of the blacks and stressed their agreement with southerners on innate black inferiority whenever they discussed black suffrage. Indeed racism was a peculiarly useful issue, for while northern Democrats found it more and more difficult to agree with their southern counterparts on the manner of slavery's expansion into the west, they certainly could find some common ground in their contempt for the black race.

The new polarization of party leaders on black suffrage was quite visible in the legislatures of the late 1850s. The only two sessions in which the Republicans did not have a majority were also the only ones in which equal suffrage resolutions failed to pass. In the remaining sessions such resolutions were adopted by almost completely partisan votes. The 1856 legislature, the first in which the newly emerging political coalitions appeared, was one of those that failed to act, but it gave indications of what was to come. No party had a majority in the Assembly, and the Republicans had only a scant lead in the Senate (seventeen of thirty-two seats). In the Senate, Samuel Cuyler, a western New York Republican, at the request of Stephen Myers, introduced a resolution to amend the constitu-

35. Holt, *Political Crisis*, p. 216.

tion by removing the property qualification for blacks. It proceeded as far as committee of the whole, where three Republicans besides Cuyler defended it and a Democrat and a Know Nothing opposed it. It was not reported out, however.[36] In the Assembly, a New York Know Nothing introduced a resolution similar to Cuyler's on which no action was taken.[37] After the session, Frederick Douglass claimed that the Assembly's Judiciary Committee (composed of two Republicans, three Democrats, and two Americans) was to blame. Its chairman, a Republican, favored the reform, but only one other committeeman had supported him, and he thought it best not to report under these circumstances.[38]

In the following year, however, when the Republicans had won a substantial majority in the Assembly, the story was different. Cuyler reintroduced his resolution in the Senate. Again only Republicans backed him in debate, but the resolution easily passed, 21–5.[39] All of the Republicans who voted favored the measure, while two of the three Democrats opposed it. The Know Nothings had the greatest difficulty reaching a uniform position. Able to unite easily on strict literacy and citizenship qualifications (which one of them had proposed as a substitute to Cuyler's measure), they divided five to three in favor of suffrage for the black man. The black, although native born, was not like other men, some Know Nothings argued. One asked, "Will they [suffrage advocates] place the colored man upon a social equality with themselves, and their families? Will they invite the colored man into their parlors and treat him as an equal, or will they sit down at the tavern table, side by side with him, and feel contented?"[40] The Senate's resolution had no difficulty in the Assembly, passing 75–27.[41] No Democrats favored it, and only one Re-

36. New York State Senate, *Journal*, 79th Sess., 1856, p. 378; *Albany Argus*, Mar. 19, 1856.

37. Myers claimed responsibility for initiating this resolution also. Myers to Smith, Mar. 22, 1856, Smith Papers; New York State Assembly, *Journal*, 79th Sess., 1856, p. 887.

38. Foner, *Douglass*, 2:389–90.

39. New York State Senate, *Journal*, 80th Sess., 1857, pp. 67, 131, 262–63, 283, 310, 353–54.

40. *Albany Argus*, Mar. 4, 1857. See also ibid., Feb. 27, 1857.

41. Immediately preceding this vote was one to put the main question (that is, stop debate and vote on the bill). It passed 65–38 with nine Republicans voting with the Democrats in opposition. Most of these Republicans were from western New York and do not appear to have been conservative. They may well have wished a chance to speak on the resolution, the first opportunity to do so since the Dred Scott decision. Two were members of the Assembly committee considering the suffrage question. New York Assembly, *Journal*, 80th Sess., 1857, pp. 862–64.

publican opposed it. All four Americans supported the measure. One legislature had now approved the amendment, but approval by a second was still needed.

The suffrage effort again stalled in 1858 when the Republicans failed to win a majority in either house. Although resolutions providing for equal suffrage were presented in each house (one by an antislavery Democrat who wanted to test the sincerity of the Republicans), they never came to a vote.[42] In 1859 and 1860, however, the difficult task of obtaining the approval of two legislatures for the proposed amendment was at last accomplished. In every instance the votes were overwhelmingly partisan.[43] (See Tables 3.10–3.13.) Only *one* Democrat in the two houses of the legislature in the two sessions voted in favor of the resolutions, and from eighty-nine to one hundred per cent of the Republicans who voted endorsed equal suffrage.[44]

A growing consciousness of the importance of party unity on the issue was also apparent in both parties. Republicans utilized the Assembly debate in 1859 to resolve the lingering doubts of some of their number on the subject. Hatred of the Democratic Party brought some of the undecided into line. Democrats opposed equal suffrage, it was argued, not on its merits but because they selfishly believed that their party would benefit from black exclusion from the ballot box. They might claim to object to unqualified blacks voting but would themselves "vote to admit everybody else from all quarters of the globe."[45] Similarly, those uncertain about equal suffrage learned that a yes vote on the resolution did not necessarily commit them to a position favoring "inferior" races. Thus when one

42. New York State Assembly, *Journal*, 81st Sess., 1858, p. 515; New York State Senate, *Journal*, 81st Sess., 1858, p. 601; *Albany Argus*, Apr. 10, 1858.

43. New York State Assembly, *Journal*, 82nd Sess., 1859, p. 732; New York State Senate, *Journal*, 82nd Sess., 1859, pp. 633, 701; New York State Assemby, *Journal*, 83rd Sess., 1860, p. 332; New York State Senate, *Journal*, 83rd Sess., 1860, p. 468. The party affiliations in the tables are taken from the Albany newspapers, which often listed the members of the legislature on the eve of its opening. Many legislators (particularly Republicans) in the later sessions were endorsed by the Know Nothings. A death, a resignation, and an official challenge account for the fact that the Senate, which had no Republican majority in 1858, had one in 1859.

44. Another Democrat, James J. Reilly of New York was listed as voting for equal suffrage in the 1859 Assembly according to the *Journal* of that body. Every press account, however, mentions only one dissenting Democrat, William C. Lamont, and the *Albany Argus*, Mar. 24, 1859, which also recorded the vote, lists Rider (a Republican), not Reilly, as casting a yes vote. It seems probable that the *Journal* was in error on this point.

45. *Albany Evening Journal*, Mar. 23, 1859.

TABLE 3.10.

Votes on equal suffrage resolution, Assembly, 1859, by party

Position	Republican			Democrat			American	
	Number	Per cent[a]		Number	Per cent[a]		Number	Per cent[a]
For	82	84	(98)	1	3	(5)	0	0
Against	2	2	(2)	19	66	(95)	0	0
Absent	14	14		9	31		1	100
Total	98	100	(100)	29	100	(100)	1	100

$\chi^2 = 86.9$ for 1 d.f. Significant at .001.
[a]Figures in parentheses are percentages excluding absentees.

TABLE 3.11.

Votes on equal suffrage resolution, Senate, 1859, by party

Position	Republican			Democrat			American		
	Number	Per cent[a]		Number	Per cent[a]		Number	Per cent[a]	
For	18	95	(100)	0	0	(0)	0	0	
Against	0	0		11	92	(100)	1	100	(100)
Absent	1	5		1	8		0	0	
Total	19	100	(100)	12	100	(100)	1	100	(100)

$\chi^2 = 30.6$ for 2 d.f. Significant at .001.
[a]Figures in parentheses are percentages excluding absentees.

TABLE 3.12.

Votes on equal suffrage resolution, Assembly, 1860, by party

Position	Republican			Democrat		
	Number	Per cent[a]		Number	Per cent[a]	
For	70	77	(93)	0	0	
Against	5	5	(7)	31	84	(100)
Absent	16	18		6	16	
Total	91	100	(100)	37	100	(100)

$\chi^2 = 80.4$ for 1 d.f. Significant at .001.
[a]Figures in parentheses are percentages excluding absentees.

TABLE 3.13.

Votes on equal suffrage resolution, Senate, 1860, by party

	Republican		Democrat	
Position	Number	Per cent[a]	Number	Per cent[a]
For	17	74 (89)	0	0
Against	2	9 (11)	7	78 (100)
Absent	4	17	2	22
Total	23	100 (100)	9	100 (100)

$\chi^2 = 23.2$ for 1 d.f. Significant at .001.

[a]Figures in parentheses are percentages excluding absentees.

Republican asked it if were not dangerous to allow Chinese to vote, he was reminded that the ultimate decision was in the hands of the voters and that it was unnecessary to insist that one's constituents vote for the measure. Indeed another Republican praised the resolution precisely because it offered the voters a chance to rule on the composition of the electorate.[46]

Those Republicans who continued to object to equal suffrage met open opposition. When in 1860 a Republican (Judiah Ellsworth of Saratoga) not only voted against black suffrage, but spoke against it as well, other Assembly Republicans bitterly condemned him, accusing him of being submissive to the wishes of southern guests at the Saratoga spas.[47]

The Democrats, too, felt the pressures of party. Thus in 1857 Senator James Wadsworth of Buffalo admitted that he personally disliked the property qualification but opposed the suffrage resolution on the grounds that the question should be left to a constitutional convention rather than to the amendment procedure.[48] Democrats who disagreed with their party on equal suffrage were indeed a rarity, however. In fact, those (both Republicans and Democrats) who voted against the majority of their parties on equal suffrage were isolated and insignificant politically. They formed no permanent or consistent factions. On the Republican side (where they were numerous enough to categorize) they tended to come from eastern New York, and some at least had very strong personal antipathies toward blacks. One senator likened blacks without property to

46. *Albany Argus*, Mar. 24, 1859.
47. Ibid., Feb. 11, 1860; *Albany Evening Journal*, Feb. 20, 1860.
48. *Albany Argus*, Feb. 27, 1857.

"cattle," and an assemblyman insisted that blacks were inferior and degraded beings.[49] Yet neither party in the legislature had a strong core of active opposition to its position on black suffrage.

Those who participated in the suffrage debates often indicated that they saw the issue as intimately connected with the other major partisan issues of the day. Republican Samuel Cuyler asked in 1857, "With what consistency . . . can we wage war even against American Slavery, or endeavor to preserve our institutions from the touch of the foul monster, and yet allow in our Constitution the very principles upon which slavery lives and breathes?"[50] In 1856 the debate on equal suffrage developed into a bitter exchange over Stephen A. Douglas's "prosouthern" popular sovereignty proposals for Kansas, a controversial subject still in 1857. In 1860 the suffrage question sparked a Republican denunciation of the Fugitive Slave Law.[51] The status of the immigrant received attention, too. The blacks of New York City, said one speaker, were "better qualified to vote than are the mass of ignorant foreigners who have no knowledge of, or regard for the institutions of the country," and there were other complaints about the poor quality of naturalized voters.[52]

The typical strategy of the Democrats in the face of Republican partisan attacks is well illustrated in a speech given by a Saratoga Democrat, George G. Scott, in 1857. Scott was a member of the Assembly committee that had considered the petitions for equal suffrage and hoped to establish his reputation on this issue.[53] He tried to keep the question of black suffrage distinct from the question of the South and slavery and to stress that the real issue was that of race. Thus he argued that voting was a matter of social expediency, not natural right; while white males over twenty-one were generally qualified to vote, blacks were not. Although a *property* qualification

49. Ibid., Apr. 10, 1860; see also Feb. 11. The sole Democratic dissenter in 1857 was a Soft who was also the only Democrat to favor any portion of the resolutions which the Republicans proposed on the Dred Scott decision. The minority Democrat in 1859 was known not to "cherish very strong party preferences." William D. Murphy, *Biographical Sketches of the State Officers and Members of the Legislature of the State of New York in 1859* (Albany: C. Van Benthuysen, 1859), p. 179.

50. *Albany Evening Journal*, Feb. 18, 1857.

51. *Albany Argus*, Mar. 19, 1856; *Albany Evening Journal*, Mar. 7, 1857, Feb. 10, 1860. No official record of the legislature's debates was kept. The Albany newspapers, however, often gave brief summaries of debates on issues of interest and also reprinted in full the texts of some speeches.

52. Quote from *Albany Argus*, Feb. 11, 1860. See also *Albany Evening Journal*, Mar. 7, 1857.

53. William D. Murphy, *Biographical Sketches of the State Officers and Members of the Legislature of the State of New York, in 1858* (Albany: J. Munsell, 1858), p. 93.

for them was not ideal, it was better than no qualification at all. Blacks were basically different from whites, inferior in intellect and morals, and equality with them was impossible, he argued. The rights of blacks were protected without the vote and should they obtain it, they would unite on political questions and support the party that would "'stoop the lowest' to secure their votes." Indeed he believed that the suffrage measure was a Republican plot to recruit black voters.[54]

Because of the connection Republicans made between black suffrage and the slavery issue nationally, specific events in the sectional controversy affected New York's actions on equal suffrage. One such event was the Dred Scott decision of 1857. Republican and Democratic responses to this event increased dramatically the awareness of the equal suffrage resolutions and the attention the general public gave to them.

The partisan press had commented only briefly when the Senate had passed its equal suffrage resolution in February, 1857, the Democratic *Albany Argus* complaining about the lack of attention to matters concerning whites and the Republican *Albany Evening Journal* calling the property qualification an "anomaly" but cautiously noting there was no need to fear "precipitate" action.[55] Then on March 6, the Supreme Court announced its Dred Scott decision. Not only did five justices declare that it was unconstitutional to exclude slavery from a territory, but three insisted blacks were not even citizens. Chief Justice Roger Taney himself argued that historically blacks had had no rights which whites were bound to respect.[56] Many leading New York Republicans reacted angrily, arguing that the decision showed the complete subservience of the Democratic majority on the court to southern slaveholders. The legislature appointed a joint committee on the Dred Scott decision which eventually presented a blistering report and a series of resolutions condemning the court. These passed both houses. In March also the Assembly adopted the equal suffrage resolutions by the most nearly unanimous vote of Assembly Republicans in the prewar years.

The Democrats took the opportunity of the passage of the suffrage resolution to launch a counteroffensive of their own. If the

54. *Albany Argus*, Mar. 14, 1857.
55. *Albany Argus*, Feb. 18, 1857; *Albany Evening Journal*, Feb. 18, 1857.
56. Allan Nevins, *The Emergence of Lincoln* (New York: Charles Scribner's Sons, 1950), 1:91–95.

Republicans wished to lament the plight of Dred Scott and excoriate the Slave Power, the Democrats had a different explanation for the Republicans' behavior, one that would appeal to deeply felt racial prejudices. On the day after the Assembly's passage of the suffrage resolution, the *New York Herald,* a Democratic paper whose editor was contemptuous of the black race and had not deigned to follow at all the legislature's suffrage efforts, observed scornfully that the Republicans were aiding their "colored brethren" by placing them on a "perfect equality" with whites at the polls. Revealing its lack of attention to the Senate's passage of the resolution, it predicted the Republican Senate would soon concur with the Assembly's endorsement of equal suffrage. To the *Herald* the measure was sheer "political clap trap," a theme to which it returned shortly thereafter when it criticized the legislature's joint committee on Dred Scott for using blacks "for party purposes, and no further" by hypocritically ignoring the property qualification for black voters. When informed by the *Tribune* that the legislature had already acted on this matter, the *Herald* passed over its blunder and launched into a violent attack on racial equality and a defense of the Supreme Court.[57]

The *Albany Argus* took the same approach but was far less clumsy. In a series of lengthy editorials from March through May, it attacked black suffrage from all vantage points. The measure was, it announced, a new plank in the "Black Republican" platform. The Republicans had seized upon the Dred Scott excitement to enact it, but their real aim was "to add ten thousand voters to the ranks of the Black Republicans of the State, to assist them in their failing fortunes. It is to recruit a Black Regiment, which shall march through the breach in the State Constitution!"[58] The Democratic members of the legislature picked up this theme and carried it further in their address to the people at the end of the legislative session. Linking the suffrage resolution to the Dred Scott resolutions and a bill to secure freedom for slaves brought into the state, they argued that the combined effect of these proposals would be: "an invitation to the negro slaves of the South to escape to this State, to be protected here against its [*sic*] the reclamation of their owners, if need be, by armed power, and to be incorporated into the mass of voters, and into the militia, to enter into the organization of Juries, and to be eligible to all the offices and functions of Magistracy, within the

57. *New York Herald,* Mar. 26, Apr. 12, 14, 1857.
58. *Albany Argus,* Mar. 27, 31, Apr. 1, 1857.

State."[59] By late May the *Argus* was arguing that historically the chief object of the property qualification had been to prevent an influx of free blacks. The Republican Party was a threat to the racial status quo, it insisted, but Republicans were in no sense sincere. They wished to force on the masses an association which they themselves avoided. Indeed they hated ordinary people, opposing the rights of certain white groups, especially the naturalized citizen. The *Argus* welcomed suffrage as a political issue and warned the Republicans that the next Senate and Assembly would be chosen on the issue.[60]

The Democrats' attack exposed the Achilles heel of the equal suffrage movement. Many Republicans did not want to campaign on the race issue. In the legislature the issue was useful. It served to reassure equal rights advocates that the party respected their position. When soliciting votes in prosuffrage areas, a party leader could cite the party's positive steps to secure voting rights for blacks. But to let the Democrats control when and where the issue would be raised could be disastrous. The Republican coalition was not made up solely of egalitarians. The more the Democrats flaunted the race question, the less willing Republicans were to take an open, straightforward stand on equal franchise rights for blacks. The party press, for instance, chose to avoid the issue or to link it to sentiment on Dred Scott. The *New York Tribune* began its editorial on the legislature's passage of the equal suffrage resolution with the statement:

> Amid the shame and sorrow to which we are subjected by the efforts of the slaveholding majority of the Supreme Court of the United States, in bold defiance of historical truths, as well as of the plainest and most universally admitted principles of legal interpretation, to force upon the Constitution of the United States a neological interpretation, we are not left without consolation.

That the "consolation" was black suffrage was not mentioned until well into the article and then it was disguised as:

> [an effort] to carry back the State Constitutions to those principles of equal rights upon which they were originally established, principles abandoned at a comparatively recent period through slaveholding influence, and out of an illjudged complaisance to our Southern brethren; a complaisance from which we have reaped no fruits except the grossest indignities and humiliations, and a spirit

59. Ibid., Apr. 24, 1857. To stress the importance of the point the original quotation was printed entirely in italics.
60. Ibid., Mar. 31, Apr. 1, May 24, 1857.

of usurpation on the part of the slaveholders which has culminated in the extraordinary judicial pronunciamiento above referred to.[61]

The *Albany Evening Journal's* only comment was to stress that black suffrage was not an innovation and had proved safe in the New England states.[62] While the Democrats played upon racial fears and resentments, the Republicans did little to assuage them. To do so would further identify the party as "Black Republicans."

On September 4, 1857, Greeley revealed that "somebody" at Albany had neglected to publish the proposed black suffrage amendment to the state constitution three months before the general election as the state constitution required. The governor's explanation was that the resolution had been sent to the executive chamber with bills requiring his signature. Separated from these, it went unnoticed and was not called for by the official who should have published it.[63] This meant that the amendment process the 1857 legislature had begun was now ended and that the procedure would have to be started all over again for equal suffrage to be adopted. The Democratic consensus was that the error had been intentional; the *Argus* hoped Republicans would take a position on the issue. The Democratic state convention meeting the following week condemned equal suffrage in its platform and called upon voters "not to be deceived by the device or accident of a supression of this amendment in the pigeon holes of the Executive Chamber into the belief that our opponents have relinquished this scheme, but to interrogate the candidates for the Senate and Assembly in regard to it, and to hold them to strict accountability."[64]

Blacks, needless to say, felt cheated and expressed their anger and frustration at a convention in New York. Greeley publicly scolded this group for believing that Republicans had it in their power to grant the suffrage. (He seemed particularly eager to demonstrate to the world that Republicans held no "peculiar regard" for blacks.) He reminded blacks that popular sentiment still opposed equal suffrage and that not more than two-thirds of Republican voters favored it. The Democrats, not blacks, were the real losers since they would have to surrender the issue. "And although the issue is lost,

61. *New York Tribune,* Mar. 28, 1857.
62. *Albany Evening Journal,* Mar. 26, 1857.
63. *New York Tribune,* Sept. 4, 1857; New York State Senate, *Documents,* 81st Sess., 1858, No. 3, p. 11.
64. *Albany Argus,* Sept. 7, 14, 1857.

they are determined to raise the cry [Down with Negro Suffrage!] with all the force of their leathern lungs and whiskey-perfumed voices."[65]

As the Republicans had hoped, the rest of the campaign was relatively free from the suffrage issue. The new Republican governor, John A. King, did explain to the 1858 legislature how the suffrage resolution had been overlooked, announce his concurrence with its aim, and ask the legislature to reconsider the matter.[66] This, however, was one of the legislatures lacking a Republican majority, and no action was taken. In 1859, when the Republicans had reclaimed the legislature, King's Republican successor, Edwin Morgan (for whom the blacks had actively campaigned), failed to mention the suffrage question in his message to the legislature. Frederick Douglass was so disappointed that he questioned whether blacks were *any* closer to their goal than in 1837 when the first suffrage campaign had been undertaken.[67] Even some of the prosuffrage advocates in the legislature felt uncertain. Senator John J. Foote, a friend of Gerrit Smith from Madison County, persuaded the Assembly to act before the Senate on equal suffrage in 1859 because the Republicans had a larger majority in the Assembly.[68] When Republicans in the legislature were actually confronted with making a decision on equal suffrage, however, they favored it. One of the results of the partisan sparring over the matter had been to make it difficult for Republicans to disavow it without great political embarrassment.

The Democrats still were not completely committed to exploiting the suffrage issue at this time. Their response to the passage of the equal suffrage resolution in 1859 by both houses was much less hysterical than it had been in 1857. The *Argus* linked black suffrage to the Republican support of the registry law which, it said, was designed to keep laborers and adopted citizens of German and Irish birth from voting while blacks were encouraged to do so. (The registry law required personal voter registration in cities, but not rural areas, before elections, thereby increasing the inconvenience and difficulty of voting.) The Democratic legislators in their address to the people in April, 1859, also denounced the equal suffrage measure as a purely "party device."[69] But in the fall the Democratic state

65. *New York Tribune*, Sept. 26, 1857.
66. New York State Senate, *Documents*, 81st Sess., 1858, No. 3, p. 12.
67. *Douglass' Monthly*, Mar. 1859.
68. John J. Foote to Gerrit Smith, Apr. 9, 1859, Smith Papers.
69. *Albany Argus*, Apr. 11, 21, 1859.

convention had nothing to say about black voting, and the Demo-
crats conducted the campaign on such issues as the registry law and
John Brown's raid without reference to black voting equality.[70] The
Republicans also steered clear of the issue.

The potentially harmful effects of the race issue on their party
were still of grave concern to the Republicans, however, particularly
as the presidential election year 1860 approached.[71] The Democrats
were aware of their opportunity to label the Republicans as extrem-
ists. The *Argus* now stressed that black suffrage was a "radical"
change in policy and would involve the blacks in *control* of the government:

> ... the Republican party now proposes ... to establish ... the
> theory of a government controlled and conducted by an intermix-
> ture of races, which shall place the Negro, the Indian, the Feejee
> [*sic*] Islander, and every other race of men, of whatever grade of
> civilization alongside of the whites, at the ballot-box, in our munici-
> pal and local boards, in the legislative hall, and in the Executive
> Chair, and admit them to an equal share in shaping the political
> destiny of this Republic.[72]

It added to its old conspiratorial theory of Republican motivation
the idea that Republicans hoped to use black voters to help pass laws
limiting the suffrage rights of the foreign born as Massachusetts (a
state where blacks could vote) had recently done. The Democrats in
their legislative address also stressed the radicalism of black suffrage
and expressed their confidence that the state's electors would "rally
to the side of the Democrats, and vote down the proposed amendment, which is intended to recruit the ranks of fanatic abolitionism
and sectionalism."[73]

The Republicans responded once again not by opposing equal
suffrage (although the proportion of Republicans voting against it
was a little larger) but by shying away from open advocacy of it outside the legislature. The most the *Albany Evening Journal* could manage after the passage of the suffrage resolution was a brief rebuttal
of the radicalism charge on the grounds that there were already
fifteen hundred black voters.[74] The *New York Tribune* made no com-

---

70. Ibid., Sept 16, 1859.
71. Editorials in the *Albany Evening Journal*, Jan. 17. 1860, and the *New York Tribune*,
Feb. 11, 1860, went to great pains to demonstrate that Republicans were not abolitionists. Cf. *National Anti-Slavery Standard*, Mar. 31, 1860.
72. *Albany Argus*, Feb. 12, 1860.
73. Ibid., Feb. 12, Apr. 18, 1860.
74. *Albany Evening Journal*, Feb. 13, 1860.

ment whatever. Toward the end of the session there was a brief alarm among the black lobbyists when it was discovered that no bill had been introduced to arrange the procedural details for the submission of the proposed suffrage amendment to the electorate.[75] (In 1850 a constitutional amendment approved by two legislatures had died when such a bill had failed to pass.) Once the lapse had been pointed out, an appropriate bill was introduced and approved.[76] It was another reminder, however, that the Republicans were not carefully shepherding the equal suffrage measure through legislative obstacles.

By the close of the 1860 legislative session all that remained to make equal suffrage part of the New York constitution was ratification of the amendment by the people in the 1860 election. Judging by surface appearances, much had been accomplished since the day fourteen years before when suffrage had been discredited at the polls. Action by the legislature had replaced initial inertia on black rights. Most immediately the restructuring of the state's political system seemed responsible. The new interest in suffrage came precisely at that point when the Republican Party replaced the old Whig Party in New York. The former was far less dependent than the Whigs on support from southeastern New York, the area of near unanimous opposition to black suffrage in 1846, and it was relatively stronger in the prosuffrage parts of western New York. The ideological significance of equal suffrage had also begun to change. Although hardly the national issue it was to become in the 1860s, suffrage was already being linked to party stands on slavery extension and the role of the immigrant in America. It was possible to view prejudice as a slavery-induced sin and the discriminatory property qualification as a sign of submission to the Slave Power. Many Republicans also saw the need to articulate some of the anxieties felt over the rapid increase of the antiblack and pro-Democratic immigrants from Ireland and Germany and to assert the rights of native-born blacks. Thus under the prodding of a largely black lobbying group, Republican legislators finally adopted resolutions amending the constitution on equal suffrage.

75. *Weekly Anglo-African* (New York), Apr. 21, 28, 1860. The blacks tended to blame the Democrats since they had opposed the bill once it was introduced. Certainly the Republicans had been surprisingly careless, however. The paper (Mar. 31, 1860) also reported that Myers had had to pressure the Republican-controlled committee considering the original resolution to report it out.

76. Lincoln, *Constitutional History*, 2:226; New York State Assembly, *Journal*, 83rd Sess., 1860, p. 1263; New York State Senate, *Journal*, 83rd Sess., 1860, p. 737.

The emergence of the parties as participants was the most important event of the 1846–1860 period for the suffrage struggle. Political parties played a central role in American society. In their efforts to mold majority coalitions, they stressed issues they felt would have key symbolic meaning to the electorate. During this time these issues centered around social conflict, a natural result of the heightened concern over both blacks and aliens. Parties had great potential influence. They virtually monopolized the major medium of communication on political topics, the newspapers, and they were part of a political tradition that stressed the reliance upon party regularity and partisanship to achieve political goals. The transformation of equal suffrage into a *political* issue, therefore, meant that it would be treated differently than it had been in 1846. Powerful new organizations were now involved in the shaping of the suffrage struggle.

But parties were also coalitions subject to internal divisions. Frank Sorauf has argued that political parties consist of the organization proper, the party in the legislature, and the party in the electorate.[77] In the case of the Democrats, all three of these elements were united in opposition to equal suffrage by 1860. The party articulated fears of black political power, thereby defining this issue for those who considered themselves Democrats and organizing their opposition to it. The Republicans, on the other hand, chose to get involved with suffrage only in the legislature. There they worked out an interpretation of the issue that linked it to the vital social concerns of the day—the dual threat posed by the southern slaveholder and the Catholic immigrant.

There was, however, a fundamental tension within the Republican Party on the question of equal voting privileges for blacks. On the one hand stood men such as Samuel Cuyler, committed to nineteenth century ideals of reform. To such men the property qualification was an unjust, unfair barrier that limited the progress of black men toward individual perfection.[78] The question was a moral one arousing almost missionary zeal: "Come, then, legislators, let us rise above the drivelling cant of conservatism and miserable cells of fossil ages, and breathe the better air of a living age, an age of great thoughts and philanthropic deeds."[79] On the other hand were those

77. Frank J. Sorauf, "Political Parties and Political Analysis," in William Nisbet Chambers and Walter Dean Burnham, eds., *The American Party Systems* (New York: Oxford University Press, 1967), pp. 37–38.
78. *Albany Evening Journal*, Feb. 18, 1857.
79. Ibid., Feb. 20, 1860.

who did not see voting equality and, indeed, racial equality as a moral imperative. Pragmatic considerations concerned them. The conservative Republican *New York Times* in early 1860 forecast that "the admission of any large numbers of blacks to political equality with the whites, so far from healing the breach between the two races, would only widen it." Prejudice would continue, said the *Times,* because blacks were in fact inferior (due to their condition in life rather than innate racial characteristics). Given political influence, they would try to avenge their wrongs creating disorder. The only answer for the *Times* was colonization.[80]

Some Republicans who had no strong objection to black voting in New York were still concerned about its practical impact on the Republican Party. In 1857 the Democrats had tried to turn public attention from Dred Scott to black suffrage, and in 1860 they had attempted to make the Republicans appear a dangerously radical party that could not be trusted with national power. Of course, occasional Democratic apologies that they did not oppose equal *civil* rights for blacks, did not want to be unjust to them, and even did not deny their equality under "favorable" conditions suggested that some considered blatant racism to be in poor taste.[81] Still, Democrats were exploiting white fears by exaggerating the possible consequences of equal suffrage. For Republicans to answer the fantastic charges of the Democrats was to allow them to make race an issue when many Republicans believed that Democrats were most vulnerable on other matters. For Horace Greeley and other Republicans it seemed enough that they were submitting the question to the people for their decision.[82] Thus while the Democrats were willing to foster prejudice for the party (and, in their eyes, national) good, many practical-minded Republicans were reluctant to challenge it directly.

The near unanimity of the Republicans in the legislature on equal suffrage was in one sense very impressive yet in another quite misleading. Not only were there practical limits to some Republicans' support of equal suffrage, but the legislators were not representative of Republicans (even Republican leaders) as a whole. The realignment had made much of western and northern New York a Republican bastion. While in the pre-1854 period most counties had been competitive (in 1844 only one county had given over sixty-

80. *New York Times,* Feb. 17, 1860.
81. *Albany Argus,* Mar. 14, 27, 1857, Feb. 12, 1860.
82. *New York Tribune,* Sept. 7, 1857.

five per cent of its vote to any candidate), after that period many counties gave lopsided majorities to one party or another. (In the three-way race for governor in 1856, eight counties gave the Republicans more than sixty-five per cent of their vote and nine more between sixty and sixty-five per cent.) As a result, many Republican legislators came from solidly Republican districts where a small amount of Republican opposition to equal suffrage was not a real threat to party control.[83] The views of Republicans in the more racially conservative eastern portion of the state were less well represented in the legislature. Yet the state could not be carried without their help. Some concessions had to be made to their views.

The Republican Party, like any major party, had to try to satisfy all its constituent elements. Its linkage of equal rights to the Kansas-Nebraska Act, Dred Scott decision, and other national events; its attractiveness to moral reformers; and its desperate need for the energy, hard work, and enthusiasm that the prosuffrage element brought to the party—all had a positive effect on black voting rights. But the presence of strong racial prejudice in much of the electorate and indeed part of the party's own leadership militated against the vigorous advocacy of equal rights on any and all occasions. Prosuffrage actions in the legislature helped to reassure one group, while indifference to it during electoral contests answered the need for party expediency. Once again the fate of equal suffrage in New York was tied to unpleasant political realities. Parties, even those increasingly polarized on equal rights, could be expected to go so far and no further on the issue. What effect the actions of party elites would have on public perceptions of the suffrage question would become clear only in 1860 as the issue was once again presented to the voters.

83. *The Evening Journal Almanac for 1861*, pp. 44–49, classified twenty-seven counties containing fifty-one Assembly seats as either Republican or strongly Republican.

CHAPTER FOUR

Black Suffrage and
the Electorate, 1860

Black suffrage was an unusual issue in that politicians could debate it endlessly, but the ultimate responsibility for its enactment or rejection could always be passed to others. Thus in 1846 Whigs could impress Liberty men with their denunciations of the property qualification while letting the popular vote show that in a practical sense change was impossible. The same was true in 1860. A victory in the legislature meant nothing unless it could also be translated into success in the popular referendum. The political climate in 1860 differed, of course, from that in 1846. An upstate Republican editor voiced the opinion that because "such a change has been made in political creeds and political parties," equal suffrage was sure to be adopted.[1] Certainly if voters responded solely as partisans, the measure would indeed have an excellent chance of success. But would they? The 1860 referendum on equal suffrage serves as a measure of the changes that had occurred since 1846 and, above all, the extent to which black rights had become politicized even before the outbreak of the Civil War. But it also indicates how little Republican politicians *wanted* to be identified as black suffrage advocates and suggests why, despite legislative action, equal rights remained such an elusive goal.

The political context of the referendum in 1860 was all impor-

1. *Cortland Republican Banner,* Oct. 3, 1860.

tant. Although the suffrage amendment was technically a proposition wholly separate from the important electoral campaign for president (and a variety of other state and local offices) under way at the time, in a practical sense it was impossible to separate the two. It was, therefore, crucial that politicians pursue strategies that would use the race issue to its best advantage to help and not to hurt their electoral chances. The ways in which politicians approached this task are quite revealing, for they indicate their perceptions of public opinion on the race issue and how that opinion could be manipulated to partisan advantage.

The Democrats were in an unenviable position in 1860. Nationally their party had split along sectional lines, the southern portion supporting John C. Breckenridge for president and the northern, Stephen A. Douglas. While the opposition to Abraham Lincoln, consisting of the Democratic factions and the Constitutional Unionists (supporters of John Bell), had united on a common electoral slate in New York, Republicans still seemed well on their way to winning the presidency for the first time in their history.[2] The Democrats' best hope seemed to be to try to convince the public that the Republicans were too extreme in their views to be trusted with national power. Ever since the formation of the Republican Party, Democrats had shown a willingness to confuse that party's opposition to slavery extension with advocacy of abolition and black equality. With black suffrage actually on the ballot, that tactic seemed even more useful.

Whereas in 1846 the discussion of the race issue had been rather haphazard, in 1860 Democrats systematically exploited it along with other "proofs" of Republican radicalism. Republicans, they insisted, were obsessed with the black man. "It is negro here, negro there, and negro everywhere. They [Republicans] have got but one idea. All their statesmen and all their leaders, in every speech, dwell upon the eternal negro."[3] They depicted Republican leaders as enthusiastic advocates of Negro suffrage and always referred to the amendment as a Republican-sponsored one. In their party platform they condemned equal suffrage and linked it with Republican "misrule," resolving:

> that instead of listening to the proposition of the Abolition agitators and Republican politicians, further to subjugate the people of this state in the name of freedom, by tampering with the suffrage and introducing a large negro element to aid in controlling our elections,

2. Gerrit Smith was also a minor-party candidate for president.
3. *New York Herald*, Oct. 9, 1860.

we demand emancipation for the white men of the State—emancipation from unreasonable taxation, from corrupt legislation and
from the oppression with which Republican misrule is crushing
them.[4]

A Democratic journal in Steuben County insisted that all Republicans *had* to favor equal rights for blacks:

> You that are for negro suffrage, will please vote the Republican
> ticket—you who are not for it will of course go the Democratic ticket.
> Negro suffrage is a part of Republicanism. The Democrats claim no
> share in it and will not vote for it. You who intend to vote for Lin-
> coln, remember this is a part of the creed—don't split the ticket.[5]

The *Sag Harbor Corrector* went one step further declaring " . . . if
you vote for the Republican ticket, you vote for universal negro suffrage in the State of New York!"[6]

In discussing the suffrage question Democrats dwelled on many
of the same points as they had in previous years—the threats of
black political power, job competition, and social equality, for example. But now they strove for even greater realism by giving vivid
examples of precisely what they meant and by developing the implications of voting equality to their fullest possible extent. The *Albany Argus* pointed out that the Democratic Party would have lost
many close elections in the past fifteen years had all blacks voted.[7]
Blacks who held political power would be "consulted, conciliated,
represented and rewarded" by the grateful Republicans. "The era
of mixed Negro government in the United States—a government of
hybrids, like that of Mexico and of Jamaica, and other West Indian
islands" would result. Blacks might become "Jurors, Sheriffs, Alder-
men, Representatives and Governors."[8] Republicans, if successful,
would then undoubtedly try to compel by law all state-supported
schools to admit black children. A voter might be asked to cast his
ballot "cheek by jowl with a large 'buck nigger.'"[9] Concern about the

4. *Albany Argus*, Aug. 17, 1860. The Democrats consciously manipulated the suf-
frage issue to their partisan advantage. See, for example, Charles G. Halpine to
Samuel J. Tilden, Sept. 10, 1860, Samuel J. Tilden Papers, New York Public Library,
New York City.
    5. *Steuben Farmer's Advocate* (Bath), Oct. 31, 1860.
    6. *Sag Harbor Corrector*, Sept. 15, 1860.
    7. *Albany Argus*, Aug. 27, Nov. 1, 1860. See also *New York Herald*, Sept. 18, 1860.
    8. Quotes, in order, from *Albany Argus*, Sept. 5, 7, Aug. 27, 1860. See also *Buffalo
Daily Courier*, Nov. 5, 1860.
    9. *Albany Argus*, Sept. 7, 1860. Quote from *Brooklyn City News*, Oct. 25, 1860. For
further racist characterizations of blacks see *New York Herald*, Apr. 1, Sept. 18, Nov. 6,

alleged sexual aggressiveness of black males, rarely mentioned in 1846, was never far from the surface. The *New York Herald* opined:

> "Liberty, fraternity, equality," is their [blacks'] motto, and they calculate that African amalgamation with the fair daughters of the Anglo Saxon, Celtic and Teutonic races will soon be their portion under the millenium [*sic*] of Republican rule which will be inaugurated by the election of Lincoln. Like the Mahomedan, who looks forward to houris in Paradise, so do the negroes of Five Points long for the day when they will be privileged to take to their arms the palefaced beauties of the Caucasian race in the city of New York. Already the waiters and whitewashers and bootblacks have grown impudent in anticipation of the bright prospect before them.[10]

Words alone were not enough for the Democrats. In preelection Democratic parades in Brooklyn and New York they made their point more graphically. "Great cheers" greeted a cart containing a likeness of Horace Greeley. "At his side was placed a large and good looking nigger wench, whom he caressed with all the affection of a true Republican." The Seventh Ward Rangers, a local Democratic club, had a wagon representing a boat filled with whites and blacks. Greeley stood at the helm saying "Free love and free niggers will certainly elect Old Abe if he pilots us safe. Colored folks have preference of state rooms."[11]

As befitted their growing numbers and importance to the Democratic Party, immigrants, especially immigrant laborers, were given special attention. The poor white working man was proudest of his right to vote, a Democratic paper noted. "It is the mark of his citizenship; and when you associate with him in it [the act of voting], a class that you regard as inferior, you evidently seek to degrade him."[12] The Republican advocates of black rights never socialized with blacks, the Democrats insisted. Why then, they asked, did Republicans try to force such behavior on the "masses" if they were not trying to humiliate and insult them? New York was in danger of becoming a "political paradise of free Negroes and self-emancipated slaves."[13] A half million black laborers might come North either taking jobs from whites or becoming a public burden if they

---

1860; *New York News* quoted in *Steuben Farmer's Advocate*, Sept. 19, 1860; *Rochester Union and Advertiser*, Nov. 2, 1860.

10. *New York Herald*, Nov. 6, 1860. See also *Buffalo Daily Courier*, Nov. 5, 1860.

11. *New York Herald*, Oct. 24, 1860. See also *Brooklyn City News*, Nov. 2, 1860.

12. *Albany Argus*, Aug. 27, 1860. See also *ibid.*, Sept. 14, 1860; *Brooklyn City News*, Nov. 3, 1860; *Schenectady Democrat*, Nov. 1, 1860.

13. *Albany Argus*, Oct. 1, Aug. 27, 1860. (Quote from issue of Aug. 27.)

remained unemployed, the Democrats argued. They reiterated the charge that Republican blacks would probably support nativist legislation. A black fresh from a southern plantation might soon be able to vote after one year, while an Irishman or German would have to wait at least five (i.e., become a citizen).[14] Democrats in Seneca County even tried to get the local Irish to vote for a former Know Nothing on their ticket by observing that his opponent "belongs to a party that says *a nigger is better than an Irishman.*"[15]

To appeal too openly to the foreign (especially Catholic) voter was also dangerous for the Democrats, however. The Democratic Party had native-born Protestant supporters who were uncomfortable with the increasingly alien character of their party. By arguing that voting was a "privilege" that should not be granted to "every being having the human form," thus hinting that some whites were also not worthy of the vote, Democratic leaders helped reassure such voters.[16]

Democrats also introduced the charge that equal suffrage was a serious threat to the Union itself. It was part of a Republican scheme to sectionalize the country as a prelude to the "irrepressible conflict." The *Argus* innocently referred to "the movement which has begun in this State, to endow the 300,000 free negroes of the Union with the right of suffrage," thereby implying that Republicans intended to extend equal suffrage to free blacks throughout the United States—including the South. According to the Democrats, blacks would naturally approve John Brown-type incursions on the South, personal liberty laws, and other sectional measures:

> Shall we, knowing the character of these negroes—knowing that if not their best qualities, at least their attachments and affections would lead them to take part against the country and the Constitution, in behalf of their own race—and knowing the ulterior designs of the demagogues who propose to marshal them as a political host and arm them with the elective franchise—shall we assist in giving them this power? . . . You must choose between negroes and nullification on one hand and the rights of white citizens and the perpetuation of the Constitution, on the other![17]

14. *American Citizen* (Ithaca), Nov. 7, 1860; *Albany Argus,* Nov. 1, 1860; *Rochester Union and Advertiser,* Nov. 2, 1860.

15. *Ovid Bee,* Nov. 7, 1860. For typical attempts to exploit Republican nativism see *Rochester Union and Advertiser,* Oct. 24, 30, 31, Nov. 3, 1860; *Buffalo Daily Courier,* Nov. 5, 1860.

16. *Newburgh Telegraph,* Sept. 13, Nov. 1, 1860.

17. *Albany Argus,* Sept. 5, 1860. See also *Plattsburgh Republican,* Oct. 13, 1860.

Thus throughout the campaign the Democrats tried to mobilize white antipathy for blacks and link the outcome of the suffrage referendum with that of the general election. They played on the social and economic insecurities of the voters and stressed the alien nature of the black, the traditional justification for exclusion and discrimination. Because of the importance of the issue to the party, there was almost no regional variation in the types of appeals made as there had been before the 1846 convention. The New York and Brooklyn papers were especially racist in their rhetoric, but their editorials and political reports were often reprinted in upstate journals.[18] In 1860 all good Democrats used the race issue.

Despite this concerted effort, the Democrats waged an uphill battle. For all their attempts to be direct and concrete, they were essentially dealing with hypothetical dangers, and the Republicans stubbornly refused to act radical. This prompted frequent Democratic cries that Republicans were behaving hypocritically by not *really* treating blacks as equals. In the heat of the campaign the tension between moral and pragmatic concerns within the Republican Party was firmly resolved in favor of the latter. Republicans tried with much success to make issues other than race salient to the electorate. Thus even before the campaign, George Templeton Strong complained of politicians who put themselves forward as "Cuffee's [the black man's] champion" but in almost the same breath he declared, "The South is so utterly barbaric and absurd that I'm constantly tempted to ally myself with Cheever and George Curtis."[19] He eventually voted for Lincoln. The "sins" of the South weighed more heavily in Republican voters' minds than the fear of blacks. As a result, Lincoln carried New York State with ease, despite the defeat of equal suffrage.

Most Republican editors eventually endorsed black suffrage, but they did so in ways that minimized the dangers to their party. Like the Democrats, they seemed to assume that a crucial portion of the electorate was prejudiced and would be alarmed at any substantive change in black political position. To various degrees they attempted to deny specific Republican involvement in equal suffrage and play down the significance of any changes that would result should the

18. See, for example, *Madison Observer* (Morrisville), Aug. 9, Sept. 27, 1860. This paper was in a county that had been prosuffrage in 1846.

19. Allan Nevins and Milton Halsey Thomas, eds., *The Diary of George Templeton Strong* (New York: Macmillan Co., 1952), 3:3–4. Cheever was an antislavery clergyman, Curtis an antislavery journalist.

amendment pass. The party leadership encouraged such a strategy by completely ignoring the suffrage question at the state convention, preferring instead to follow the lead of Republicans nationally in emphasizing the party's moderate character. Horace Greeley set the tone of the campaign when he warned his fellow partisans in mid-September that it was a "common mistake of Republicans to suppose that they must answer all the slang of their opponents and dispute all their bugaboo stories." The party was responsible *only* for the doctrines in its platform (which had not mentioned black suffrage at all). Advocacy of anything else was purely an *individual* affair. Denials forced Republicans to get away from the "main" issues of the campaign. Greeley himself endorsed the proposed amendment, but he insisted that it did not constitute the essence of the Republican cause.[20]

Some Republicans labored to show that Democrats, too, favored black rights, and a few even labeled the Democracy as the "black" party. They informed the voters that Democrats (by being the majority party in the 1821 and 1846 conventions) were responsible for the fact that blacks with a $250 freehold could vote. Democrats also had controlled several constitutional conventions in the New England states which had failed to disfranchise any blacks. A black Democratic club in Clifton Springs was continually mentioned as an illustration of the fondness of blacks for the Democratic Party.[21]

Rather than shunning racism, some Republican politicians used it as part of their own stock in trade. One paper recounted the remark of an Illinois Republican upon seeing a Democratic parade featuring a white man kissing a black woman: "'Thank God! [Stephen A.] Douglas has at last found his mother!'"[22] Another reprinted a *Chicago Press and Tribune* editorial recalling, with racial slurs, that in 1836 the Democrats had nominated as vice president Richard M. Johnson, who was married to a black woman.[23] The suffrage issue spurred Republican defensive tactics as far away as Missouri, where

20. *New York Tribune,* Sept. 15, 17, 1860. The *Roman Citizen,* Oct. 17, 1860, was one of the few Republican papers insisting that *all* Republicans should favor equal suffrage.
21. *Albany Evening Journal,* Aug. 27, Sept. 21, 1860; *Roman Citizen,* Oct. 31, 1860. See also F. Marvin to Thurlow Weed, Oct. 25, 1860, Thurlow Weed Papers, University of Rochester Library, Rochester, New York.
22. *Long Islander* (Huntington), Nov. 2, 1860.
23. *Owego Times,* Nov. 1, 1860. Although Johnson had lived openly with his black family, he never actually married his black mistress.

a Republican paper argued after the New York referendum that the results showed that "some" Democrats had joined the "great body" of Republicans in opposing equal suffrage.[24]

As they had traditionally done, Republicans tried to deny that race was the central question in the referendum. The point at issue, insisted Thurlow Weed's *Albany Evening Journal*, was *not* extending to blacks the right to vote but rather making that right dependent on a $250 property qualification. Voters were simply deciding whether to "place all men of color on an equality *with each other*, and so far as the naked right to vote is equality, on a level with whites."[25] (Emphasis added.) All the old arguments used against property qualifications for whites in previous decades were summoned forth again.[26]

The Democrats' racist onslaught led some Republicans to deny or qualify their support for black equality. When Herschel V. Johnson, the vice presidential candidate on the Douglas ticket, made a speaking tour through New York in which, according to a Republican paper, he "confined himself to a blackguardism of Abolitionism and the 'nigger,'"[27] he elicited this response from a Republican paper in Utica:

> Does he suppose that the veriest zany who heard him did not *know* that he was uttering a stupid falsehood in charging that the cardinal principle in the platform of the Republican party was the "political, civil and *social* equality of the negro race?" Whence does he derive his information? Upon what word uttered by Republican platforms, press or speakers, does he base his silly charges? Who has contended for the *social* equality of the negro? Who has claimed that he shall be admitted to our houses—shall associate with our wives and our daughters—should sit at our tables and partake of all the comforts of our domestic fireside?[28]

The *New York Times* explained that "the sentiment which pervades the great mass of the people of the Northern and Western States,

24. *St. Louis Democrat* quoted in *National Anti-Slavery Standard* (New York), Dec. 1, 1860.
25. *Albany Evening Journal*, Oct. 26, 1860; *New York Reformer* (Watertown), Sept. 27, 1860.
26. See *Albany Evening Journal*, Oct. 26, 1860; *New York Evening Post*, Oct. 19, 1860; *Elmira Weekly Advertiser*, Sept. 8, 1860; *New York Tribune*, Sept. 17, 1860; *Cortland Republican Banner*, Oct. 24, 1860; *Oneida Weekly Herald*, Oct. 30, 1860; *St. Lawrence Republican* (Ogdensburg), Nov. 6, 1860.
27. *Herkimer County Journal* (Little Falls), Oct. 25, 1860.
28. *Oneida Weekly Herald*, Oct. 23, 1860.

and which has organized the Republican Party, rests on a more substantial basis than that of mere philanthropy [toward blacks], and aims at broader results than relieving the condition of any class."[29]

The party reassured voters in other ways as well. When the black population was mentioned, Republicans stressed that it was small and insignificant.[30] A Buffalo paper remarked that "there is no danger of his [the black man's] ever attaining positions of distinction in society or government."[31] Occasionally Republicans admitted that the the perception of blacks as inferior was probably due to white prejudice and discrimination, but this belief was never seen as a reason to intervene and give blacks compensatory benefits. Instead these editors praised blacks for achieving as much as they had after starting with so little. Blacks could indeed become good citizens, they insisted, and would certainly vote no more unwisely than portions of the present electorate. As the Whigs had argued in 1846, simple justice and equity dictated that blacks be trusted with the franchise.[32]

Republicans continued to rely on the technique of relating equal suffrage to other issues (the South, slavery) or groups (Democrats, immigrants) upon which party members could agree more readily. They particularly emphasized the Democrats' partisan motives in attacking black suffrage. The New York Democrats really wanted all blacks to be slaves in order to please their southern allies, Republicans asserted. They feared that blacks might help Republicans to win elections.[33] The latter was a dangerous admission to make since it recalled Democratic warnings that blacks might become politically influential. To avoid this association, a Suffolk Republican paper asserted that blacks would vote for Gerrit Smith, the Radical Abolitionist presidential candidate. Another Suffolk editor simply stated that blacks would vote *against* Democrats implying that if they voted

29. *New York Times*, Sept. 28, 1860.

30. *Oneida Sachem*, Oct. 25, 1860; *New York Evening Post*, Oct. 19, 1860; *New York Times*, Sept. 17, 1860.

31. *Buffalo Morning Express*, Oct. 24, 1860. Blacks themselves sometimes tried to foster this illusion by deliberately refraining from endorsing some of their noted leaders for elective office. See Philip S. Foner and George E. Walker, eds., *Proceedings of the Black State Conventions, 1840–1865* (Philadelphia: Temple University Press, 1979-), 1:92.

32. *New York Evening Post*, Oct. 19, 1860; *Oneida Sachem*, Oct. 25, 1860; *Roman Citizen*, Oct. 17, 1860; *Buffalo Morning Express*, Oct. 22, 1860.

33. *Suffolk Herald* (Patchogue), Nov. 2, 1860; *Long Islander*, Nov. 2, 1860; *Albany Evening Journal*, Nov. 1, 1860.

Republican it was merely because Republicans were the Democrats' chief opponents.[34]

The need to win at least a portion of the German vote in several midwestern states kept the Republicans from contrasting native blacks with European immigrants as they had done in 1846. Few papers went as far as the *Independent,* a religious weekly, which preyed on anti-Irish sentiment the same way the Democrats had exploited antiblack feelings. Having noted that life in the "piggery" had made the Irish eager to debase blacks to their own level, it declared:

> The question to be submitted to the Christian people of this State next Tuesday, is not whether the Irish and negro races shall be permitted to intermarry if their tastes shall so incline, nor whether the Paddy race shall be kept as distinct as possible from the African race in our hospitals, jails and alms houses; but whether this State shall continue to exact of its native colored citizens a money qualification for voting, which it does not demand of the ignorant, foul, priest-ridden Paddy just landed upon the dock at Castle Garden. We say, away with a restriction so senseless, so mean, so unjust.[35]

One thing that Republicans did *not* do was to insist that all loyal Republicans support equal suffrage. Certainly, however, due to the Democrats' efforts and the endorsement (even if lukewarm) of the amendment by many Republicans, the distinction between the parties on the issue was far clearer than it had been in 1846. A new political awareness of the issue had developed over the past half decade and was quite evident in the debate over the suffrage amendment. The Democrats wished to exploit white anxieties about any change in the racial status quo to defeat the Republicans. The latter were equally determined to defuse the race issue by means of denials, reassurances, and directing voter attention to other matters. Unlike the Whigs, the Republicans did not have to fear the possible loss of disgusted racial liberals to a third party. (Compared to the Liberty Party, the Radical Abolitionists posed *no* threat whatever to Republican ascendancy.)[36] Thus the Republicans were free to move toward the center of the political spectrum, deemphasize black suffrage, and pick up conservative support at will. They did not repu-

---

34. *Suffolk Herald,* Nov. 2, 1860; *Long Islander,* Nov. 2, 1860.

35. *Independent* (New York) quoted in *Buffalo Daily Courier,* Nov. 5, 1860.

36. James M. McPherson, *The Struggle for Equality: Abolitionists and the Negro in the Civil War and Reconstruction* (Princeton: Princeton University Press, 1964), p. 20, estimates that the Radical Abolitionists received no more than two thousand or three thousand votes nationally.

diate equal suffrage except in rare instances. (The *New York World,* a fledgling Republican paper at this time, and another Republican journal in Montgomery County opposed modifying the property qualification.) By and large, however, Republicans avoided the embarrassment of contradicting their state legislators. They either maintained a decorous silence on the proposed amendment or explained it in the already noted ways.

Thus what had changed most since 1846 were political perceptions of equal suffrage. Party spokesmen discussed black voting increasingly in terms of the central themes of the 1850s—nativism, slavery, the South, and Union. And just as those concerns had become crucial in differentiating the political parties, so too they had helped to politicize the suffrage issue. Racism remained an all-important consideration, of course. In 1860 as in 1846 no one dared to challenge directly voters' prejudices. It was both simpler and safer for the Republicans to work around them.[37] White voters were encouraged to support black suffrage in order to uphold justice and the guarantees of the Declaration of Independence for the "downtrodden Ethiopian" or indirectly to annoy the Democrats, the Irish, and the South, but that was all. It was left primarily to the Democrats to point out the political gains that might accrue to the Republicans from black voters, an indication perhaps that Republican leaders felt that such gains were highly unlikely since black suffrage was sure to be defeated.[38] The white advocates of equal suffrage had other concerns to worry about. For the Republican leadership, electing their national and state tickets in 1860 was the highest priority; black suffrage did not take precedence.

Black leaders reluctantly admitted the truth. Frederick Douglass angrily noted that white Republicans and even abolitionists were ignoring equal suffrage while only blacks were campaigning actively for it.[39] Blacks indeed worked feverishly, once again using the organizational techniques they had developed to lobby the legislature.

37. Some Democrats thought that Republicans were very worried about voter backlash. See *New York Herald,* Nov. 6, 1860; *Rochester Union and Advertiser,* Oct. 20, 1860; *American Citizen* (Ithaca), Oct. 17, 1860.

38. Blacks also believed that Republicans were anxious to get black voters (see *Weekly Anglo-African* [New York], Apr. 21, 1860), but Republicans themselves almost never mentioned the need for black support.

39. *Douglass' Monthly* (Rochester), Nov. 1860. Many white abolitionists saw Lincoln's election as necessary to halt further southern aggression. If equal suffrage might hurt the Republican cause, it had to be sidestepped for the moment.

A free-suffrage convention, which had representatives from eleven counties, met in New York on May 10 to outline a general plan of action. The group appointed a central committee of thirty-five to direct the prosuffrage campaign and designated six agents to canvass the state to speak in behalf of equal suffrage and accept donations for the cause. At the local level blacks formed suffrage clubs and associations to distribute tracts and ballots.[40] There were forty-eight such clubs in New York City alone and eighteen in Brooklyn. The New York City and County Suffrage Committee issued at least seven thousand copies of an address to blacks urging them to organize and work for equal suffrage and five thousand copies of a pamphlet appealing for voter approval of black suffrage.[41] William C. Nell, a well-known black abolitionist, published a pamphlet detailing the reasons all blacks should vote. The general assumption of this literature seemed to be that whites were anxious primarily over the qualifications of blacks to vote. They feared blacks because they knew nothing about them. The pamphlets recounted the accomplishments of New York blacks in military service, business, social organizations, etc., and raised the question, "are not these patriotic, industrious, provident, exemplary citizens deserving equal rights at the ballot box?"[42] Simple justice demanded a positive response.

Reversing the strategy they had employed in working with the legislature, many blacks asked voters to disregard their party affiliations in voting on equal suffrage and tried themselves to avoid partisan actions. They feared that to take a party position would help mobilize sentiment against equal suffrage among Democrats, especially among foreign-born Democrats, and perhaps cost the amendment some stray Democratic votes. Indeed blacks circulated foreign-language literature on behalf of equal suffrage, and one black leader advised against a large suffrage convention on the eve of the referendum for fear of alienating foreign voters. Some black lead-

40. *Douglass' Monthly,* Oct. 1860; Rhoda Golden Freeman, "The Free Negro in New York City in the Era before the Civil War" (Ph.D. diss., Columbia University, 1966), p. 149; S. Holmes to Gerrit Smith, Oct. 20, 1860, Gerrit Smith Collection, George Arents Research Library for Special Collections at Syracuse University, Syracuse, New York; *Weekly Anglo-African,* Apr. 28, May 5, 19, 26, 1860.

41. George Walker, "The Afro-American in New York City, 1827–1860" (Ph.D. diss., Columbia University, 1975), p. 186; B. Shieffelin to Gerrit Smith, Sept. 24, 1860, with enclosures, Smith Papers.

42. William C. Nell, *Property Qualification or No Property Qualification* (New York: n.p., 1860), pp. 20–22.

ers, however, continued to act as Republicans with the expectation that this loyalty would be rewarded later.[43]

Blacks also disagreed on whether to argue against the suffrage discrimination as a form of racial or of class oppression. The militant Henry Highland Garnet favored the directness of the former approach, but others hoped to win more support by emphasizing that the amendment was aimed at men without a $250 freehold.[44] Like white Republicans, some blacks were afraid to challenge racial prejudices head on.

Disagreements on strategy, however, caused fewer problems to the movement than the simple lack of resources for agitating. With little help from abolitionists and Republicans, both money and workers were in short supply. Reports of "apathy" among the black masses were common, and wealthy abolitionists like Gerrit Smith had to be solicited for funds at critical junctures. All too often blacks had to cut back their campaign efforts.[45] The task of mobilizing sympathizers and converting the undecided was difficult enough to begin with; without resources it was impossible.

On November 6, 1860, voters finally went to the polls to decide the fate of equal suffrage in New York State. At last it would be known how the gradual politicization of the issue had affected the nature of support and opposition to it. Was race still a political hazard that must be avoided at all costs? As in 1846, there was a separate ballot on the suffrage question. Its wording was a little more ambiguous than in the earlier year: "Proposed Amendment in Relation to Suffrage," to be marked either for or against. No confusion seems to have resulted, however. The percentage of those at the polls participating in the referendum was actually four per cent higher than in 1846 (80.3 per cent). (The average participation in five referenda since the 1846 constitution had been adopted was only 63.7 per cent.) Many voters were apparently aware of and interested in the proposed change.[46]

43. Jane H. Pease and William H. Pease, *They Who Would Be Free: Blacks' Search for Freedom, 1830–1861* (New York: Atheneum, 1974), p. 147. Part of the debate on the wisdom of a partisan approach may be followed in the *Weekly Anglo-African*, Sept. 3, Oct. 1, Nov. 26, 1859, Mar. 17, 31, May 19, 1860.

44. Freeman, "Free Negro," p. 146; *Weekly Anglo-African*, May 19, 1860.

45. *Weekly Anglo-African*, Oct. 15, 1859, May 19, June 2, 30, 1860; B. Shieffelin to Gerrit Smith, Sept. 24, 1860, Smith Papers.

46. Edgar A. Werner, *Civil List and Constitutional History of the Colony and State of New York* (Albany: Weed, Parsons & Co., 1891), p. 131. Two referenda on a free school law in 1849 and 1850 had slightly higher rates of participation, 84 and 91 per cent re-

The electorate emphatically rejected equal suffrage but by a somewhat smaller margin than in 1846. The vote was 345,791 to 197,889; 63.6 per cent of the voters opposed equal suffrage, 8.8 per cent fewer than in 1846.[47] At the same time, Lincoln carried New York with 53.7 per cent of the vote. Figure 4.1 and Table 4.1 show the gross distribution of the vote statewide, by county.

One-sided voting on equal rights was much rarer in 1860 than in 1846. While eleven counties had been less than ten per cent pro-suffrage in 1846, only four were in 1860.[48] Two counties had been

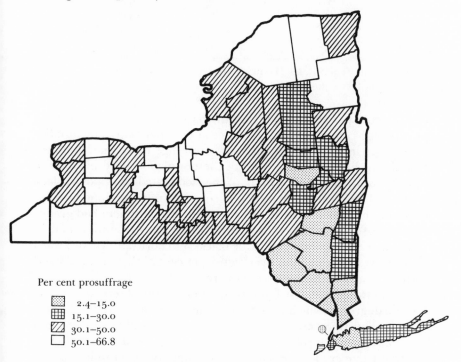

Per cent prosuffrage

- 2.4–15.0
- 15.1–30.0
- 30.1–50.0
- 50.1–66.8

FIGURE 4.1. Distribution of the prosuffrage vote, 1860 referendum.

spectively. The degree of interest in equal suffrage may have varied from place to place. See the report of the Rochester correspondent in the *New York Herald*, Oct. 30, 1860.

47. These totals have been adjusted to take into account some slight errors in the "official" state totals as given in the *Tribune Almanac for 1870*, p. 53. Collation with county canvasses revealed probable errors in the returns for Orange, Herkimer, and Chenango Counties. See Phyllis Frances Field, "The Struggle for Black Suffrage in New York State, 1846–1869" (Ph.D. diss., Cornell University, 1974), p. 183n.

48. Rockland (2.4 per cent) was the least prosuffrage county.

TABLE 4.1.

Prosuffrage voting by counties, 1860 referendum

Per cent prosuffrage	Counties[a]		Per cent of state population
	Number	Per cent	
2.4-10.0	4	6.8	3.1
10.1-20.0	11	18.6	39.3
20.1-30.0	4	6.8	4.9
30.1-40.0	6	10.2	11.5
40.1-50.0	16	27.1	19.8
50.1-60.0	13	22.0	15.8
60.1-66.8	5	8.5	5.6
Total	59	100.0	100.0

[a]Fulton and Hamilton are treated as one county. (See Appendix E.)

over seventy per cent prosuffrage in 1846 while in 1860 the leading prosuffrage county was St. Lawrence at 66.8 per cent. The number of counties in the forty to sixty per cent range more than doubled. Still almost half (47.3 per cent) of the population lived in counties where seventy per cent or more of the electorate had opposed black voting.[49] The greatest opposition to equal suffrage continued to center in southeastern New York, but prosuffrage sentiment had gradually increased in western New York. Eight more counties than in 1846 gave equal voting rights for blacks a majority. Town and ward returns are available from over eighty per cent of these counties and form the basis of the analysis in the rest of this chapter.[50]

The point of greatest interest to referendum observers in 1860 was the degree to which Republican voters had supported equal suffrage.[51] The Democrats had hoped the issue would cause the Republicans serious problems. As early as 1857 Horace Greeley had thought Democratic voters to be ninety-nine per cent united in opposition to equal suffrage, the American Party voters only a little less so (ninety-two per cent), while only two-thirds of the Republicans could be counted on to favor such a reform.[52] The voting pat-

49. The comparable figure in 1846 was 59.3 per cent.
50. These counties are listed in Appendix C, where they are compared to the state as a whole. The demographic data used were from the *New York State Census for 1855*. See Appendix E for other details of the data analysis.
51. This is clear from editorial comments after the referendum. See *Albany Argus*, Nov. 12, 1860; *New York Herald*, Nov. 8, 9, 1860; *New York Times*, Nov. 22, 1860.
52. *New York Tribune*, Sept. 26, 1857.

TABLE 4.2.

Correlation between prosuffrage and party voting,
1860 referendum[a]

Election and party	Correlation	Coefficient of variability
1858, governor		
Republican	.69	3.37
Democratic	−.58	2.99
American	−.36	1.03
1860, governor		
Republican	.75	4.28
Douglas Democratic	−.71	2.98
Breckenridge Democratic	−.10	0.45
1860, president		
Republican	.78	4.51
Fusion[b]	−.78	*

N = 885.
*Not available.
[a]Town-level data.
[b]Includes Breckenridge and Douglas Democrats and Constitutional Unionists.

terns generally confirm this estimate. Table 4.2 shows the correlations between party voting in 1858 (the last year the American Party ran a ticket) and 1860 and the prosuffrage vote. There was a high negative correlation between Democratic and prosuffrage strength in both 1858 and 1860, and as the Democratic coalition had solidified, the negative association had increased (from −.58 to −.78). While it had been possible in 1846 to find several townships where Democrats *must* have voted for equal suffrage, in *no* town for which returns are available did the prosuffrage vote exceed the Republican vote.[53] Nor is there any impressionistic evidence suggesting Democratic support for the amendment. The high degree of unity among the Democrats is clear.

The Americans were somewhat more difficult to deal with since they did not exist as a distinct voting bloc after 1858. Nevertheless American Party areas in that year did tend to be antisuffrage in

53. This was not literally true in two cases. In Clymer, Chautauqua County, and Smithfield, Madison County, more voted on the referendum than for the major presidential candidates. In Smithfield, voters for Gerrit Smith on the Radical Abolitionist ticket probably swelled the prosuffrage total. In neither town *must* the prosuffrage votes not given by Lincoln supporters have come from the Democrats.

1860, although not to as great a degree as the Democrats. Blacks seemingly were as alien as Irishmen in nativist areas.[54]

The Republicans, while distinctly prosuffrage, provide a striking contrast to the Democrats. The correlation between the Lincoln vote and the prosuffrage vote was quite high (.78), much higher in fact than *any* correlation found in the analysis of the 1846 referendum. Yet assuming that all the prosuffrage votes were cast by Republicans, only a little over half (54.5 per cent) of the Lincoln voters *could* have favored increased black voting. And assuming that all Democrats were antisuffrage, at least 13.8 per cent of the Repblicans *must* have joined them in opposing the constitutional amendment. Such almost certain Republican defections were widespread, occurring in a minimum of eighty-six per cent of all the towns surveyed. Every county had such towns. Yet there was a smaller percentage of Republicans definitely voting antisuffrage in 1860 than of Whigs doing the same thing in 1846. In only one-third of all towns did at least a tenth of the Republicans almost certainly oppose equal suffrage, and in only three per cent of the towns (compared to 23 per cent in 1846) did half or more do so.[55]

Most of these exceptional towns were in two counties, Ulster and Montgomery, in eastern New York. Ulster had always been conservative on racial matters, but it is not clear why it was more extreme in its reactions than its neighbors.[56] In Montgomery, however, the chief Republican paper cited racist reasons for favoring the Republican Party (e.g., to preserve the territories for free white men) and gloried in the defeat of the constitutional amendment.[57] The power of such suggestions was obvious. Local Republicans saw racial discrimination as a tenet of their party and responded accordingly.

In most areas, however, it was impossible for Republican voters not to know their party's association with black suffrage. Democratic

---

54. John L. Hammond, *The Politics of Benevolence: Revival Religion and American Voting Behavior* (Norwood, N.J.: Ablex, 1979), pp. 135–36, argues that New York's Know Nothings were even more opposed to slavery agitation than to the foreign born.

55. The minimum percentage of Republicans opposing equal suffrage was calculated by subtracting the total number of Democratic voters from the total antisuffrage vote and dividing by the Republican vote. It assumes that all Democrats are voting and voting antisuffrage and is therefore conservative in its estimate of Republican defections.

56. On the character of Ulster County see Alphonso T. Clearwater, *The History of Ulster County, New York* (Kingston, N.Y.: W. J. Van Deusen, 1907) and Nathaniel Barlett Sylvester, *History of Ulster County, New York* (Philadelphia: Everts and Peck, 1880).

57. *Montgomery Republican* (Fultonville), Oct. 20, Nov. 13, 1860.

tactics alone almost guaranteed it. Yet rather than abandon their party or openly repudiate its position, racially conservative Republicans often opted instead to abstain from voting in the referendum. Thus they refused to let their partisan and racial views come into conflict. As the map (Figure 4.2) shows, prosuffrage strength fell short of that for the Republicans by significant amounts across much of the state. In thirteen southeastern counties, for instance, the Republican and prosuffrage percentages differed by more than thirty per cent. Much of this difference was due to abstentions by antisuffrage Republicans who abstained in the referendum rather than vote against the perceived position of their party. Both the *Albany Argus* and Frederick Douglass openly accused Republicans of dodging equal suffrage. Douglass pointedly observed, "While the Democrats at the polls never failed to accompany their State and national tickets with one against the proposed amendment, Republicans—many of them—refused to touch a ticket in favor of the

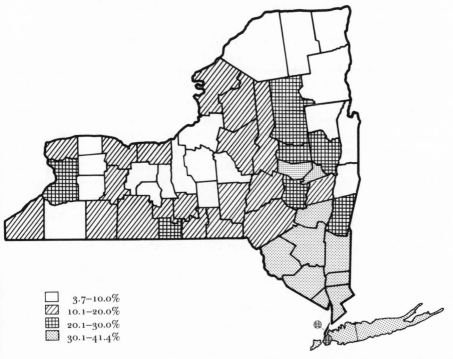

☐	3.7–10.0%
▨	10.1–20.0%
▦	20.1–30.0%
▨	30.1–41.4%

FIGURE 4.2. Percentages by which Republican votes exceeded prosuffrage votes, 1860 referendum.

amendment."[58] Republican leaders often facilitated such abstentions from voting by refusing to press prosuffrage ballots on their
followers. The *National Anti-Slavery Standard* commented that the
Democrats "provided all their voters with negative ballots" while Republicans seldom did so.[59]

The correlation between prosuffrage percentages and the percentage of voters at the polls taking a position on equal suffrage was
.53. This suggests that in areas where black suffrage was accepted
there were few abstentions, but in places such as the southeastern
counties, where it was unpopular, more people chose to avoid the
issue by not voting. That these latter were primarily Republicans is
suggested by a correlation of $-.72$ between the percentage of presidential voters voting in the suffrage referendum and the percentage
of Republicans who almost certainly abstained.[60] Where referendum participation was low, Republicans were not voting for black
suffrage.

Thus as the Democrats tried to establish black voting as an issue
between parties, two things happened. First, dissent among Democrats on the question virtually disappeared (obviously made easier
by their loss during the 1850s realignment of a great deal of support
in areas now favorable to equal suffrage). Second, Republicans an-
tagonistic to both equal suffrage and the Democratic Party increasingly refused to vote on the question of suffrage at all rather than
gratify the Democrats by opposing it. That the Democrats were unable to recruit Republicans who were conservative on the race issue
is an indication that Republicans paid more attention to their own
leaders' reassurances than to Democratic scare stories. Republicans had been able to blunt the sword of Democratic racism. They
had, however, only minimized defections and done little to reduce
the prejudice some of their followers felt toward blacks. This prejudice would come back to haunt them later in the 1860s, when they
had to explain emancipation and Reconstruction to these same followers.

In 1846 some factors unrelated to party affiliation, such as ethnic
or cultural background, had had an independent influence on the
pattern of voting on black suffrage. These same factors may have
influenced voting in the 1860 referendum as well. Table 4.3 sum-

58. *Albany Argus*, Nov. 12, 1860; *Douglass' Monthly*, Dec. 1860.
59. *National Anti-Slavery Standard*, Feb. 2, 1861. The *Albany Argus*, Nov. 2, 1860,
urged all Democratic leaders to provide only antisuffrage ballots to their followers.
60. The latter variable was calculated by taking the difference between the Republican and prosuffrage votes and dividing by the Republican vote.

TABLE 4.3.

Correlation between various population subgroups and prosuffrage and
Republican votes, 1860 referendum[a]

Variable	Per cent Republican (correlation)	Per cent prosuffrage (correlation)	Coefficient of variability
Per cent born New England	.52	.58	1.62
Per cent born Ireland	−.48	−.34	1.01
Per cent born Germany	−.32	−.25	0.52
Per cent born Ireland and Germany	−.53	−.39	1.00
Per cent Dutch Reformed of communicants	−.23	−.37	0.32
Per cent nonevangelical of communicants	−.37	−.44	0.64
Per cent black	−.29	−.40	0.58
Average value of dwelling per family	−.31	−.28	1.01

N = 885.
[a]Town-level data.

marizes the relationships between various population groups and
both the Republican and prosuffrage voting in 1860. In general, the
correlations were similar to 1846.

As in the earlier referendum, areas recently settled by New Englanders disproportionately favored equal suffrage, compared with
other areas. The reforming zeal of New Englanders apparently had
abated little. The political preferences of areas of Yankee settlement, however, had undergone a transformation. Such regions now
tended to be solidly Republican in contrast to 1846, when they had
shown a slight trend toward the Whigs.[61] Towns with more Yankees
than the average for all townships still dominated the prosuffrage
forces but not to the extent that they had in 1846. In that year
eighty-eight per cent of the prosuffrage towns had had more than
the mean proportion of New Englanders; in 1860 the corresponding figure was seventy-five per cent. The relative number of prosuffrage towns, of course, had also increased in the interim. Thus while
some Republicans disapproved of equal suffrage, it is clear that as
the issue had become more partisan, its appeal had broadened to

61. Per cent Yankee in 1845 correlated .05 with per cent Whig in 1844 and .26 with
per cent Whig and Liberty Party combined.

include more than just Yankee moralists and had intensified, involving a larger proportion of the groups that favored it.

English, Scotch, and Welsh towns that had been Whig and prosuffrage in 1846 were Republican and prosuffrage by 1860.[62] Over ninety per cent of the towns where ten per cent or more of the residents were born in England or Scotland were more than the mean per cent prosuffrage for all towns. The figure for towns more than ten per cent Welsh was almost as high.[63] Again, however, such towns were no longer as distinctive as in 1846. Many other Republican towns favored equal suffrage to the same degree.

Not all areas increased their support for black voting rights. In 1846 one of the strongest prosuffrage regions had been a section of northern New York bordering on Vermont and Canada. The Liberty Party had considerable strength there, and Democrats had frequently taken stands favorable to equal rights. In Clinton County, for example, the proportion of voters favoring equal suffrage for blacks in 1846 had far exceeded that supporting the Whig and Liberty tickets. This area, still largely a wilderness in 1846, had drawn residents first from New England and later Canada. By 1860 a number of Irish immigrants had also ventured into the area to work in forestry and mining. Support for equal suffrage changed dramatically. Clinton, Essex, and Franklin Counties experienced some of the sharpest prosuffrage declines in the state. Part of this decline may be traced to shifts in the electorate. By 1860 many Canadians (and Irish) were naturalized and eligible to vote in the referendum. In the township of Clinton, for instance, where 78.4 per cent of the eligible voters were naturalized in 1855 and the majority of these eligibles were Canadian (most of the rest being Irish), the Democratic vote in 1860 was eighty-five per cent and the antisuffrage vote 93.5 per cent. But party pressures were a factor too. In 1846 many eligible Canadians had apparently abstained in the referendum as had many Democrats in general. One probable reason for the high rate of abstention is that party leaders had offered little advice on how to vote. Another is that the area had the highest illiteracy rate in the state, which presumably made learning about the issue diffi-

62. On the political proclivities of these groups see also Rowland Tappan Berthoff, *British Immigrants in Industrial America, 1790–1950* (Cambridge: Harvard University Press, 1953), pp. 195–96.

63. Usually ethnic groups were far more heavily represented in the total population than the census figures suggest, since the latter did not take into account second- and third-generation residents.

cult.[64] In 1860, however, there were clear party cues on the suffrage question, and opposition to the proposed amendment was easily mobilized. Political parties did indeed affect some group voting.

Many important groups apparently opposed black voting in 1860 as vigorously as in 1846. Areas where Dutch influence could be established by the presence of Dutch Reformed churches and communicants were as solidly antisuffrage as ever. Ninety per cent of all towns containing Dutch Reformed church communicants rejected equal suffrage, and the larger the percentage of such communicants among all communicants, the larger the proportion opposing it.[65] All seven towns surveyed that contained *only* Dutch Reformed churches were antisuffrage, and six of these seven were more than eighty per cent opposed to it. The Democrats normally held an edge in the Lower Hudson "Dutch" towns, but antisuffrage voting was especially likely to cross party lines there. Although many of these towns were slightly more prosuffrage in 1860 than in 1846, their gains were some of the lowest in the state. (See Figure 4.3.) It would appear that the events of the 1850s had done relatively little to alter the outlook of this area on suffrage reform.

Similarly, most immigrant groups remained firmly ensconced in the Democratic Party and in the legions opposed to equal rights for blacks. Much partisan propaganda had been directed toward the threats posed to the foreign born (especially Catholics) by the Republicans and blacks. The last-minute efforts of blacks to counter such attacks proved useless. After the referendum Frederick Douglass lamented over the "drunken Irishmen, and ignorant Dutchmen, controlled by sham Democrats," who had spurned the suffrage amendment.[66] The referendum returns strongly confirmed the existence of a black/Irish antagonism.[67] Of the ten most Irish towns and wards in the sample, none was more than 34.2 per cent prosuffrage. And despite the fact that only a minority of towns and wards had been heavily settled by the Irish, the correlation between per cent Irish and per cent prosuffrage voting was −.34.

64. Most of the Canadians in this area and New York generally were of French descent. *Census of the State of New York for 1855*, p. 16.
65. The religious data, although superior to those in the 1845 census, are still difficult to interpret. See Appendix E on the problems involved in measuring religious preference.
66. Philip S. Foner, *The Life and Writings of Frederick Douglass* (New York: International Publishers, 1950–1955), 2:532.
67. See Florence E. Gibson, *The Attitude of the New York Irish toward State and National Affairs, 1848–1892* (New York: Columbia University Press, 1951), p. 142.

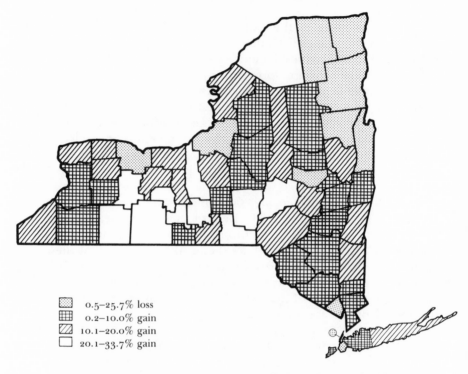

FIGURE 4.3. Losses and gains in prosuffrage voting, 1846–1860.

German towns, too, tended to be opposed to suffrage reform, but there was greater variation among them and they were generally less one-sided than their Irish counterparts. The behavior of towns or wards with the highest percentage of German-born residents is recorded in Table 4.4. All but one of these was opposed to equal suffrage, and the overall correlation between per cent German and per cent favoring equal suffrage was −.25. The German responses to the black rights problem seemed to parallel roughly their partisan outlook and perhaps reflect the often-noted difference between Germans of pietistic and liturgical religious backgrounds.[68] The former sometimes displayed the reforming zeal of American Yankees and found the Catholicism of some of their own compatriots disturbing. The two most prosuffrage towns and wards were also predominantly pietistic. The liturgical Prussian Lutherans of Wheat-

68. See Paul Kleppner, *The Third Electoral System, 1853–1892: Parties, Voters, and Political Cultures* (Chapel Hill: University of North Carolina Press, 1979), pp. 153–63.

TABLE 4.4.

Voting patterns of German towns and wards, 1860 referendum

Town or ward	Per cent German[a]	Per cent natural- ized	Per cent Republi- can	Per cent prosuf- frage
Syracuse, Ward 2	59.5	80.6	55.6	50.8
West Seneca, Erie	57.3	81.5	35.5	3.0
Buffalo, Ward 7	51.9	87.2	59.0	42.8
Wheatfield, Niagara	47.2	60.9	41.7	19.0
Buffalo, Ward 5	45.0	78.8	47.2	23.5
Buffalo, Ward 6	43.1[b]	94.0	48.9	16.6

[a]Total German and Prussian.

[b]Figure based on 1865 census. German total omitted from 1855 census.

field, however, were largely antisuffrage.[69] For immigrants especially, parties helped explain and rationalize the world of American politics. Even newcomers were soon able to perceive the apparent relevance to their interests and values of black suffrage.

While the Irish bolstered the antisuffrage forces, certain other native-born groups moved in the opposite direction.[70] Indeed, since most immigrants were antisuffrage and the foreign-born population was increasing, prosuffrage gains in the state must be largely attributed to native voters. In 1846 the residual class of Americans who were not born in New York or New England (mainly from Pennsylvania or New Jersey) lived in predominantly antisuffrage towns. By 1860, however, the situation had changed. The lower New York counties of Jersey settlement did remain solidly opposed to equal suffrage, but the Southern Tier, along the Pennsylvania border, one of the areas most affected by the partisan realignment in the 1850s, greatly increased its prosuffrage support, although it still remained somewhat more antisuffrage than the rest of western New York. Twenty towns where more than ten per cent of the population was of Pennsylvanian origin were an average 43.4 per cent prosuffrage.

69. Henry Perry Smith, *History of the City of Buffalo and Erie County* (Syracuse: D. Mason, 1884), 2:151. See Dwight H. Bruce, *Memorial History of Syracuse, N.Y.* (Syracuse, N.Y.: H. P. Smith & Co., 1891), pp. 351, 357–58, for suggestions of conflicts among Syracuse Germans stemming from religion. Again the paucity of hard evidence on religious preference makes these observations suggestive rather than conclusive.

70. This was not true of the older native groups of eastern New York. The Huguenot, Palatine, and Old British towns cited by Benson (see Chapter 2 at note 89) were with one exception all at least eighty-five per cent antisuffrage.

The average increase in support for equal suffrage over 1846 in fourteen of these towns where returns were available for both years was 26.8 per cent. A portion of the population of Pennsylvania origin probably supported equal suffrage although at not nearly as high a rate as did, for instance, Yankees.

There was a clear sectional cast to both the suffrage and party votes in 1860. Western New York was already gaining a reputation as a Republican stronghold, and it had also favored equal suffrage. Using a dummy variable that distinguishes the area of pre-1790 settlement from that settled thereafter (as in Chapter 2), one finds the area of earliest settlement more heavily antisuffrage and Democratic. Thus there was a tendency for groups in the more recently settled parts of New York to favor both the Republicans and voting rights for blacks.

This sectional cast to the vote was noted by both Democrats and Republicans. The *Albany Argus* thought the explanation simple: counties in which there were no free Negroes voted for black suffrage and those where there were opposed it. The paper further insisted that should the black population of the state be shifted, counties receiving blacks would then reject all forms of equality.[71] Indeed the correlation between per cent black and per cent supporting equal suffrage was $-.40$. All but one of the towns where blacks constituted six per cent or more of the population rejected the amendment. (The average prosuffrage percentage for those towns was only 13.9.)

The sole prosuffrage town among towns more than six per cent black was North Elba in Essex County in the Adirondacks. When Gerrit Smith in the 1840s had given some of his property in this town to blacks expressing a willingness to farm it, a small black community had grown up there. John Brown also lived in North Elba for a time before his ill-fated Harper's Ferry expedition.[72] That North Elba and twelve other of the eighteen towns in the county voted for equal suffrage in 1860 is an indication that an influx of blacks into an area did not always mean instant disaster for equal suffrage as the *Argus* had predicted. Although the county's prosuffrage vote declined from 1846, that of the entire northern region

71. *Albany Argus*, Dec. 31, 1860.
72. H. P. Smith, ed., *History of Essex County* (Syracuse: D. Mason & Co., 1885), pp. 188–89.

generally did as well. And even with the decrease, most whites still continued to support equal voting rights for blacks.

As in 1846 many towns with few blacks showed great hostility towards the race. Sixty-four per cent of the towns where more than three quarters of the voters were opposed to extending black voting rights had black populations of two per cent or less. Such towns were not as widely dispersed throughout the state as in 1846 although all but eleven counties of the forty-nine surveyed had such towns.[73] Knowing the racial balance in a community, therefore, was not a sure way to predict its prosuffrage affinities, although, in general, whites in areas with many blacks opposed their advancement. The Democratic Party's insistence on the potential dangers of the black community perhaps facilitated this result.

The Republican *Albany Evening Journal* thought that the distinguishing characteristic of the prosuffrage section was not its lack of blacks but rather the "morality and intelligence" of its citizens.[74] Such a conclusion was certainly a reflection of the editor's own values. Yet it raises again the question whether culturally determined definitions of "morality" were involved in the suffrage struggle. Certainly both in 1846 and in 1860 in some quarters, one of the chief arguments for the reform had been a moral one—that blacks must be free to improve themselves without hindrance from the government. This concept of morality, however, was more likely to be stressed by the evangelical sects who believed in taking an activist role in perfecting society and who were generally hostile to social hierarchy.[75] It is difficult to determine which towns were largely nonevangelical and which not, even though the 1855 state census provided more information on the religious makeup of towns than did that in 1845.[76] Still, if one examines the proportion of communicants who were Catholic, Dutch Reformed, Episcopalian, or of other definitely nonevangelical sects, it appears that towns with

73. The exceptional counties were Allegany, Cayuga, Chautauqua, Cortland, Madison, Onondaga, Oswego, Tioga, Tompkins, Washington, and Yates. In addition, Queens and Suffolk had no towns that were less than two per cent black.

74. *Albany Evening Journal*, Dec. 29, 1860.

75. See Richard Jensen, "The Religious and Occupational Roots of Party Identification: Illinois and Indiana in the 1870's," *Civil War History*, 16 (Dec. 1970), 325–43, and Ronald P. Formisano, *The Birth of Mass Political Parties: Michigan, 1827–1861* (Princeton: Princeton University Press, 1971), p. 328.

76. Given the difficulties of measuring religious preference the figures in this paragraph should be interpreted as indicating a trend rather than precisely measuring that trend.

larger fractions of this nonevangelical population were indeed disproportionately antisuffrage (and Democratic) and hence "immoral" in the eyes of certain righteous Republicans.[77]

Both parties in 1860 directed appeals toward the poor. The Republicans urged the rejection of a property qualification that discriminated against poor men while the Democrats raised alarm over job competition between black and white workingmen. Yet such arguments seemed to spur few voters to cross party lines. If one actually differentiates the towns of New York according to their economic well-being (determined by the average value of dwelling per family), there is a slight, negative relationship between prosperity and prosuffrage voting.[78] Even controlling for the level of urbanization of an area makes little difference.[79] Areas most favorable to equal suffrage remained somewhat poorer than average, which suggests that the Democrats' appeals to the working class were not widely heeded unless the workers were already Democrats.

As has been shown above, areas where groups who favored equal suffrage dominated also tended to be Republican and, conversely, areas heavily antisuffrage tended to be Democratic. Yet there were

TABLE 4.5.
Variables explaining votes for equal
suffrage, 1860 referendum
(partial regression coefficients)[a]

Variable	Beta
Per cent Republican, 1860	.60
Per cent born New England	.20
Per cent American Party, 1858	−.16
Per cent black	−.15

N = 885.
Fraction of explained variance, 70.0%.
[a]Town-level data.

77. The actual correlation is −.44. Other sects included the Calvinist Methodists and Old School Baptists.
78. The correlation was −.28. The variable is calculated by dividing the total value of dwellings by the total number of families adjusting for the proportion of dwellings for which no values were given. No towns were classified unless values were given for at least eighty per cent of all dwellings.
79. In general, urban areas tended to have higher property values than rural areas. The control was performed by differentiating towns according to whether they had urban areas (cities or villages) over 50,000 in population; between 10,000 and 50,000; between 5,000 and 10,000; between 1,500 and 5,000; or under 1,500 and then looking at the relationship between prosperity and suffrage voting in each group.

exceptions to this general rule. By multiple regression analysis it is possible to determine which characteristics of a community exerted an independent influence on the suffrage vote and how important each was in predicting support for the suffrage amendment. Table 4.5 shows the partial regression coefficients obtained in a stepwise multiple regression.[80] Together the four variables listed explain seventy per cent of the variation in the prosuffrage vote. The tremendous importance of party is immediately apparent. The most salient feature of towns willing to support equal suffrage was their Republicanness, and towns with other prosuffrage characteristics were still Republican above all else. Unlike the situation in 1846, party groupings, more than cultural groupings, were basic to conflicts over suffrage rights for blacks. Only three other variables had slight but independent influences.[81] Areas recently settled by New Englanders (as in 1846) were particularly likely to be prosuffrage, while those with many blacks and where opposition to the Democrats had first centered in the American rather than the Republican Party were apt to be opposed to black voting.

One may summarize the characteristics of places where Republicans were least likely to vote for equal suffrage (i.e., voted against it or abstained) in a slightly different way. Table 4.6 displays the simple correlations between the percentage of Republicans not voting in favor of suffrage and various social and demographic variables.[82] Again, it is clear that Republicans failed to support equal suffrage in those areas where Republicanism itself and the primary groups upon which it was based were likewise weak—eastern New York, for instance, or places where New Englanders were few, but Dutch, nativists, and blacks were more common. The Republican Party had

80. The variables used for the regression were per cent New England born, per cent born Ireland and Germany, value of dwelling per family, per cent American Party 1858, per cent Republican for president in 1860, per cent nonevangelical of communicants, and area settled before 1790. For the criteria for selection of these variables see Appendix E. The variables listed in the table added at least one per cent to explained variance.

81. The residuals from a simple regression using per cent Republican as the independent variable were examined to see if small, concentrated groups that could hardly influence the statewide vote were disproportionately represented (thereby indicating their independent influence in those towns). They were not.

82. The percentage of Republicans not voting for suffrage is calculated by subtracting the prosuffrage from the Republican vote and dividing by the latter. One could use other measures, of course, such as the residuals from the party-suffrage regression or the arithmetic difference between the Republican and prosuffrage percentages. These variables are so highly correlated with each other that essentially the same conclusions come from the study of any of them.

TABLE 4.6.

Correlation between per cent Republicans not voting for
equal suffrage in the 1860 referendum and
population characteristics[a]

Variable	Correlation
Per cent born New England	−.49
Per cent black	.39
Per cent prosuffrage	−.91
Per cent Republican, 1860	−.49
Per cent Dutch Reformed of communicants	.37
Per cent nonevangelical of communicants	.39
Per cent American Party, 1858	.34

N = 885.
[a]Town-level data.

coalesced from diverse elements, and it was not ideologically united
on the question of racial equality. Realizing this, Republican leaders
had deemphasizd the suffrage question in conservative areas,
thereby making suppport for the amendment even more unlikely.
Republicans had little hope of actually carrying such places by this
stratagem; nevertheless, for their candidates to win statewide it was
necessary to avoid alienating these voters. The influence such areas
could exert on future party policy was closely circumscribed, however. The dissident Republican voters, unlike the disaffected Whigs
of 1846, were a minority in the party and concentrated in normally
Democratic areas. They had been among the last to join the Republican coalition and were its least influential members. They lacked,
therefore, the leverage to reverse their party's stand on black suffrage.

Having established the general contours of support and opposition to equal suffrage in 1860, it is possible to categorize the types
of shifts that had occurred since 1846. Figure 4.3 and Table 4.7
show some of these changes. Counties were quite disparate in their
behavior. Eleven counties showed declines in prosuffrage voting,
and in one, Clinton, the loss was over twenty-five per cent. Yet
eleven other counties had gains of more than twenty per cent, the
largest increase being 33.7 per cent in Cayuga. Almost half the
population of the state, however, lived in counties that had shifted
less than five per cent in either direction since 1846. The counties
that had favored equal suffrage in 1846 experienced the smallest

TABLE 4.7.
Losses and gains in prosuffrage voting, 1846-1860,
by county

Per cent change	Counties		Per cent of state population
	Number	Per cent	
Loss, 5.1-25.7	4	6.8	3.2
Loss, 0.5- 5.0	7	11.9	35.3
Gain, 0.2- 5.0	10	16.9	12.6
Gain, 5.1-10.0	11	18.6	17.0
Gain, 10.1-15.0	10	16.9	13.3
Gain, 15.1-20.0	6	10.2	6.1
Gain, 20.1-25.0	6	10.2	5.6
Gain, 25.1-33.7	5	8.5	6.9
Total	59	100.0	100.0

gains in their support for it fourteen years later. Six of these ten counties suffered losses, and the other four registered only slight increases. The most substantial growth in prosuffrage support took place in western New York. One of the few contemporary analyses comparing the two referenda (done by the *National Anti-Slavery Standard)* saw changes developing along a rural/urban continuum with "right sentiment" growing in the rural areas while cities and large towns "where prejudice is rampant and grogshops abound, and large masses of voters are ignorant and degraded" generally swelled their antisuffrage vote.[83] Indeed prosuffrage sentiment did decline in Monroe (Rochester), Kings (Brooklyn), and New York Counties (due mostly to the increase in Democratic immigrant groups). However, some rural areas, too, lost enthusiasm for equal suffrage, and even gains in rural areas were far from uniform. Town returns for twenty-nine counties (containing 486 towns) are available for both the 1846 and 1860 referenda, and using these data, one may examine more closely the changes that occurred.

The percentage voting prosuffrage in the two referenda correlate at .61 at the township level, indicating a substantial amount of continuity. Taking the arithmetic difference between the prosuffrage percentages in the referenda as the dependent variable, one may perform a stepwise multiple regression to begin to analyze their dif-

83. *National Anti-Slavery Standard,* Feb. 2, 1861.

ferences.[84] Table 4.8 records the partial regression coefficients obtained.[85] The eight variables listed account for sixty-one per cent of the variance in the dependent variable. As noted earlier, there was a general tendency for antisuffrage areas to become gradually more favorable to black voting and extremely prosuffrage areas to retreat from their advanced position. Both shifts were partially related to the increasing voter acceptance of party as a cue in voting on the referendum. That is, more Republicans than Whigs saw the obligation to vote for equal suffrage, while practically all Democrats came to oppose it. The realignment, too, had had an impact. Areas shifting toward the Republicans increased their backing for equal suffrage. Changes were also related to specific demographic shifts, especially in the cities. An increase in Irish and German voters and a corresponding decrease in support for equal suffrage occurred in New York, Rochester, Troy, and Schenectady.[86] In general, areas that failed to add to their prosuffrage vote or where it actually declined tended to be in the older regions of the state, where the Democratic Party had been well entrenched in 1846, where blacks were numerous, and where the American Party had attracted adherents as late as 1858. The greatest gains for equal suffrage were likely to be concentrated in towns moving toward the Republican Party, where the Whig and Free Soil Parties had obtained a preponderance of support in 1848, and where New Englanders predominated. Thus where the changing composition of the population was not a factor, political and cultural differences sometimes were. Again there was a basic difference in behavior between Yankee, reformist, antisouthern, increasingly Republican areas and non-Yankee, solidly Democratic ones.

In 1846 black suffrage had been decisively defeated, and it had

84. This variable was calculated by subtracting a town's prosuffrage percentage in 1846 from the comparable figure for 1860. All other variables measuring change over time have been calculated similarly—the earlier figure has been subtracted from the later one.

85. The variables used in the regression were per cent prosuffrage 1846, average value of dwelling per family, per cent black 1855, per cent voters naturalized 1855, per cent American Party for governor in 1858, per cent born New England 1845, per cent Democrat/Nativist for governor in 1846, per cent Whig/Free Soil for governor in 1848, change per cent Democratic 1844–1860, per cent nonevangelical communicants, and area of pre-1790 settlement. Since no highly correlated independent variables may be used in a regression, choices had to be made among such variables, which accounts for the absence of per cent Republican, per cent Irish and German, etc.

86. Rural towns were also affected. Florence, Oneida County, turned decisively antisuffrage as its Irish inhabitants obtained the vote.

TABLE 4.8.
Variables explaining equal suffrage voting shifts, 1846-1860 (partial
regression coefficients)[a]

Variable	Beta	Coefficient of variability
Percent prosuffrage, 1846	−.92	1.25
Change per cent Democratic, 1844-1860	−.29	0.61
Per cent born New England, 1845	.19	1.54
Per cent Whig/Free Soil for governor, 1848	.17	1.70
Area of pre-1790 settlement	−.16	0.86
Per cent Democrat/Nativist, 1846	−.14	3.55
Per cent black, 1855	−.13	0.61
Per cent American Party, 1858	−.12	0.98

N = 486.
Fraction of explained variance, 61%.
[a]Town-level data.

seemed that little progress could be made until the issue received more political backing. That increased support was visible in 1860, even before the trauma of Civil War and Reconstruction had been felt. The typical prosuffrage town in 1860 was above all else Republican. It also was somewhat more likely to be Yankee in origin, to have few blacks, and to have rejected the American Party as an alternative to the Republican in the 1850s. In essence, the conflict that had started in 1846 as one between a relatively small group of Yankee reformers and the rest of the state had now blossomed into one between the majority wing of the Republican Party and the Democrats aided by a portion of the more conservative Republicans. Although the same fundamental forces were in some cases still involved (Yankees, for instance, seem to have been the heart of the prosuffrage movement in both referenda), the conflict could now most accurately be described in *political* terms. The partisan realignment of the 1850s had affected the behavior of citizens, as well as legislative leaders, toward suffrage. While the issue of black voting per se was not critical in bringing about the realignment, it was increasingly seen as intimately connected with the social and ideological factors that did. Thus more and more voters responded to equal suffrage in a partisan fashion.

Yet the emerging party split on equal suffrage had other implications for the suffrage struggle as well. After the realignment, the Democratic Party no longer had significant support in prosuffrage areas. Because the Democrats no longer had to compete for Liberty

Party or other antisouthern or antislavery voters and because they became increasingly dependent on immigrants whose fears of blacks could easily be exploited, they were able to unleash violent attacks against the suffrage amendment and New York's black community. They rallied their own supporters, even those (in northern New York, for example) who had hitherto been neutral or somewhat favorable to equal suffrage, into a solid phalanx of opposition to the proposed amendment. Aware that there was another crucial portion of the electorate that was affected by racism but had until now been repelled from the Democratic Party by its presumed association with the twin demons of popery and the Slave Power, Democrats waged a vigorous campaign to make race, not the South or the Catholic church, the deciding issue for such voters.

This Democratic tactic placed Republican leaders in a quandary. They had mobilized large numbers of the traditional prosuffrage groups such as the Yankees of western New York. Yet they still needed support from groups in eastern New York opposed to equal rights for blacks. Such Republicans, they knew, had joined the Republican coalition for reasons having little to do with the black man. The Republican leaders took the course of least resistance under these circumstances. They avoided the race issue (especially where it was most unpopular) and reassured their voters about it elsewhere. They did *not* actively marshal support in behalf of the amendment.

Republicans avoided the consequences of being identified as the "black" party, and events aided them. There was little real proof that the traditional subordination of the black in New York had changed in any way. Voters became more deeply involved with other partisan issues, and Republican candidates swept on to victory. Their party, of course, remained divided, vulnerable if the race issue again surfaced. But once again the defeat of equal suffrage in a popular referendum would seemingly prevent the issue being raised again soon. It had been buried once more. The Democrats had mobilized to promote racism, but the Republicans had failed to find the unity to counter it. In November, 1860, New York was still far from granting political rights to its black citizens.

CHAPTER FIVE

War, Reconstruction,
and the Politics of Race

Under normal conditions the decisive defeat of equal suffrage at the polls in 1860 would have quieted the issue's advocates for several years at least. But the 1860s proved to be anything but normal. National events intervened to give black rights an obvious new relevance. The outbreak of war provided black and white abolitionists with the chance of a lifetime to discredit the South and its conservative northern allies and to push decisively toward the abolition of slavery and the end of legalized discrimination against blacks in America. These events also furnished Democrats with the long-awaited opportunity to exploit the racial divisions within the Republican ranks. In short, war and later Reconstruction dramatically altered the political significance of black suffrage. Politicians were forced to make new calculations concerning the race question and to develop new strategies appropriate to the changing political realities. What remained constant amid the rapid developments of this period was the obvious desire of political leaders to maintain control over the race issue and to keep their parties from being overwhelmed by it. Both partisan coalitions ultimately faced dilemmas growing out of the political exploitation of racial change, and both tried to protect their parties' interests. The fate of equal rights once again hinged in part on the nature of American politics.

Two changes confronted New York Republicans in the 1860s.

First, it was increasingly difficult to leave support of or opposition to black rights up to an individual, as had been done in the 1860 referendum. As the party in power nationally, Republicans were responsible for the manner in which the war was carried on (including wartime emancipation and the use of black troops) and for the formulation of the terms of reunion after the war (which eventually included civil and political rights for blacks). The party *had* to seek common ground on racial matters or face division and defeat at the polls.

Second, Republicans had to recognize and respond to the tenuous base of their political power in New York. The electoral volatility that had characterized the 1850s was passing. As the correlation matrix in Table 5.1 shows, the basis of partisan polarization changed little in the 1860s. Republicans and Democrats could count on the same groups for support year after year. Only in 1861, when there was a general patriotic rallying around the national government following the outbreak of the war, was there any exception to this rule. By 1862 the bipartisan spirit had dissipated, and, although Republicans enthusiastically touted themselves as "Unionists" for the remainder of the war, they seemingly made little impression on Democrats. The war confirmed rather than dissolved partisan allegiances.

Stability did not indicate tranquility, however. In New York, as in many other northern states, only a razor-thin margin separated the two parties. Between 1862 and 1869, for instance, the Republicans averaged 49.99 per cent of the vote, winning four elections and losing four. As the *Nation* pointed out in 1867, "ardent" Republicans alone could never carry an election. The party had to depend on the "lukewarm . . . whose political feelings are not strong, who are affected in voting by divers [*sic*] collateral considerations, and who, unless they are well looked after are as likely as not to go over to the enemy on the day of battle."[1] A few disgruntled individuals who simply stayed home on election day could decide an election. Strategies to deal with this element had to be devised. There was no easy answer. Discussions, rivalries, and policy disputes naturally developed.

The New York Democracy inevitably sought to exploit the divisions among its opponents. To leave the Republicans unchallenged was to face possible defeat at every election. The 1860 referendum had proved that Republican leaders lacked confidence on racial issues and that the rank and file were also less united on them than

1. *Nation* (New York), Sept. 19, 1867.

TABLE 5.1.

Correlation matrix of the per cent Democratic vote, 1860-1869[a]

	1860	1861	1862	1863	1864	1865	1866	1867	1868
1861	.74								
1862	.97	.77							
1863	.96	.81	.98						
1864	.96	.78	.98	.98					
1865	.93	.79	.95	.96	.97				
1866	.94	.70	.97	.95	.97	.96			
1867	.95	.69	.95	.94	.95	.93	.97		
1868	.96	.74	.97	.96	.98	.97	.98	.97	
1869	.94	.78	.96	.97	.96	.96	.96	.94	.97

[a]County-level data.

on most other matters. As the war developed and Republican radicals began to push for emancipation and equal rights, therefore, the Democrats protested every such move. Republicans were thus forced to define how far they were willing to go to support legislation that benefited blacks. Democrats also compelled their opponents to come up with new ways to explain racial change to their wide range of followers. When the question of equal suffrage did arise again later in the decade, it would be debated in these new terms.

Emancipation was the first issue to threaten the Republican coalition. From the outset, Democrats promised firm opposition to it. Any endeavor to "pervert" the war into one for emancipation, warned the 1861 New York Democratic platform, would be "fatal to all the hopes of the restoration of the Union."[2] Republicans at first, both nationally and locally, showed signs of indecision. A number of Republicans in the House of Representatives, including the nineteen from New York who voted, favored the Crittenden Resolution in July 1861. It made reunion the sole object of the war and promised not to interfere with "established institutions" in the South. New York's Republican newspapers generally avoided the issue of the slave.[3] It soon became obvious, however, that a war against a

2. *New York Herald*, Sept. 6, 1861.

3. *Congressional Globe*, 37th Cong., 1st Sess., 223. Four other New York Republicans did not vote. Mary P. Hodnett, "Civil War Issues in New York State Politics" (Ph.D. diss., St. Johns University, 1970), p. 38. Also useful on the race issue during the war are Forrest G. Wood, *Black Scare: The Racist Response to Emancipation and Reconstruction* (Berkeley: University of California Press, 1968) and V. Jacque Voegeli, *Free but Not Equal: The Midwest and the Negro during the Civil War* (Chicago: University of Chicago Press, 1967), which touches on many themes common to New York.

slaveholding region could not be carried on without seriously disrupting that institution. Escaped slaves sought refuge within the Union lines. Sometimes the army returned them, but on other occasions it kept them as "contraband" of war. In August of 1861 John C. Fremont attempted to free the slaves of disloyal Missourians by military decree. He justified his action (which was disallowed by Lincoln) on the grounds of military necessity.[4] This association of emancipation with wartime needs was a crucial one. It linked a policy many Northerners had previously regarded with apprehension with the fulfillment of patriotic objectives. Republicans had found an important means to enlarge support for controversial racial measures.

Several of the more radical New York Republican papers such as the *New York Tribune* and the *Evening Post* began to call for emancipation as a military measure in 1861 as well. The party as a whole took no position, however, until forced to do so by Lincoln's issuance of the preliminary emancipation proclamation in September, 1862.[5] This came at a critical juncture for New York Republicans, the opening of the fall campaign to elect a governor.

The Democrats, who had long awaited this opportunity, made an all out attack on the proclamation. The *Tribune* testily observed:

> It is evident that one of the principal resources of the opposition, during the present canvass, is an appeal to that cruel and ungenerous prejudice against color which still remains to disgrace our civilization and to impeach our Christianity. It is astonishing with how much stolidity men, who call themselves gentlemen, resort, at a pinch, to the intolerance and arrogance of caste; and, to satisfy the exigencies of an election, imitate, to the best of their ability those atrocities which are the stigma of history.[6]

According to the Democrats, the Republicans intended to make the war a "negro crusade."[7] A vote for Democratic gubernatorial candidate Horatio Seymour, said the *New York World*, now the leading Democratic journal in New York City, was a vote "to protect our white laborers against the association and competition of Southern negroes," while a vote for his Republican opponent, James S. Wadsworth, was one to prolong the war, to destroy the southern social system, and "to elbow aside our white immigrant population and

4. Allan Nevins, *The War for the Union* (New York: Charles Scribner's Sons, 1959), 1:331–34.
5. Hodnett, "Civil War Issues," pp. 42, 51–53.
6. *New York Tribune*, Oct. 16, 1862.
7. *Albany Argus*, Sept. 24, 1862. See also *New York World*, Oct. 7, 1862.

repel it from our shores."[8] Emancipation, Democrats insisted, would certainly lead to disaster: an increased determination on the part of white southerners never to give in, an influx of blacks into the North, or a servile revolution at the South.[9]

Faced with this onslaught, Republicans fought back, but in ways they thought would preserve party unity. They refused to repudiate the president's action. Indeed most Republican leaders gave the proclamation immediate and complete support. The state convention and numerous Republican meetings throughout the state endorsed it. Even Thurlow Weed, the editor of the influential *Albany Evening Journal*, who personally doubted the political, and indeed military, wisdom of emancipation, continued loyally to support the party's abolitionist platform and gubernatorial candidate throughout the election campaign.[10]

But Republicans tried to make the Emancipation Proclamation seem important and desirable to all party members, not just the Yankee moralist wing. While some radical journals did point out the evils of slavery and the justice of abolishing it, many other papers stressed expedient reasons for freeing the slaves and indeed relied upon common stereotypes of the black man in defending emancipation. In this way racial conservatives could be cajoled into supporting the measure. Wadsworth, for instance, declared that he did not consider freeing the slaves dangerous because "the blacks are the most docile people on the face of the earth; they will make the most innocent if not the most industrious peasantry, and we shall recover from the shock sooner than we dare to hope."[11] Similarly, Daniel S. Dickinson, a "War" Democrat supporting Lincoln and the Republicans because of the war, argued that emancipation would help rid the North of its black population: "When slavery is no longer recognized in the Southern States, the colored race will not struggle for the cold North to compete with our laborers, but those

8. *New York World*, Nov. 4, 1862.

9. Sidney David Brummer, *Political History of New York State during the Period of the Civil War*, Columbia University Studies in History, Economics, and Public Law, 39, No. 2 (New York, 1911), p. 239. Democrats also attacked the constitutionality of the proclamation.

10. *The American Annual Cyclopaedia and Register of Important Events of the Year 1862* (New York: D. Appleton & Co., 1863), p. 655; Brummer, *Political History*, pp. 238–39; Glyndon G. Van Deusen, *Thurlow Weed, Wizard of the Lobby* (Boston: Little Brown and Co., 1947), pp. 299–302.

11. James Wadsworth to James C. Smith, Sept. 13, 1862 in Henry Greenleaf Pearson, *James S. Wadsworth of Geneseo* (London: John Murray, 1913), p. 153.

now with us will seek a more congenial clime in the sunny South." [12] Republican speakers and editors praised Lincoln's proclamation for its military, rather than its moral, implications. Slavery, they urged, had to be challenged because it was upholding the rebellion and prolonging the war. The government's decision, insisted John K. Porter, was whether to "weaken the public enemy by emancipating those who dig trenches for Northern blood—or strengthen them by keeping four millions of men in chains." [13]

The outcome of the election tested the effectiveness of the Republicans' strategy. They lost the state by some eleven thousand votes in a total of more than 600,000. Their share of the vote in every county but one declined from 1860. Undoubtedly a lack of enthusiasm for emancipation was one factor that kept erstwhile Republicans at home or led them to cast Democratic ballots. [14] Yet what is perhaps most interesting is that Republican losses were no more severe in racially conservative areas than in others. And even with "proof" of Republican extremism, the overwhelming majority of Republicans continued to reject the Democratic alternative. The average decline in support for the Republicans in counties where there had been more than thirty per cent fewer prosuffrage votes than Republican votes in 1860 was 4.5 per cent; where there had been less than thirty per cent fewer prosuffrage votes, the decline was actually greater: 4.8 per cent in counties with a ten to thirty per cent difference and 4.6 per cent in counties where the difference had been less than ten per cent. In fact, there was almost no correlation (.10) between Republican losses 1860–1862 and the difference between the Republican and prosuffrage percentages in 1860. [15] Thus it seems that a substantial number of Republicans who had been alarmed in 1860 by the prospect of black voting in New York were not sufficiently upset by the thought of three million blacks being freed in the South

12. Daniel S. Dickinson, *The Duty of Loyal Men. Speech of Daniel S. Dickinson, at the Union Meeting in New York, Oct. 9, 1862* (n.p., 1862), p. 9.

13. Brummer, *Political History*, p. 239; Hodnett, "Civil War Issues," p. 64; John K. Porter, *Speech of John K. Porter at the Union Ratification Meeting Held at Glens Falls October 21* (Albany: Weed, Parsons & Co., 1862), p. 14.

14. Paul Kleppner, *The Third Electoral System, 1853–1892: Parties, Voters, and Political Cultures* (Chapel Hill: University of North Carolina Press, 1979), p. 83, found Republican losses nationwide in 1862 to be centered in Yankee and German areas. This does not seem to be true for New York. The German population was far too concentrated to account for the statewide declines, and per cent Yankee and per cent decline in the Republican vote correlated at only − .12 in towns for which returns were available.

15. This correlation was based on county-level data. At the town level the correlation was even lower, .05.

to switch to the Democrats. The race issue *was* dangerous to the Republicans, but losses could be minimized and perhaps later recouped if the matter were handled with sufficient skill and care.

After the 1862 defeat, Republicans made more extensive efforts to neutralize the impact of the race question. Throughout the following year they tried to accommodate the views of conservatives on emancipation while still supporting the president. The Republican-controlled state Senate, for example, considered several emancipation resolutions in 1863 in response to Governor Horatio Seymour's denunciation of abolition in his annual message. The one that eventually passed proposed to sustain the president in his use of his executive powers as commander-in-chief to suppress the rebellion (the legal justification for the Emancipation Proclamation).[16] Republicans were able to unite in support of this measure, which *did* back the president but did *not* require the sanctioning of emancipation as a war *aim* or even the defense of it as the *best* means for ending the war. Speakers again emphasized expedient reasons for freeing the slaves. In the fall, conservatives on the resolutions committee at the Republican convention actually omitted any reference to the Emancipation Proclamation in their proposed platform. To radicals this was too great a concession, however, for it implied the victory of the conservative wing. Aroused delegates insisted on including an endorsement of the proclamation "as a war measure thoroughly legal and justifiable."[17]

The New York Republicans' ability to demonstrate that the "worst" elements among the Democrats were the most loudly and violently racist also helped them to maintain a high degree of unity. Many Republicans believed that Democratic criticism of the war effort bordered on treason at the very least and to associate with such men on any grounds was most difficult. Republicans quickly noted, for instance, that the chief organizer of a large antiabolition rally in New York City was Fernando Wood, a Democrat who, as mayor in 1861, had called for the secession of the city. Resolutions passed at the rally condemned the "continual pressing of the negro question," asserted that the government "was established exclusively for the white race," and concluded that blacks (an "inferior and dependent

16. New York State Senate, *Journal*, 86th Sess., 1863, pp. 81, 95–97, 101, 106–107, 136. Emancipation resolutions were also introduced in the Assembly, but none proceeded to a final vote in the evenly divided chamber. New York State Assembly, *Journal*, 86th Sess., 1863, pp. 223, 232–33, 473.

17. Brummer, *Political History*, p. 339.

race") were entitled to neither political nor social equality. To participate in such a meeting was to risk being labeled as one of "questionable loyalty."[18]

Republicans were also able to exploit the antagonism between
Irishmen and the native born to reinforce support for their party.
The 1860 referendum had shown Republican weakness on the suffrage issue in nativist (American Party) areas. The Republican press,
therefore, strove to establish disloyalty and racist behavior as peculiarly Irish characteristics. Often the actions of the Irish played directly into the hands of their opponents. Maria Daly, the wife of a
well-to-do Irish-born Democratic judge in New York, explained why
some Irishmen avoided the army: "They [the Irish] have no idea of
fighting for the blacks. The abolitionists, they say, tell them that
soon they will have good, faithful, colored servants, and that these
Irish will then have to go back to their poorhouses. The Irish believe
the abolitionists hate both Irish and Catholic and want to kill them
off. The abolitionists always, the Irish say, put them in front of the
battle."[19]

In several cases Irishmen attacked blacks as their enemies. In
1863 mobs of striking Irish longshoremen fought with blacks who
had been hired to replace them. In July of that year, too, many Irish
participated in the so-called draft riots, which soon developed into
a general terrorization of New York's black community.[20] The *New
York Times* charged: "Hundreds of them [blacks] have been killed in
the public streets with atrocities such as we have never before heard
of in a civilized country. . . ; hundreds of them have had their
houses sacked and burned, and their little all forcibly taken from
them; thousands of them have fled from the city in abject terror;
and nearly all of them have been thrown out of employment."[21]

Some Republicans even believed that the riots had been deliberately staged to help the Confederates by diverting troops to New

18. Jerome Mushkat, *Tammany: The Evolution of a Political Machine, 1789–1865* (Syracuse: Syracuse University Press, 1971), p. 340. Quotes are from *New York Herald,* July
2, 1862 and *Harper's Weekly* (New York), Oct. 4, 1862.

19. Harold Earl Hammond, ed., *Diary of a Union Lady, 1861–1865* (New York: Funk
& Wagnalls Co., 1962), pp. 182–83.

20. Brother Basil Leo Lee, F.S.C., *Discontent in New York City, 1861–1865* (Washing-
ton, D.C.: Catholic University of America Press, 1943), pp. 140–41; *New York Times,*
Aug. 7, 1862. On the riots see Adrian Cook, *The Armies of the Streets: The New York City
Draft Riots of 1863* (Lexington, Ky.: University Press of Kentucky, 1973).

21. *New York Times,* July 17, 1863.

York when they were badly needed elsewhere. In the wake of such horrors, sympathy for the blacks and contempt for the Irish rapidly crystallized. A committee of New York merchants agreed to provide relief for black families while the Republican press had a field day linking the violent disorders to Democrats and disloyalists. The riots, of course, did not necessarily reduce prejudice among all conservatives. In some cases they probably increased it. Maria Daly, for example, regretted the "cruelties" inflicted but hoped they would "give the Negroes a lesson, for since the war commenced, they have been so insolent as to be unbearable."[22] What New York's bloody uprising did do, however, was to give the Republicans a nearly perfect example of what they had been telling their adherents for the past two years: that opposition to emancipation and the black was intimately associated with opposition to the war, riot, disorder, and treason—all embraced in the Democratic Party and its steadfast Irish Catholic adherents.

Thus the Republicans' endorsement of emancipation left a fundamental uneasiness in the party over the advocacy of black rights. Although many Republicans hated slavery and legal discrimination and welcomed emancipation as a long-sought goal, the party lacked unanimity and had to treat racial issues carefully. The broader agreement within the party on southerners, the Irish, and the disloyalty of Democrats could be used, however, to coalesce support for black freedom. Other implications of emancipation, as time would soon show, would be harder to deal with.

Yet the changes set in motion by the Republicans' emancipation policy had a logic of their own. The longer it remained in effect, the harder it became to restore slavery as it had been. Opposition to emancipation began to lack meaning. Even the Democrats, who since the 1850s had had little difficulty in agreeing on a racial strategy, now showed tentative signs of division. Should they continue to oppose abolition because they considered it a disastrous and unconstitutional policy, or should they bow to reality and accept it as a *fait accompli?*

The Democrats were experiencing a factional dispute along what Joel Silbey has termed "purist" and "legitimist" lines. The purists saw opposition to emancipation as a basic tenet of the Democratic faith which could never be surrendered or compromised. The le-

22. Hammond, *Diary,* p. 251.

gitimists were more intent on winning elections and wished to play down issues that were doubtful vote getters.[23] Thus in the New York Assembly in 1864 a Democrat (Carolan Bryant of New York City) went so far as to introduce a resolution calling for a constitutional amendment outlawing slavery. The Republicans passed such a measure late in the session, but apparently few Democrats joined them in the end.[24] In the national House of Representatives two New York Democrats in 1864 and six in 1865 favored the proposed Thirteenth Amendment abolishing slavery. These were a minority of New York's Democratic delegation, of course, but even some of the others felt that there was little likelihood of preventing emancipation.[25] In the 1864 presidential contest, the Republicans took firm ground in favor of the Thirteenth Amendment while the Democrats officially opposed it. Already, however, they faced the charge of defending a corpse.[26] In 1860 the Democrats had been rabidly antiabolitionist, the Republicans desperate to dissociate themselves from the unpopular antislavery minority. Now not only had Republicans accepted emancipation, but even some Democrats were considering that possibility.[27]

Yet anxieties about race itself did not die down. They rapidly became embodied in other issues. The eventual passage of four million human beings from slavery into freedom raised immediate questions of the role they and their brethren in the North were now

23. Joel H. Silbey, *A Respectable Minority: The Resurrection of the Democratic Party* (New York: W. W. Norton, 1977), pp. 96–114. Prior to emancipation the Democrats had perhaps been more united on race than any other issue. See Jean H. Baker, "A Loyal Opposition: Northern Democrats in the Thirty-seventh Congress," *Civil War History*, 25 (June 1979), 146–48.

24. New York State Assembly, *Journal*, 87th Sess., 1864, pp. 496, 737, 1418; *New York Herald*, Apr. 27, 1864. The resolution was passed by voice vote. For a general analysis of the Democrats' problems during the war years see Silbey, *Respectable Minority*.

25. For the views of a diehard see John V. S. L. Pruyn, Personal Journal 4, June 14, 1864, Jan. 7, 1865, New York State Library, Albany. The Democratic defectors in 1864 were John Griswold of Troy and Moses F. Odell of Brooklyn. (Griswold became a Republican shortly thereafter.) In 1865 the six were Odell, John Gansen of Buffalo, Ansom Herrick of New York City, Homer A. Nelson of Poughkeepsie, William Radforth of Yonkers, and John B. Steele of Kingston.

26. William Frank Zornow, *Lincoln & the Party Divided* (Norman, Okla.: University of Oklahoma Press, 1954), pp. 167–69.

27. A complete reversal was, of course, impossible. Republicans were still cautious. Theodore Tilton complained during the 1864 campaign that Republicans were pushing aside the Thirteenth Amendment for "prudential reasons." *New York Tribune*, Oct. 12, 1864. Similarly, Democrats used antiabolitionist literature, but it seemed to be aimed primarily at traditional Democrats.

to play within American society. Again the parties had to decide how to react. One of the first points of disagreement came over military service. Blacks had fought in every previous American war on a limited scale, but many white soldiers were unhappy with the government's decision in 1862 to enroll large numbers of black troops. Some New York recruits swore never to fight beside the "damned nigger."[28] The Democrats played freely on this prejudice. Annoyed by the demand that black soldiers be paid the same as their white counterparts, the *World* insisted:

> After we have spent millions of money and spilt useless torrents of blood in pursuit of this negro-equality chimera, we, too will discover that it is the supreme of folly to hold blacks to be the equal of the whites for warlike purposes.
>
> It is a gross injustice to the white soldier to pay him no better than you do the black. . . . As a race the blacks lack the brightness, smartness, persistence and enterprise of the whites.[29]

Yet Republicans could defend black recruitment, as they had emancipation, without upsetting traditional stereotypes or prejudices. One advocate of black troops wrote, "I believe in making the negroes fight to preserve the Union—It is not so great a loss if they are killed—and there is no danger of their being sun struck."[30] Another thought blacks would make good soldiers because they "possess strong imitative powers, which readily enable them to acquire a proficiency in drill—conform willingly to habits of discipline and obedience—and above all are stimulated by the motive of emulating the example of their white comrades in arms."[31] Even some Democrats could see advantages to black military service. At a private political gathering John V. S. L. Pruyn, a Democratic congressman, found Horatio Seymour opposed to black enlistments while Amasa J. Parker, another Democratic leader, argued for them, "preferring that the white men should not be taken away from their homes & the *ballotbox*, in the November election, and that as the war was for the blacks, they should participate in it as far as possible."[32]

Some Republicans welcomed black service, but most preferred to

---

28. Lee, *Discontent*, p. 150.
29. *New York World*, Dec. 18, 1863.
30. Lee, *Discontent*, p. 152.
31. Quoted in Henry O'Rielly, *First Organization of Colored Troops in the State of New York, to Aid in Suppressing the Slaveholders' Rebellion* (New York: Baker & Godwin, 1864), p. 23. See also William Seraile, "The Struggle to Raise Black Regiments in New York State, 1861–1864," *New York Historical Society Quarterly*, 58 (July 1974), 215–33.
32. John V. S. L. Pruyn, Journal 3, July 20, 1864.

use appeals to white self-interest to justify it rather than to argue that black men should serve for the same reasons that white men did.[33] To have done so would have invited needless opposition. Yet the mere appearance of black *soldiers* among civilians accustomed to honoring and even exalting their "protectors" served to shake some individuals' assumptions about blacks. Observing the first black regiment depart New York, Maria Daly commented, "Though I am very little Negrophilish and would always prefer the commonest white that lives to a Negro, still I could not but feel moved."[34] A Republican who had opposed equal suffrage in 1860 witnessed a similar sight and admitted later: "I am not ashamed to say that from that hour, I had an affection for the man who when everything else was dark and gloomy would go forth to protect me and my wife and children, and my friends and society, and above all, his country. . . . And men who have done that for me I believe . . . to be men."[35] The warm public response to the troops frankly amazed the *New York Times,* which had been unenthusiastic when the subject of black enlistments had first been broached.[36]

A few months after the first black troops left, a great furor erupted when a streetcar conductor on the Eighth Avenue line ejected the widow of a black soldier from a car reserved for whites. The Union League rallied behind her and prepared to take the case to court. The company quickly capitulated, ordering an end to all further discrimination. When the Sixth Avenue line followed suit a few days later, Jim Crow came to an end (at least on paper) on the streetcars of New York.[37] Increasingly, whites, especially very patriotic ones, were reconsidering their attitudes toward the black man.

Where discrimination was less clearly related to the conduct of the war, however, it proved harder to eradicate. The continued em-

33. Louis S. Gerteis, *From Contraband to Freedman: Federal Policy toward Southern Blacks, 1861–1865* (Westport, Conn.: Greenwood Press, 1973), pp. 183, 185, concludes that in their entire racial policy Republicans considered military needs first and foremost and never ventured into policies that could be justified only on humanitarian grounds. See also Mary Frances Berry, *Military Necessity and Civil Rights Policy: Black Citizenship and the Constitution, 1861–1868* (Port Washington, N.Y.: Kennikat Press, 1977).

34. Hammond, *Diary,* p. 278.

35. *Proceedings and Debates of the Constitutional Convention of the State of New York* (Albany: Weed, Parsons & Co., 1868), 1:270. (Hereafter cited as *Convention Proceedings.*)

36. *New York Times,* Mar. 7, 1864. New York sent over 4,000 black troops to the front, fourteen per cent of whom died in the war. See Seraile, "Black Regiments," pp. 231–33.

37. Lee, *Discontent,* pp. 136–37.

phasis on expediency when introducing emancipation and black military service laid no groundwork for general racial reform. Andrew D. White struggled in vain to remove a provision permitting segregated schools from an act consolidating school laws in 1864. Complaints about the property qualification for black voters similarly went unheeded. Following Illinois's repeal of its discriminatory black laws in 1865, *Harper's Weekly*, an outspoken radical journal, insisted that the "same mean and inhuman prejudice" had inspired New York's property qualification, which should now be removed. For the first time since 1861, petitions to repeal the property qualification were introduced into the legislature in 1864 and 1865.[38]

To the disappointment of suffrage advocates, however, white New Yorkers still seemed willing to discriminate. Many Republican political leaders had deferred to, rather than challenged, white bigotry during the war. They had sidestepped the race question altogether when possible and concentrated their fire on the Democrats' weakest point, alleged disloyalty and copperheadism within their ranks. As for the black man, Horace Greeley admitted:

> We have . . . liberated him from galling and grinding bondage, not specially for *his* sake, not because we pitied him as weak, downtrodden and terribly abused, but because the life of the nation hung upon a course of simple justice to this long-suffering race—because it was for our advantage, our peace, our safety and our prosperity to acknowledge the manhood of the Black, who involuntarily has become the greatest benefactor of this nation, since through him we have been able to strike a blow at faction and to assert the supremacy of the Constitution.[39]

Greeley realized, nevertheless, that in freeing the slaves the Republicans had started a chain reaction that could not be easily stopped. Having destroyed one system of race relations in the South, they had to substitute another; having alienated southern whites and befriended southern blacks, they had to acknowledge this state of affairs in any plan for peace; and having accepted black soldiers as partners in winning the war, they could not ignore their oppression without appearing singularly ungrateful. Yet if blacks in the seceded states were to be guaranteed basic rights, could northern states continue to withhold these same rights from their own

38. Gilbert T. Stephenson, *Race Distinctions in American Law* (New York: D. Appleton and Co., 1910), p. 185; *Harper's Weekly*, Feb. 11, 1865; New York State Assembly, *Journal*, 87th Sess., 1864, pp. 32, 487; 88th Sess., 1865, p. 129.
39. *New York Tribune*, June 14, 1865.

black populations? The Republicans confronted a dilemma. To permit southern whites to resurrect antebellum society seemed foolhardy. Yet to intervene in the blacks' behalf might offend northern racial sensibilities.

Over the next few years Democrats, both nationally and in New York, tried to take advantage of the Republican dilemma by forcing them to defend racially liberal policies before the voters. The New York Democracy chose black suffrage as their principal point of attack. (Civil rights for blacks were less controversial since the state did not officially restrict them.[40]) The endorsement of black suffrage in the South by some radicals who thought the time was now ripe seemed to offer Democrats an opening. Frederick Douglass for one was proclaiming: "Our streets are in mourning, tears are falling at every fireside, and under the chastisement of this Rebellion we have almost come up to the point of conceding this great, this all-important right of suffrage. I fear that if we fail to do it now, if abolitionists fail to press it now, we may not see, for centuries to come, the same disposition that exists at this moment."[41] Blacks had formed a National Equal Rights League in 1864 with auxiliaries in many states including New York. Their purpose was to labor for equal rights and equal opportunities for all blacks.[42] The airing of such issues, Democrats hoped, would help their cause.

The Democrats eagerly anticipated a battle on the black suffrage issue. Although Horace Greeley estimated that seven-eighths of all Republicans in New York now favored black voting, he still had to admit ". . . so long as a tenth, or even a twentieth, of the Republicans vote with the Copperheads on this point, we, who stand for Equal Rights, must struggle in vain."[43] Black suffrage had proved unpopular in other states as well. In 1865 and 1866 voters rejected it in Connecticut, Wisconsin, Minnesota, the District of Columbia, and the territories of Colorado and Nebraska.[44]

The Democrats made a valiant effort in those years to win over

40. Democratic leaders in New York tended to accept the idea of equality before the law and object only to the Republican methods for assuring it. See *New York World*, Oct. 21, 1865; *New York Herald*, Feb. 12, 1866.

41. [George Luther Stearns], compiler, *Equality of All Men before the Law Claimed and Defended* (Boston: Press of Geo. C. Rand & Avery, 1865), pp. 36–37.

42. James M. McPherson, *The Negro's Civil War* (New York: Pantheon Books, 1965), pp. 286–87.

43. *New York Tribune*, Oct. 13, 1865.

44. William Gillette, *The Right to Vote: Politics and the Passage of the Fifteenth Amendment* (Baltimore: Johns Hopkins Press, 1969), pp. 25–26.

conservative Republicans. They accepted the finality of the Thirteenth Amendment abolishing slavery and endorsed Andrew Johnson's Reconstruction proposals in an attempt to dispel their copperhead image and show their fundamental loyalty. And they portrayed the Republicans as favoring a "radical" reconstruction of the South which included the imposition of black rule by government fiat. Thus Republicans would appear as the real threat to the Constitution, peace, and reunion. To bolster its new "loyal" image the party even went so far as to include several disgruntled Republicans on its state ticket in 1865, and in 1866 it was heavily involved in the National Union movement, a "new" conservative political organization backing the president.[45]

As they had during the war, however, Republicans treated the racial question cautiously and managed to keep their party united. Outraged purists among the Democrats unintentionally helped the Republican cause by emphatically rejecting their party's new strategy, which called on them to support former Republicans and even Lincoln's running mate as though they were among the party faithful.[46] Compared to the Republicans, proportionately fewer Democrats turned out to support their party's "loyal" candidates in 1865 and 1866 than in 1864 when McClellan had run for president on a "copperhead" peace platform. The Democratic vote in 1865 was 75.3 per cent of that in 1864, the Republican, 81.4 per cent. In 1866 the corresponding figures were 97.4 per cent and 99.3 per cent. The Democrats new strategy had not worked because it appealed to only one faction in the party while offending the other.

Although New York Republicans did disagree on the merits of black suffrage in the South, they did so in ways that did not create insurmountable problems for their party. Even in 1865 very few Republican leaders desired blacks to be excluded from the suffrage solely on account of their race.[47] They differed mainly over *how*

45. Edward Lee Gambill, "Northern Democrats and Reconstruction, 1865–1868," (Ph.D. diss., University of Iowa, 1969), pp. 13, 46, chapter 3 passim; Silbey, *Respectable Minority*, chapter 8; LaWanda and John H. Cox, *Politics, Principle, and Prejudice, 1865–1866: Dilemma of Reconstruction America* (New York: Free Press of Glencoe, 1963), chapter 4; Homer Adolph Stebbins, *A Political History of the State of New York, 1865–1868* (New York: Columbia University, 1913), pp. 49–50; *Albany Argus*, Sept. 23, 1865.

46. For a humorist's version of the problem the new strategy caused the Democrats see David Ross Locke, *The Struggles of Petroleum V. Nasby* (1872; abridged ed., Boston: Beacon Press, 1963), pp. 111–13. See also *New York Times*, Oct. 25, 1865.

47. *New York Times*, Sept. 27, 1865; Walter G. Hannahs, "The Attitude of *The New York Tribune* towards the Negro in Reconstruction" (M.A. thesis, University of Roch-

many blacks should vote, a token few or a substantial number. Racial fears were, of course, involved in the advocacy of requirements which would in fact disfranchise most blacks. As Greeley remarked, "If the Blacks by some magic process could all be bleached to-day, and rise to-morrow with fair cheeks and straight hair, nobody would admit that any difficult problem existed at all."[48] However, the point at issue often appeared to be general suffrage requirements rather than race per se.

At election time Republicans took common, conservative positions. In the 1865 state party convention a plank favoring black suffrage was scuttled.[49] Democrats' charges that the Republicans were adamant on this point were thus made to seem even more ridiculous.

Nationally, too, the party took limited stands, which helped matters in New York. In early 1866 the House of Representatives passed a bill permitting blacks in the District of Columbia to vote, but the Senate failed to act until after the 1866 elections. In mid-1866 Congress proposed the Fourteenth Amendment, which reduced the representation of any state that denied the vote to a portion of its male citizens. Both of these measures revealed essential caution. In the House a majority of Republicans (including fourteen of nineteen New York Republicans who voted) had wanted only former soldiers or literate blacks to vote in the District of Columbia. Only when Democrats joined radicals to reject this proposal did Republicans unite to give all blacks in the District the ballot. The Joint Committee on Reconstruction also did not include an explicit grant of suffrage to blacks in the Fourteenth Amendment, partly on the advice of the New York Republican caucus.[50]

As had occurred with the Emancipation Proclamation, state Re-

---

ester, 1951), pp. 28, 36, 47ff; *Harper's Weekly*, May 20, 1865; B. F. Camp to Thurlow Weed, Sept. 13, 1865, Thurlow Weed Papers, University of Rochester Library, Rochester, New York. See also Eric L. McKitrick, *Andrew Johnson and Reconstruction* (Chicago: University of Chicago Press, 1960), pp. 55–59.

48. *New York Tribune*, May 30, 1865.

49. The platform did express the hope that the southern states would grant "all their people" the "full rights of citizenship." *American Annual Cyclopaedia . . . of the Year 1865*, p. 614; Stebbins, *Political History*, pp. 61–63; Dorothy Dodd, *Henry J. Raymond and the* New York Times *during Reconstruction* (private edition distributed by the University of Chicago Libraries, 1936), p. 32.

50. Edward McPherson, *The Political History of the United States of America during the Period of Reconstruction, 1865–1870*, 2nd ed. (Washington, D. C.: Solomons & Chapman, 1871), pp. 114–15; *New York Times*, Jan. 22, 1866; Joseph B. James, *The Framing of the Fourteenth Amendment* (Urbana, Ill.: University of Illinois Press, 1956), p. 110.

publican leaders showed a willingness to support their party's actions nationally even when these seemed unwise to some. In 1866 the state legislature passed resolutions approving the congressional approach to Reconstruction. A joint Republican caucus agreed to endorse black suffrage in the District of Columbia as part of one of these resolutions, even though some Republicans reportedly considered this clause inexpedient. In the Assembly the resolutions passed by a strictly partisan vote, the debate centering on clauses unrelated to suffrage. The Senate, however, voted on suffrage in the District separately, and several substitutes were offered from the floor. Of the twenty-seven Republicans in that body, twenty-one wanted all blacks in the District to vote; two would have preferred a literacy or war service requirement but accepted full suffrage when those amendments failed, and four others would have granted the right to vote *only* to veterans or the literate.[51] Most Republicans, therefore, supported the House of Representatives' action on black suffrage.

When facing the electorate, however, New York Republicans continued to minimize popular discontent over their racial policies in the South by stressing expedient and even racist arguments for them. Roscoe Conkling, a congressman from Utica who had helped frame the Fourteenth Amendment, told his constituents that the amendment would equalize political power between northern and southern *whites* and that granting civil rights to southern blacks would encourage them to stay in the South and not to venture north.[52] Whites were frankly assured, "There are to be no negro Presidents or Governors, or Senators in the future."[53]

By treating racial questions rather gingerly in 1865 and 1866, Republicans allowed Andrew Johnson's reconstruction proposals to become the focal point of public discussion. Here they had a distinct advantage. Many Republicans were deeply concerned that the Democrats, aided by Johnson, would restore unrepentant southerners to a dominant position in national politics. "The masses of the Union Party are praying, God fearing men, who look upon Rebels

---

51. *New York Herald*, Mar. 9, 1866; New York State Assembly, *Journal*, 89th Sess., 1866, pp. 655–57; *Albany Argus*, Mar. 10, 1866; New York State Senate, *Journal*, 89th Sess., 1866, pp. 679–81.

52. Alfred R. Conkling, *The Life and Letters of Roscoe Conkling, Orator, Statesman, Advocate* (New York: Charles L. Webster & Co., 1889), p. 277. See also *Albany Evening Journal*, Sept 22, Oct. 30, 1866.

53. *Albany Evening Journal*, May 14, 1866.

and Copperheads as agents of the Devil and enemies of human progress," wrote one Republican.[54] Severe provocation would be necessary to persuade such men even to consider casting a Democratic ballot. In 1866 the Democratic plans with regard to the South seemed more dangerous than unrestricted black suffrage throughout the country (which Republicans had not endorsed in any case).[55] As a result the Republicans carried New York in both 1865 and 1866.

In 1867, however, the situation changed dramatically. Once again events on the national scene forced New York Republicans to rethink their racial strategy. Hoping for better terms, southern legislatures rejected the Fourteenth Amendment. Congressional Republicans did not back down. Instead they instituted military rule in the southern states to be followed by new constitutional conventions chosen by both blacks and whites.[56] This momentous and far-reaching decision promised to enfranchise nearly all the nation's blacks for the first time. It forced the Republican Party as a whole to face the subject of black political power directly and to see that their party's fate hinged upon it. It prepared the way for the Fifteenth Amendment two years later. The national party had in effect officially endorsed black voting in a real rather than token sense; the period of agonizing indecision was over.

New York Republicans accepted the new state of affairs. Once more there were signs of a determination to create a unified, viable position on the issue. The party leadership rapidly assimilated the implications of southern black voting. "For good or ill, for weal or woe, the Republican party is committed to the principle of negro suffrage. It cannot evade the issue; and it should not if it could. To do so would indicate such supreme cowardice and injustice as to prove the party unworthy of trust or control; and would result, as it should, in its overthrow and disgrace," stated the *Albany Evening Journal* which had hitherto been very cautious on the issue.[57] Even

54. Ransom Balcom to William Henry Seward, Mar. 2, 1866, William Henry Seward Papers, University of Rochester Library, Rochester, New York.
55. Many Republicans believed the Philadelphia Convention that formed the National Union movement to be dominated by disloyal elements. See D. H. Cole to Thurlow Weed, July 19, 1866; Anthony F. Campbell to Weed, July 10, 1866; Samuel W. Smith to Weed, Aug. 23, 1866, Weed Papers; George Dawson to Frederick Seward, July 14, 1866, Seward Papers.
56. George Selden Henry, Jr., "Radical Republican Policy toward the Negro during Reconstruction, 1862–1872" (Ph.D. diss., Yale University, 1963), p. 204.
57. *Albany Evening Journal*, Mar. 19, 1867.

the conservative *New York Times* objected only to the tactics of the radicals and frankly accepted the inevitability of black suffrage. The New York legislature adopted resolutions approving the repassage of the bill granting full suffrage to the blacks of the District of Columbia over the president's veto. Not a single Republican dissented, although four senators had opposed full suffrage for the District's blacks the previous year.[58]

But Republicans soon demonstrated that they intended to control the partisan consequences of black suffrage even if they would not dream of rejecting the reform. The 1846 state constitution contained a provision that required that the question whether to hold a new constitutional convention be submitted to the voters every twenty years. In the fall elections of 1866 the voters expressed the wish for such a convention. The legislature had to make the arrangements. Controversy immediately erupted over the manner of electing delegates to the gathering. The Senate's convention bill granted equal suffrage to all blacks in the election of delegates while the Assembly's did not. Since the convention would create a new governmental compact, it was argued, the provisions of the old document should not be binding upon it. (There was some precedent for this position.) Both the *New York Tribune* and the *Albany Evening Journal*, however, advised care, expressing fears that the Senate's version would needlessly excite prejudice.[59]

On February 27, 1867, Charles S. Hoyt introduced an amendment to the Assembly bill which would have followed the Senate in granting equal suffrage to blacks to elect delegates to the convention while also disfranchising anyone who had engaged in rebellion or bribery. The parallel to what was going on in the South (enfranchisement of blacks, restrictions on ex-rebel voters) was unmistakable. Yet Republican after Republican rose to claim that while he personally favored black voting, the reform should be incorporated in the new constitution and not in advance of it. Hoyt replied that "technical constitutional objections" should not stand in the way of justice; a few argued that the proposal was completely constitutional in any case. Yet the amendment was rejected 33–90 with a majority

58. *New York Times*, May 3, June 13, July 3, 1867; New York State Assembly, *Journal*, 90th Sess., 1867, p. 248; Senate, *Journal*, 90th Sess., 1867, pp. 181–82. Two of the four senators were absent.

59. *New York Tribune*, Feb. 8, 1867; *Albany Evening Journal*, Feb. 4, 8, 1867. For a somewhat different interpretation of the black suffrage issue and the 1867 convention see James C. Mohr, *The Radical Republicans and Reform in New York during Reconstruction* (Ithaca, N.Y.: Cornell University Press, 1973), chapters 7–8.

of Republicans opposed.[60] (See Table 5.2.) Senate Republicans were also divided but succeeded in defeating an amendment which would have restored the voting qualifications under the 1846 constitution.[61]

A conference committee of both houses (which had to adjudicate several other disagreements as well) eventually sent in a report favoring black suffrage for the delegate election. The Assembly again rejected that provision, however, although a slight majority of Republicans favored it this time.[62] (The Democrats with one exception were at all times united in opposition to black suffrage.[63]) A second conference committee finally eliminated equal suffrage, and the convention bill passed both houses with only three Republicans in the Assembly and four in the Senate opposed.[64]

Although the Republican opponents of equal suffrage in the delegate elections mostly claimed that they favored black voting, their adversaries considered them simply illiberal. One of the senators who was on the Republican State Committee went so far as to introduce resolutions in that body condemning the Assembly's factious behavior in rejecting impartial suffrage. The resolves were tabled on procedural grounds but only by two votes.[65]

Clearly some Republicans thought equal rights a more viable issue than others. This was later confirmed in the convention when several Republican delegates expressed a strong belief that opinion on equal suffrage had, as one remarked, made "rapid advances" because of the war.[66] Yet not all Republicans were so confident of public opinion and apparently were reluctant to act for just that reason.

60. *Albany Argus*, Feb. 27, 28, 1867; New York State Assembly, *Journal*, 90th Sess., 1867, pp. 438–39. The best statement of the constitutional argument may be found in Andrew Dickson White, *Remarks of Hon. Andrew D. White, of Onondaga in the Senate* (Albany: Weed, Parsons, and Co., 1867).

61. New York State Senate, *Journal*, 90th Sess., 1867, p. 297. Stephen K. Williams, a Republican, was incorrectly listed as voting both ways. From the debates it is clear that he favored equal suffrage in the delegate election.

62. New York State Assembly, *Journal*, 90th Sess., 1867, pp. 854–55.

63. The exception was Smith M. Weed of Clinton County. An unusual Democrat, he came from Quaker and Yankee stock and had been an early supporter of the Thirteenth Amendment. Other Democrats bitterly attacked his action. S. R. Harlow and H. H. Boone, *Life Sketches of the State Officers, Senators, and Members of the Assembly of the State of New York in 1867* (Albany: Weed, Parsons, and Co., 1867), pp. 382–83; *Albany Evening Journal*, Feb. 15, 1867; *New York Herald*, Feb. 15, 1867.

64. New York State Senate, *Journal*, 90th Sess., 1867, p. 549; Assembly, *Journal*, 90th Sess., 1867, p. 974.

65. See F. B. Sanborn to Andrew D. White, Mar. 25, 1867; Eugene Schuyler to White, May 22, 1867, Andrew D. White Papers, Cornell University Library, Ithaca, New York. *New York Tribune*, Mar. 23, 1867. See also *Harper's Weekly*, Apr. 6, 1867.

66. *Convention Proceedings*, 1:258, 270, 317, 331.

TABLE 5.2.

Republican legislators' votes on equal suffrage in electing delegates to the state convention, 1867

	Assembly votes				First Senate vote[c]	
	First[a]		Second[b]			
Position	Number	Per cent	Number	Per cent	Number	Per cent
For suffrage	32	38.5	44	53.0	16	59.3
Against suffrage	47	56.5	32	38.5	8	29.6
Absent	4	4.8	7	8.4	3	11.1
Total	83	99.9	83	99.9	27	100.0

[a]Hoyt amendment to permit voting "without distinction of color" for convention delegates.

[b]Motion to approve section 2 of conference committee report permitting black suffrage in electing convention delegates.

[c]Murphy amendment to restore voting qualifications of the present constitution.

If one divides the Assembly Republicans into groups according to whether they supported equal suffrage in one, both, or neither of the direct votes on the question, it appears that those most opposed to blacks voting for convention delegates were also somewhat more likely to come from counties that rejected black suffrage in 1869. (See Table 5.3.) The same pattern appears in the vote of the Senate Republicans. (See Table 5.4.)

Yet in the end virtually *every* Republican accepted the convention bill without equal suffrage for blacks.[67] The party remained united. What it had proved was that it was not willing to go to *any* lengths to assert the black man's right to the franchise. Party harmony was just as vital. Indeed according to the Albany correspondent of the *New York Tribune,* it was a partisan Democratic attack on the Republican Party which finally convinced prosuffrage Republicans in the Assembly to accept the compromise version of the convention bill which the Democrats opposed. Republicans in general showed renewed concern about their party's practical needs. When a few Republicans suggested (the Democrats joyfully concurring) that Frederick Douglass be nominated as a Republican delegate-at-large to the convention—a position tantamount to election since these seats were to be uncontested, each party naming sixteen men as at-large

67. Only one Republican voted against the final bill in the Assembly because of the suffrage provision. *New York Tribune,* Mar. 28, 1867.

Table 5.3.

Suffrage votes of Republican assemblymen, 1867, by suffrage position of their home counties, 1869[a]

Position of Republicans on suffrage	Position of home county on suffrage, 1869					
	For		Against		Total	
	Number	Per cent	Number	Per cent	Number	Per cer
Opposed on both votes	14	43.9	18	56.1	32	100.0
Opposed, then favored	7	58.7	8	41.3	15	100.0
Favored on both votes	24	82.9	5	17.1	29	100.0

$\chi^2 = 11.3$ for 2 d.f. Significant at .01.

[a]Only Republicans participating on both votes are included. Assembly districts were some times smaller than counties.

Table 5.4.

Suffrage votes of Republican state senators, 1867, by suffrage position of their districts, 1869

Position of Republicans on suffrage	Position of districts on suffrage, 1869					
	For		Against		Total	
	Number	Per cent	Number	Per cent	Number	Per cent
Opposed	2[a]	25.0	6	75.0	8	100.0
Favored	12	75.0	4	25.0	16	100.0

$\chi^2 = 7.1$ for 1 d.f. Significant at .01.

[a]One of these was from Erie County, whose prosuffrage vote in 1869 was probably overestimated. (See Chapter 6, note 48.)

delegates—not only did Douglass not get the nod, but he also was decisively rejected as a regular candidate from his home district.[68]

The legislature's action was not a rejection of black suffrage per se, but rather an expression of a determination to control the political consequences of it. Indeed the Republicans specifically reasserted their commitment to black voting at their state convention held to nominate the at-large delegates. They unanimously adopted a resolution instructing the new nominees to support "an amendment to the Constitution, giving to the black man the same rights of ballot as the white man."[69]

68. Ibid.; *Albany Argus*, Mar. 16, Apr. 5, 6, 10, 20, 1867; *New York Herald*, Apr. 1, 1867; D. W. Fiske to Andrew D. White, Mar. 16, 1867, White Papers.
69. *Albany Argus*, Apr. 12, 1867.

The constitutional convention of 1867 became the apparent vehicle for a Republican demonstration of their solidarity on the principle of equal suffrage. Unfortunately, the character of the convention itself made the likelihood of this outcome problematical. The delegates who assembled in Albany on June 4 faced serious problems almost from the outset.[70] Although the Republicans had a healthy majority (ninety-seven of one hundred sixty delegates) and could create a constitution of their choosing, their work would be wasted without voter ratification.[71] The state was closely divided politically and there were numerous indications that the Democrats, in contrast to 1846, saw no need for reform and would oppose most suggested changes. Republicans had the will and power to act but the frustration of knowing they were most likely to fail. The convention lacked vigorous and skilled political leadership too and quickly bogged down.[72] In the end the body met months longer than any previous convention (almost nine months including recesses), considered innumerable reforms, and yet came up with a document that was not markedly different from the 1846 constitution. Worries about the convention's effectiveness would have an impact on the fate of equal suffrage in it.

In the convention, as in the legislature, Republicans agreed on the *principle* of black suffrage but divided on how much they were willing to risk politically in its behalf. William Gillette has argued that Republicans generally supported black suffrage because it offered them the important political advantage of more voters in closely divided northern states like New York. In New York, however, the potential political advantage was probably at most only one element in Republican calculations.[73] Certainly New York had a long tradition of close elections, which made the question of voter eligi-

70. For a general outline of the convention see Stebbins, *Political History*, chapter 9.
71. Due to the manner of selecting delegates, the Republicans' heavy majority was not representative of the party's statewide strength. In addition to the thirty-two at-large delegates, four delegates had been chosen from each of the thirty-two Senate districts (malapportioned to favor the Republicans). The race issue played a less prominent part in the delegate elections than in 1846 when the Liberty Party was a factor. But the issue did come up in conservative Greene County. See *Albany Argus*, Apr. 20, 1867.
72. Ibid., Sept. 2, 1867.
73. Gillette, *Right to Vote*. Republicans rarely mentioned the subject of black additions to the Republican Party in connection with New York, but see *New York Times*, Sept. 26, 1867. Horace Greeley often talked of the need for black voters in Connecticut but never mentioned it as crucial for New York. See *New York Tribune*, Apr. 4, 1866, Apr. 4, 1867.

bility crucial. But the black vote was hardly the key to future Republican success. Black male adults in the state numbered no more than 10,000, and some of these were already able to vote under the property qualification. Estimates of new voters under equal suffrage usually ranged from five thousand to seven thousand.[74] (The last previous Republican loss in the gubernatorial race of 1862 had been by eleven thousand votes.) In addition, the proportion of blacks in the population was shrinking in contrast to the foreign born, who were typically Democratic and whose numbers were rapidly increasing. The black vote would help but could not be a panacea for the Republicans.

In fact, Republican legislators had already begun to experiment with other means of changing the structure of the electorate. They had passed voter registration laws which applied only to cities (where most immigrants lived) and which tended to reduce participation by making it more difficult. *Harper's Weekly* suggested another alternative. Alarmed by the growing and increasingly decisive political influence of the "profoundly ignorant" Irish, whom it contrasted to the "intelligent, industrious" native blacks, it suggested that the convention should consider equal but *qualified* suffrage, which would "encourage" education among the populace.[75] At the convention literally *every* provision of the suffrage article produced a battle, from an increase in the period before naturalized citizens could vote to the method for determining which voters were mentally deranged. In sum, the Republicans had more than the black suffrage option to consider.[76]

Even though the black vote was not a sufficient inducement to account for strong Republican support for it, a moral commitment to equal rights among all the Republican delegates is not the only other possible explanation for their actions. A moral concern was definitely there, as it always had been. But, after the enactment of black suffrage in the South by the Republican U.S. Congress, party loyalty itself dictated support for equal rights. The *Nation* insisted that the issue assumed its chief importance at the convention "because of its bearing on the course of reconstruction at the South."[77]

74. *New York World*, Apr. 6, 1867; *New York Times*, Sept. 26, 1867; *Albany Argus*, June 20, 1867.
75. *Harper's Weekly*, Nov. 24, 1866.
76. For an indication that Democrats were similarly concerned with all aspects of suffrage see William Cassidy to Samuel J. Tilden, Nov. 12, 1867, Samuel J. Tilden Papers, New York Public Library, New York City.
77. *Nation*, Oct. 3, 1867.

For black suffrage to fail would be a reflection on both the party and its Reconstruction program. In five votes on various Democratic alternatives to equal suffrage at the convention, not a single Republican dissented from his party's position.[78]

As in the earlier battles for suffrage in 1846 and 1860, the preferred way to rally support for the measure proved to be to relate it to issues of broader partisan appeal—in this case the war and slavery. Republicans portrayed equal rights as a natural outcome of the war. The majority report of the convention's suffrage committee asserted:

> Slavery, the vital source and only plausible ground of such invidious discrimination [the property qualification], being dead, . . . we can imagine no tolerable excuse for perpetuating the existing proscription. . . . Whites and blacks were indiscriminately drafted and held to service to fill our State's quotas in the war whereby the Republic was saved from disruption. We trust that we are henceforth to deal with men according to their conduct, without regard to their color.[79]

While some Republicans *were* staunch believers in complete racial equality, others, while approving black suffrage, implicitly or explicitly avowed the superiority of the white race.[80] Certainly some did not feel a *moral* compulsion to remove racial distinctions. Some in fact showed little interest in the problems of black people. A potential for discord within the party thus existed, especially if the black suffrage issue were suddenly to appear politically risky. This potential remained unrealized during the first half of the convention. The Democrats urged that the suffrage proposition be separately submitted to the electorate as in 1846, but the Republicans were determined that this time it should not be. Suffrage supporters believed that inclusion of it in the body of the constitution would forestall the massive Republican abstentions on the question that had occurred in the 1860 referendum. And many Republicans seemed to believe

78. *Journal of the Convention of the State of New York* (Albany: Weed, Parsons, and Co., 1867), pp. 287–92, 303–306, 979–80. (Hereafter cited as *Convention Journal.*) Two would have allowed all whites plus the blacks eligible under the 1846 convention to vote. One would have allowed those blacks plus those subsequently born in the state and meeting other qualifications to vote. One would have established a discriminatory residency requirement for blacks only. Another alternative would have changed the preface of the section to indicate that only New York could control its franchise provisions.

79. *Documents of the Convention of the State of New York* (Albany: Weed, Parsons and Co., 1868), Doc. 15, p. 4.

80. Examples of the former were Martin I. Townsend and Seth Wakeman; of the latter, Horace E. Smith, Patrick Corbet, and Judson Landen.

that concealing the change in the body of the constitution would also make it less subject to political attack.[81] In fact, there was a notable amount of optimism, apparently spurred by the Republican triumphs in 1865 and 1866, that public opinion itself had changed significantly.[82]

The rather uncharacteristic behavior of certain Democratic leaders encouraged this view. Soon after congressional passage of black suffrage in the South several Democratic editors, including Manton Marble of New York's major Democratic daily, the *World*, began to consider the proper Democratic response. Marble, a member of the legitimist faction, thought that it would be difficult to overturn the Reconstruction Acts and that the best course for the Democratic Party to pursue would be to accept the acts for the moment and try to win over a portion of the black vote in the South. Reconstruction as an issue would then die down to be superseded by issues, such as financial policy, on which Marble felt sure the Republicans were vulnerable.[83] Since the party had failed to win over the racial conservatives in the Republican ranks in 1865 and 1866, perhaps it would have an easier time winning back former Democrats who had joined the Republicans out of disgust with the Democrats' position on slavery and the South. In accordance with this strategy, Marble wanted the Democrats at the constitutional convention to support equal suffrage or at least insist on separate submission without making their position clear. The minority report of the Suffrage Committee indeed followed the latter course, and three Democrats out of sixty-three at the convention eventually endorsed equal suffrage.[84] Such

81. *Independent* (New York), Aug. 1, 1867; *Convention Proceedings*, 1: 247, 248, 292. See also *New York World*, July 18, 1867.

82. Four petitions were received specifically favoring black suffrage, only one against it. These did not represent the total sentiment on the subject. Many more petitions were received on "universal suffrage." Although the primary effect of these would be to enfranchise women, some black suffrage advocates preferred the more general suffrage endorsement. See *Convention Journal*, index. On the joint effort to solicit support for female and black suffrage see Ellen Carol Dubois, *Feminism and Suffrage: The Emergence of an Independent Women's Movement in America, 1848–1869* (Ithaca, N.Y.: Cornell University Press, 1978), p. 87.

83. J. M. Bloch, "The Rise of the New York *World* during the Civil War Decade" (Ph.D. diss., Harvard University, 1941), pp. 257–58; George Tilden McJimsey, *Genteel Partisan: Manton Marble, 1834–1917* (Ames, Iowa: Iowa State University Press, 1971), pp. 114–19; *New York World*, Mar. 4, 6, 16, 19, Apr. 6, 1867.

84. *New York World*, Apr. 6, June 14, 1867. See also Allen G. Sexton, "The Democratic Party in Western New York, 1865–1870" (M.A. thesis, University of Buffalo, 1951), p. 42. *Convention Documents*, Doc. 16. The three were George W. Clinton of Erie, Magnus Gross of New York, and Smith M. Weed of Clinton.

defections delighted the Republicans, who openly wooed the Democrats during the debates with the promise that the passage of equal suffrage would remove the race issue forever from politics.[85]

The overwhelming majority of Democrats, however, were not willing to surrender on the race issue. They believed they were right, and no amount of pleading that their position was inexpedient (which many doubted) could persuade them to abandon it. Prominent Democrats looked askance at Marble's behavior. Former President James Buchanan warned ominously from Pennsylvania that the *World's* course would have an "unhappy effect" in that state.[86] Marble's tone at first became defensive; then as the fall elections approached, he went back to making blatant appeals to prejudice.[87] The Democrats, like the Republicans, found it important to maintain a unified party position on the race question.

The revelation that the Democrats still intended to exploit racial anxieties in the electorate and moreover were successful at it alarmed Republicans at the convention. A few had thought from the beginning that inclusion of black suffrage in the constitution was a mistake and would ensure its defeat.[88] News from other states confirmed their fear of the race issue. Everywhere Democratic cries of "Negro rule" were meeting a sympathetic response in the electorate. With the passage of the military reconstruction acts and the attempts to amend state constitutions in the North to add black suffrage, the Democrats at last had ample proof of Republican "extremism." In Ohio a black suffrage referendum was in trouble. Everywhere Republican candidates were experiencing setbacks.

The impact on the constitutional convention was devastating. There could no longer be any doubt that a constitution incorporating black suffrage would be in danger if submitted. Already far behind schedule and uncertain of the public response to their labors, the Republicans at the convention caucused and agreed to adjourn the convention until after the election. On September 24, they easily turned down a Democratic proposal to submit the suffrage article and another on the Court of Appeals at the upcoming election as the final work of the convention, and then passed a resolution ad-

85. *Convention Proceedings*, 1:272, 319, 321, 499.
86. James Buchanan to Joseph B. Baker, May 2, 1867 in John Bassett Moore, ed., *The Works of James Buchanan* (Philadelphia: J. B. Lippincott Co., 1911), 11:445.
87. *New York World*, Nov. 4, 1867.
88. *Convention Proceedings*, 1:258, 299. See *Albany Argus*, July 24, 1867, for newspapers taking this view.

journing the convention until November 12. Both votes were along straight party lines except that two Democrats voted with the Republicans on both questions.[89]

Although the Democrats attacked the adjournment in their state platform as "a cowardly evasion of a paramount issue in the pending struggle," the Republican move was actually fairly shrewd under the circumstances and highly consistent with their past behavior on racial matters.[90] The party saved the constitution and its suffrage provision to put forward at a more opportune time. At the same time it failed to repudiate black suffrage. Indeed it could not, for as the *New York Times* rightly pointed out: "By no manoeuvering can it [Negro suffrage] be kept out of the election as a principle of the Republican Party. . . . Support of Congress implies support of impartial suffrage, and the party which upholds it as a measure of justice and safety for the South cannot honorably shirk it in its application to this State."[91]

The day after the convention adjourned, the Republican state convention passed a resolution declaring "that, as Republicans of the State of New York, recognizing the obligation of consistency and straightforwardness in support of the great principles we profess, we unhesitatingly declare that suffrage should be impartial, that it is a right not to be limited by property or color."[92] This was the most forthright endorsement of equal suffrage ever to appear in a New York Republican platform and was designed to reassure those morally committed to equal rights that the party shared that commitment. Yet its recommendation of impartial suffrage (both races treated the same) over universal suffrage (both races fully enfranchised) was also conciliatory to conservatives. The party at the convention was following the same course that the party in the legislature had in the early spring. While supporting black suffrage in principle, it was asserting its determination to control the political consequences of it.

The Democrats in New York instituted a hard-hitting campaign in 1867. Although the contest was for state executive officers from secretary of state on down, Democrats laid heavy stress on the theme of "black" Reconstruction in the South. "The right of the negroes to rule the whites, the Radicals are forcing upon the South with the

89. *Convention Journal*, pp. 626–31.
90. *American Annual Cyclopaedia . . . of the Year 1867*, p. 545.
91. *New York Times*, Sept. 25, 1867.
92. *American Annual Cyclopaedia . . . of the Year 1867*, p. 544.

bayonet, at the cost of millions upon millions," stated the *Albany Argus* in a typical editorial.[93]

The Republicans parried such charges feebly. They were on the defensive on other issues, too. The legislature had passed an excise law the previous year placing restrictions on the sale of alcohol. The law had alienated many German Republicans and helped to mobilize Irish and German Democrats, who feared it might be strengthened and expanded. The party also faced charges of corruption.[94] In the end, the Republicans lost the election by almost fifty thousand votes, a far larger margin than their last previous loss by eleven thousand votes in 1862. The Democrats won a majority in the state Assembly and came within two seats of doing the same in the Senate. The Republican percentage of the vote declined in all but one county. Their greatest percentage loss was in Queens County, which had the largest black population in the state. Still, as in 1862, areas that experienced Republican losses (compared to 1866) did not correlate well with areas of Republican opposition to or apathy toward black suffrage either in 1860 or 1869. This low correlation suggests that the Republican defeat was due to a variety of factors.[95]

Perhaps more important than the election results themselves was the interpretation leading Republicans gave them. The margin of defeat was a distinct shock. Before the election, predictions had been that about ten thousand to fifteen thousand votes might be lost on the suffrage issue, which would be the most damaging issue for the party.[96] The loss of New York by forty-eight thousand votes, in conjunction with the decisive defeat of black suffrage in Ohio and the reduction of Republican majorities or increases in Democratic totals in *all* of the other eighteen states holding elections in 1867,

93. *Albany Argus*, Oct. 29, 1867.

94. *New York Evening Post*, Sept. 23, 1867; Georges E. B. Clemenceau, *American Reconstruction, 1865–1870*, trans. Margaret MacVeagh (New York: Lincoln MacVeagh, 1928), pp. 97–98, 131; Allan Nevins and Milton Halsey Thomas, eds., *The Diary of George Templeton Strong* (New York: Macmillan Co., 1952), 4:152; George J. J. Barber to Thurlow Weed, Oct. 24, 1867, Weed Papers; John Birney to Schuyler Colfax, Nov. 2, 1867 (copy), William Pitt Fessenden Papers, Library of Congress, Washington, D.C.; Stebbins, *Political History*, pp. 197–99.

95. Republican opposition or apathy to equal suffrage is measured as the difference between the Republican and prosuffrage percentages. The correlation at the town level was .06 in 1860 and .04 in 1869. Dale Baum, "The Political World of Massachusetts Radicalism: Voting Behavior and Ideology in the Civil War Party System, 1854–1872" (Ph.D. diss., University of Minnesota, 1978), p. 502, found a variety of factors including the liquor question influencing the election in Massachusetts as well.

96. Stebbins, *Political History*, p. 169; John Birney to Schuyler Colfax, Nov. 2, 1867 (copy), Fessenden Papers; *New York Herald*, Oct. 25, 1867.

was a stunning blow.[97] Republican journals at both ends of the political spectrum attributed the defeats at least in part to distrust of radical leadership and dislike of black voting. Even the radical *Harper's Weekly*, which insisted that if "the policy of equal rights as the law of reconstruction had been the sole issue, the Republicans would have triumphed," nevertheless began a series of editorials immediately following the announcement of the Ohio results explaining once again the necessity of black suffrage in the South.[98] The radical press was frankly on the defensive from 1867 onwards.

The Republicans' treatment of the suffrage issue after their defeat is very revealing. Not all agreed on the best course to follow. The *New York Tribune*, insisting that political setbacks (which it believed would be temporary) were preferable to a surrender of principle, proclaimed that those who were not willing to endorse equal rights should be forced out of the party. The conservative *New York Times*, on the other hand, wanted a retreat from universal to impartial suffrage in the South, the reduction of black officeholding there, and a greater observance of proper constitutional form in promoting black rights.[99] But what changed most after the revelation of public sentiment in 1867 was not Republican *policy* but tactics. For a brief time portions of the party had acted as if the straightforward (even self-righteous) advocacy of black suffrage would be supported by all loyal members of the party. While the election showed that *most* Republicans would not bolt on the issue, it also demonstrated that the defection of even a minority (especially in conjunction with other issues damaging to the party) could be devastating.

Thereafter the party became more and more circumspect on racial matters. As they had done following their 1862 defeat, Republicans concentrated on explaining the expediency of their actions

97. Charles H. Coleman, *The Election of 1868: The Democratic Effort to Regain Control* (New York: Columbia University Press, 1933), p. 49. See also Michael Les Benedict, "The Rout of Radicalism: Republicans and the Elections of 1867," *Civil War History,* 18 (Dec. 1972), 334–44.

98. *New York Times,* Oct. 14, Nov. 7, 1867; *Independent,* Nov. 21, 1867; *New York Tribune,* Nov. 16, 1867; *New York Evening Post,* Nov. 6, 1867; *New York Commercial Advertiser* quoted in *New York Tribune,* Nov. 8, 1867. For individual Republicans making the same observation see John Birney to William Pitt Fessenden, Dec. 19, 1867, Fessenden Papers; George J. J. Barber to Thurlow Weed, Oct. 24, 1867, Weed Papers; Jesse Segoine to William Seward, Nov. 8, 1867, Seward Papers. *Harper's Weekly,* Nov. 2, 9, 23, 1867.

99. *New York Tribune,* Oct. 10, Nov. 16, 1867; *New York Times,* Oct. 15, Nov. 7, 8, Dec. 27, 1867.

rather than their inherent justness. "If the [Southern] Blacks are not enfranchised, Vallandigham could beat Gen. Grant for President," Greeley pointed out in an obvious effort to shift the focus of debate from race to copperheadism.[100]

There was less willingness to involve the party in political risks in order to advance black voting rights, as became clear when the constitutional convention reconvened on November 12. A number of Republican delegates and political analysts seemed to take it for granted at the outset that black suffrage would now be submitted separately from the constitution.[101] The choice was between giving black suffrage its best chance for adoption by incorporating it in the constitution and increasing the constitution's chances for acceptance by dissociating it from equal suffrage. By a strictly partisan vote the delegates did refuse to change the suffrage article itself. But when it came to adopting the principle of separate submission, forty-three Republicans voted in favor while only thirty-one opposed.[102] A majority of those voting placed the constitution's fate above that of equal suffrage. Two-thirds of the Republicans who favored joint submission came from areas that were prosuffrage in 1869 compared to only half of those who opposed it. Still, more than half (53.5 per cent) the Republican delegates from prosuffrage counties agreed to separate submission. They apparently believed it to be in their party's best interests.

Further disagreement arose on the proper form for the suffrage ballot. The committee studying the question recommended ballots for or against the property qualification, thus omitting any reference to race. This proposal infuriated the Democrats, who wanted a very explicit ballot similar to that in 1846, "Equal suffrage for colored men—yes or no." They apparently threatened opposition to the entire constitution on this count.[103] The convention eventually compromised on a ballot that read "for or against the property qualification for men of color." Race was mentioned, but so also was the property qualification. The Republicans once again split. While all thirty-eight Democrats voting favored the addition of the words "for men of color," forty-four Republicans voted with them on the issue

100. *New York Tribune*, Oct. 16, 1867.
101. *New York Times*, Nov. 16, 1867; *Nation*, Nov. 28, 1867; *Convention Proceedings*, 5:3560, 3885, 3887.
102. The Democrats divided 36–2 in favor of separate submission while 23 Republicans and 25 Democrats were absent. *Convention Journal*, pp. 979–80, 1185–86.
103. Ibid., p. 1183; *New York Times*, Mar. 3, 1868; *Albany Argus*, Feb. 27, 1868.

while thirty others steadfastly opposed.[104] The Republican divisions differed from those on separate submission. The minority who wished the ballot left ambiguous was made up of both those strongly in favor of equal suffrage (two-thirds came from counties that favored black voting in 1869) and those who seemingly wished to minimize its political danger by obscuring it from the voters. Once again, however, Republicans were carefully considering the political implications of any move they made on black rights.

On February 28, 1868, the convention completed its work in uncertainty and ill feeling, but the political maneuvering on equal suffrage had just begun. It was important to Republicans that the suffrage article when submitted not hurt their party. The act under which the convention had assembled had called for a submission of the proposed constitution in November, 1867. Since that date had passed, it was unclear whether the convention had the right to determine how or when the new constitution should be ratified. The prospects for the document appeared gloomy. In most areas observers did not regard it as a marked improvement on the 1846 constitution. Many Democrats opposed it, and even the Republican press seemed relatively unexcited by it.[105] There was certainly little enthusiasm for a quick submission. Eventually the state legislature managed to postpone the vote until November, 1869, a full twenty-one months after the constitution's completion.

One reason for the long delay in submitting the constitution was an unwillingness by some Republicans to have the suffrage issue become embroiled in the presidential race in 1868. After the 1867 setback, the party leaders tried very hard in 1868 to reassure the electorate on the racial question. The suffrage plank in the national Republican platform called for "loyal" suffrage in the South, while in the North voting was left to the discretion of individual states. Not only was a double standard condoned but the reference to "loyal" voters deemphasized the racial aspect of the question. The state platform went no further.[106] Republican campaign literature on Reconstruction and the black man tended to stress the modera-

104. Twenty-three Republicans and twenty-five Democrats were absent. *Convention Journal*, pp. 1186–87.

105. *New York Times*, Mar. 3, 1868; *Harper's Weekly*, Mar. 21, 1868; *New York Tribune*, Feb. 28, 1868.

106. Kirk H. Porter and Donald B. Johnson, *National Party Platforms, 1840–1964* (Urbana, Ill.: University of Illinois Press, 1966), p. 39; *American Annual Cyclopaedia . . . of the Year 1868*, p. 549.

tion of Republican moves and the extent to which southern opposition had justified them.[107]

The Republican strategy seemed to have reassured some of the lukewarm Republicans who had stayed home or defected in 1867. New York *did* fall to the Democrats in the presidential race, but by a slim margin (ten thousand votes), and evidence of massive naturalization frauds in New York City convinced many Republicans that the election had been stolen, rather than lost.[108] With their military candidate, Ulysses S. Grant, the Republicans had made war themes salient. As the *Argus* remarked soon after the election, "They [Democrats] were defeated solely because the Radicals succeeded in arousing the War feeling of the North, and that sectional hatred which preceded even the War."[109]

The Democrats' uncertainty over how to consolidate their 1867 gains also helped the Republicans. Discussion continued for months on the best strategy for the Democrats to pursue in the presidential contest. Joseph Warren, the editor of the *Buffalo Courier*, thought the party should develop policy alternatives to the Republicans. Another leader, George Curtis, on the other hand, counseled evasion: "Let us not put at hazard the continued support of those who voted with us, by permanently asking them to indorse *our* remedy."[110] Many believed opposition to black suffrage should be the keynote of Democratic efforts. Samuel J. Tilden, a prominent Democratic leader, argued:

> On no other question can we be so unanimous among ourselves. On no other question can we draw so much from the other side and from the undetermined. It appeals peculiarly to the adopted citizens, whether Irish or Germans; to all the working-men; to the young men just becoming voters. The Republican party contains large numbers who are naturally hampered by its position on this issue; and large numbers of old Federal and old Whig antecedents, who do not think that any poor man, white or black, ought to vote; and though they may go along with their party on the theory that

107. Republican Congressional Committee, *Emancipation! Enfranchisement! Reconstruction! Legislative Record of the Republican Party during and since the War* (Washington, D.C.: Union Republican Congressional Committee, 1868).

108. John L. Davenport, *The Election and Naturalization Frauds in New York City, 1860–1870* 2nd ed. (New York: n.p., 1894), pp. 107–236.

109. *Albany Argus*, Nov. 11, 1868.

110. Quote from George Curtis to Manton Marble, Nov. 7, 1867. See also Joseph Warren to Marble, Nov. 9, 1867. Both from Manton Marble Papers, Library of Congress, Washington D. C.

the blacks are a counterpoise to the adopted citizens, their hearts
misgive them. . . .
The more we concentrate the public attention on this issue so that
the people will act with reference to it,—the better our chance of
success will be.[111]

Yet the legitimist faction feared that stressing black suffrage
would inevitably lead to a general discussion of the war and Reconstruction and bring up the Democrats' copperhead past. They preferred financial questions as a campaign issue. Manton Marble of
the *World* for a time promoted the possible candidacy of Salmon P.
Chase in an effort to attract back to the party former Democrats
who had joined the Republicans during the war or earlier. Chase,
although an early antislavery advocate, a suffrage supporter, and a
long-time Republican, agreed with the Democrats on most nonracial
issues.[112] Hence while Tilden wished to appeal to racially and socially conservative "old Whigs," Marble was after relatively less conservative ex-Democrats.

The southern situation presented an additional complication. Before the war contempt for the black man had united northern and
southern Democrats. But now some South Carolina Democrats were
seeking to win over black voters in their state. The *World* suggested
at different times the omission of a suffrage plank from the national
platform or perhaps even the adoption of one recommending impartial suffrage to the states. So irate were Democratic responses to
such suggestions that the *World* dropped its support for Chase.[113]
Chase might be willing to endorse state control of suffrage (tantamount to its rejection in most cases), but this was not enough for the
party. As Marble explained it:

> While the party is compelled to recognize the existence of many un-
> welcome facts which it cannot reverse, it has not changed, and can-
> not change, its principles. The fact that the negroes [in the South]
> will vote in the coming Presidential election is a fact which the

111. John Bigelow, ed., *Letters and Literary Memorials of Samuel J. Tilden* (New York:
Harper & Brothers, 1908), 1:220. See also ibid., p. 217; S. L. M. Barlow to Samuel J.
Tilden, Sept. 21, 1868, Tilden Papers; W. J. B. [William J. Bogart] to Marble, June 15,
1868, Marble Papers; James Buchanan to Augustus Schell, Nov. 9, 1857 in Moore,
Works, 11:455.

112. William H. Ludlow to Horatio Seymour, June 26, 1868, Horatio Seymour Papers, New York State Library, Albany, New York; Irving Katz, *August Belmont: A Political Biography* (New York: Columbia University Press, 1968), p. 169; *New York World*,
Oct. 11, 1867, June 19, 1868.

113. *New York World*, June 3, 8, 17, 22, 1868; see also Ethan A. Allen to Seymour,
June 16, 1868, Seymour Papers, New York State Library.

Democratic party recognizes only on compulsion, while Chief-Justice CHASE regards it with more than complacency, with more than satisfaction, with the joy which attends the fulfilment [*sic*] of a long-cherished hope.[114]

Still, the Democratic national platform was less explicit on black suffrage than it might otherwise have been. The only reference to it came in the second resolution, which demanded "Amnesty for all past political offences, and the regulation of the elective franchise in the States by their citizens."[115] The same detachment prevailed in New York, where the national platform was simply endorsed. Some New York Democrats attacked their party early in the campaign for not being more forceful on the race issue. Horatio Seymour, the Democratic candidate for president, claimed that he had received the ill will of many Democrats for having been an early Chase supporter.[116] Thus the Democrats in 1868 were hampered not only by the evasive tactics of Republicans but also by their own inner divisions.

Of course, in the heat of the fall campaign attention to the race issue was expressed in increasingly emotional terms. The *World*, for instance, invoked the image of a "majority . . . made up against you by a thick-lipped, grinning, ignorant, Obi-worshipping crew of cotton-pickers whom your money has just set free."[117] The Democrats found themselves fully as constrained on the race issue as the Republicans after 1867. While the latter could not retreat from black suffrage very gracefully, the Democrats could not soften their position on it with any greater ease. Party lines on the issue were drawn more and more tightly even though there were some in each party who regretted this result.

Immediately after Congress reconvened following the election, it began to move toward a Fifteenth Amendment providing for black suffrage. Despite the Republicans' timidity on the question during the previous year, the move was a completely consistent one. And more was certainly involved than a partisan desire to add northern black voters to the party's dwindling ranks.[118] Passing an amend-

114. *New York World*, June 15, 1868.
115. Porter and Johnson, *National Party Platforms*, p. 37.
116. *American Annual Cyclopaedia . . . of the Year 1868*, p. 549; A. Brewster to Seymour, Sept. 1868, Seymour Papers, New York State Library; A. Beardslee to Seymour, Aug. 11, 1868; Seymour to J. D. Van Buren, Sept 8, 1868, Seymour Papers, New York Historical Society, New York City.
117. *New York World*, Sept. 18, 1868.
118. Gillette, *Right to Vote*.

ment at this time offered many advantages, particularly to those whose states would not benefit from black voting or who were not morally committed to black suffrage to the hazard of all else.

To begin with, the Republican Party was already strongly identified with black suffrage and therefore always in danger of being hurt by the issue as long as it remained salient. The presence of a significant faction who had favored the reform for years as a just and proper goal of the party and the promise of continued forceful agitation in its favor by black groups meant that the issue was unlikely to die down. Successful evasion of the issue was not always possible, especially if Democrats were determined to keep it uppermost. As the *Independent* pointed out in 1868, even if the Republicans said *nothing* in their platform on black suffrage, they would still be accused on the basis of their past actions of "negro championship."[119] To repudiate their previous endorsement of black voting would be a humiliating admission of error. It was far more attractive to Republicans to guarantee voting rights to *all* blacks, thereby removing the issue from politics altogether. Republicans seemed to believe that once discrimination by law was abolished, nothing more need be done for the blacks; hence, a Fifteenth Amendment would "take the everlasting negro question forever out of National politics."[120]

The permanent addition of blacks to the electorate would presumably force the Democrats to tone down their antiblack rhetoric. Horace Greeley had pointed out as early as 1865, "There isn't a Democrat fool enough—however unprincipled—to treat them as Democrats now do after they shall have been armed with votes."[121] The *Albany Evening Journal* in 1868 was already accusing the Democrats of inconsistency for seeking the black vote in South Carolina while spurning it elsewhere.[122]

By passing the amendment in Congress in 1869, the Republicans could minimize their risks as well. No national election would be held until 1870. There were sufficient legislatures controlled by Republicans to assure the measure's ratification. And presumably most

119. *Independent*, May 14, 1868.
120. *New York Tribune*, Feb. 27, 1869. See also Wilbert Harrell Ahern, "Laissez Faire versus Equal Rights: Liberal Republicans and the Negro, 1861–1877" (Ph.D. diss., Northwestern University, 1968), pp. 218–20; *Harper's Weekly*, Feb. 13, 1869; *Independent*, Jan. 2, 1868; *New York Times*, Mar. 19, 1869; *New York Evening Post*, July 17, 1867.
121. *New York Tribune*, June 15, 1865.
122. *Albany Evening Journal*, Aug. 5, 28, 1869. See also *Independent*, Jan. 28, 1869; *New York Tribune*, Mar. 21, 1867; *Albany Evening Journal*, Mar. 18, 1867.

rank-and-file conservatives who would not tolerate black voting were already cooperating with the Democrats. The experience of 1862 and 1867 had shown as well that Republican voters were not likely to defect *permanently* to the Democrats on racial issues, but rather to come back to the party when the issue was no longer as salient.[123] Thus any losses the Republicans might suffer as a result of the amendment would presumably be relatively short term and in less important state contests.

The passage of the Fifteenth Amendment through New York's legislature in March and April of 1869 was illustrative of how closely and automatically party lines were now drawn on the issue of suffrage. Both the arguments and the final votes on the measure were entirely predictable. The Republican Assembly caucus endorsed the amendment unanimously; it passed the Assembly (reclaimed by the Republicans in the 1868 election) 72–47 and the Senate 17–15, both strict party-line votes.[124] In the debates that preceded the vote the Democrats repeated the litany of the past ten years—the threat to constitutional government of amendments expanding federal powers, the selfish motives of the Republicans and their indifference to the hardships of immigrants, the manifold inadequacies of blacks as voters, and the failure of Republicans to heed the popular mandate against suffrage. The Republicans denied these charges but relied primarily on arguments deriving from the war. The rhetoric was highly antisouthern and anticopperhead. They praised blacks for their loyalty and portrayed their complete enfranchisement as not only a matter of justice but also a way to keep traitors in check.[125]

The debate on the Fifteenth Amendment was indicative of what had and had not changed in the struggle for equal rights in New York over the course of a decade. On one hand, the Republican Party, which in New York State had tried to deny its responsibility for the equal suffrage amendment in 1860, had now almost succeeded in extending black voting rights throughout the nation. The Democratic Party, which had exploited fears of abolition and black advancement in 1860, had come to accept the end of slavery, the recruitment of black troops, and civil rights for blacks; a few of its

123. Horace Greeley made this argument continually. See also Clemenceau, *American Reconstruction*, pp. 115–16.
124. New York State Assembly, *Journal*, 92nd Sess., 1869, p. 544; Senate, *Journal*, 92nd Sess., 1869, p. 590; *New York Tribune*, Mar. 12, 1869.
125. Full texts of many of the speeches were published in the *Albany Argus* and the *Albany Evening Journal* in March and April of 1869.

members even felt opposition to black voting a losing proposition. Under the pressure of war and Reconstruction both parties had come further in their adjustment to racial changes than either perhaps would have dreamed possible in 1860. Yet the Democratic Party had *not* surrendered its belief that the race issue could divide the Republicans. Nor had the Republicans given up their fear of it, as their far-from-daring defense of the Fifteenth Amendment showed.

Why then did Republicans pursue black voting rights in the 1860s? Controversy abounds on this point. William Gillette has argued that the party wanted to gain desperately needed black votes in the closely divided northern states.[126] John and LaWanda Cox, on the other hand, have insisted that Republican leaders had a crucial moral concern for black rights and that they committed the nation to black suffrage "not because of political expediency but *despite* political risk."[127]

The Republican Party's treatment of the black suffrage issue in New York suggests a more complex motivation. Republican ideologues did exist. Indeed equal rights enthusiasts had been an important element in the party since its formation in the 1850s. Republicans were certainly not averse to gaining more votes either. But it was the logic of national events—the war and Reconstruction—that pushed the party step by step toward the advocacy of emancipation, the arming of black troops, and ultimately black suffrage. Tremendously loyal to their party and suspicious of the Democrats, Republican leaders made every effort to accommodate the new positions. Since the breakup of their party was unthinkable, the only alternative was to try to make black rights acceptable to a wide range of Republicans. The leadership proved remarkably adept at assuaging racial fears and directing hostilities at southerners, the Irish, and copperheads rather than blacks.

Every step taken by the party showed a concern for its unity. By 1865, nearly all party spokesmen agreed that discrimination *solely* on the basis of race was wrong. While this view seemed favorable to blacks, such a position could also be upheld by those who favored "impartial" distinctions that would weigh heavily against blacks in practice as well as by those who believed blacks inferior but in need

126. Gillette, *Right to Vote*.
127. LaWanda Cox and John H. Cox, "Negro Suffrage and Republican Politics: The Problem of Motivation in Reconstruction Historiography," *Journal of Southern History*, 33 (Aug. 1967), 317.

of rights as a means of self protection.[128] Republicans tried to minimize the political fallout from their actions on race, too. When the advocacy of equal voting rights for blacks in the convention delegate races threatened to alienate nonradicals in the party, Republican legislators eventually adopted a convention bill without such a provision. At the convention all the Republicans agreed to delay completing their work until after the dangerous November elections, and, when black suffrage still proved unpopular, a majority of them favored submitting equal suffrage separately.

Many Republicans were clearly unwilling to push for black rights no matter what the cost politically. Instead, moderates and radicals seemed to work out a *modus vivendi* whereby they supported black suffrage but also considered the needs of the Republican Party. In this way the party could remain united despite internal disputes over race policy. Thus Republicans avoided the black rights issue at inopportune times and gave expedient, sometimes racist, reasons for backing it. The party also preferred that strict constitutionality be observed. (Both nationally and in New York attempts to change the suffrage by law rather than alteration of the constitution were rejected.) This deference to party needs kept both radicals and conservatives in check and prevented the fragmentation of the Republican Party on the race issue.

The decade from 1860 to 1869 was an important one for the suffrage struggle. Although even before 1860 nearly all Republican legislators had favored the abolition of the property qualification, both the nature of Republican advocacy and the importance of the suffrage issue itself changed as a result of the war and Reconstruction. In the 1850s equal suffrage had been an issue primarily of concern to New Yorkers. Because Congress passed black suffrage for the South in 1867, however, it became a national concern. The need for party consistency was thus added to other considerations when dealing with the issue. As a result, suffrage became an issue *between* the parties not only in the eyes of the Democrats (who had emphasized the point in 1860) but in the eyes of the Republicans as well. Marked deviation within either party on the topic became difficult to tolerate. The Republicans, to facilitate support for black suffrage, expanded the grounds on which it had been traditionally defended. To humanitarian arguments they added reasons growing

128. See *Albany Evening Journal*, Feb. 1, 1867; Henry Smith in *Albany Argus*, Mar. 20, 1867.

out of deeper feelings about the war: the fact that blacks had helped the Union cause and that black voting would punish the South for its arrogance and assure loyal governments throughout the region.

The Republicans had indeed handled the race issue skillfully. But in the past the cleverness of politicians had often spelled the doom of black hopes. The crucial question remained whether support for equal rights had really extended into the electorate. Did their enthusiasm match that of Republican leaders? The answer was all important, for on it would depend future Republican assessments of the practicality of the race issue. Through the control of state legislatures Republicans could almost guarantee the passage of the Fifteenth Amendment, but the true end to discrimination would depend not just on laws but on the willingness of people to uphold the spirit of those laws.

CHAPTER SIX

The Popular Verdict
on Equal Suffrage, 1869

Equal rights for blacks had always been a troublesome issue for New York politicians. Yet in 1869 when equal suffrage was presented to the voters for the third time in twenty-three years, its supporters believed the prospects for success were as promising as they had ever been in the long, frustrating struggle to enact the reform. The Republican Party was committed officially to black suffrage and indeed was well on the way to incorporating it in the U.S. Constitution. During the war Republican politicians had learned techniques for introducing racial change to the electorate. They had discovered that temporary losses on the race issue might be quickly recouped. Unlike the situation in 1860, also, only minor state offices (the highest was secretary of state), not the presidency, were at stake in 1869, thus reducing Republican risks. In contrast to 1860, too, the Democrats seemed less entranced by the black rights issue. Black suffrage itself was no longer a novelty. In 1860 only five states granted blacks the franchise; in 1869 that number had expanded to include the entire South plus Wisconsin, Minnesota, and Iowa in the North.[1]

But even with these hopeful signs, would equal suffrage really pass? Would the Republican electorate at last rally behind it? What groups would or would not shift to its support? The answers to such

1. William Gillette, *The Right to Vote: Politics and the Passage of the Fifteenth Amendment* (Baltimore: Johns Hopkins Press, 1969), pp. 25–28.

questions were very important to politicians who were naturally concerned about the continued viability of black rights legislation in the North.

As in the past, politicians devoted great care to how they presented the suffrage issue to the electorate in 1869. The referendum did not just happen; careful thought and planning went into all the arrangements. Once black suffrage became thoroughly politicized, no other result was possible. Party leaders desired that the issue be handled in a way that promoted, rather than harmed, their interests.

One example of the control exercised over the issue was the timing of the referendum. The logical date to have submitted the constitution and equal suffrage to the voters was the first general election after the completion of the convention's work, November, 1868. The Democrats favored this date, since it would allow the issue to enter the important 1868 presidential election campaign. The Democratic Assembly in 1868 tried to push through a measure to submit the constitution in November in four parts (equal suffrage, the judiciary article, the legislative article, and the remainder of the constitution). They succeeded, but in the Senate Republicans on the Judiciary Committee valiantly resisted both the constitution's dismemberment and the chosen date. Republicans defeated every effort to bring the bill to committee of the whole for debate; only three of them consistently voted for consideration. The *Albany Argus* protested, "The Radicals did not like to go to the polls and vote for Negro Suffrage. . . . They squelched a Constitutional reform in order to evade the issue which negro suffrage at home presents to them."[2]

The Republicans controlled the legislature the following year, but their margin in the Senate was a scant two seats. Republicans on the Senate Judiciary Committee wanted to present the constitution and the suffrage clause at the town elections in April, thus minimizing the impact of any backlash vote. The Democrats, however, adamantly opposed this idea. They apparently persuaded several Republicans to join them (with what inducement is not known), and in committee of the whole they succeeded in adding the judiciary and

2. New York State Assembly, *Journal*, 91st Sess., 1868, pp. 877–78, 983–84; New York State Senate, *Journal*, 91st Sess., 1868, pp. 959–63, 1073. Quote is from *Albany Argus*, May 9, 1868.

taxation articles as separate submissions and in making November, 1869, the date for submittal.[3]

Politicians also carefully considered the implications of the ballot's wording. The Democrats wanted it to emphasize the issue of race, the Republicans the notion of a property qualification. So determined were the Democrats that one Republican cynically remarked that they would not be satisfied until there was a picture of a Negro on the ballot. This time, however, the Democrats lost, and the Senate retained the ballot form suggested by the Republicans at the constitutional convention which mentioned the property qualification.[4] Even though the Democrats had obtained some concessions on the manner of submission, a majority of them in both houses eventually opposed the submission bill.[5]

Although foiled in their attempts to have the suffrage question submitted in 1868 and its racial nature emphasized, the Democrats were still determined to reap the maximum political benefit from the issue. Their main goal in 1869 was to gain control of the legislature.[6] In 1867 they had elected the lesser state officers (secretary of state, comptroller, attorney general, etc.) whom they now hoped to reelect. In 1868 they had made John T. Hoffman governor. But since the adoption of the 1846 constitution, the Democrats had *never* won a majority in both houses of the legislature.[7] Democrats also expected to benefit from the popular perception that the Republican legislature was tinged with corruption. Republicans themselves were divided over this charge, and Democrats hoped their opponents would be unable to mount an effective campaign.[8]

The suffrage issue lent itself well to a contest for the legislature. The current legislature's ratification of the Fifteenth Amendment linked national and state politics. Instead of waiting for the people

3. *Albany Argus*, Feb. 13, 1869; New York State Senate, *Journal*, 92nd Sess., 1869, p. 241.

4. *Albany Argus*, Feb. 10, 1869. On the outside of the ballot was "Constitution—Property Qualification," on the inside, "For the Property Qualification for Men of Color" or "Against the Property Qualification for Men of Color."

5. New York State Senate, *Journal*, 92nd Sess., 1869, p. 241; New York State Assembly, *Journal*, 92nd Sess., 1869, p. 1387. In the Senate four of eleven Democrats who voted favored the bill; in the Assembly, six of forty-eight.

6. *New York World*, Sept. 13, 1869.

7. In 1852 the Democrats had organized the legislature, but in the Senate the Democrats and Whigs were evenly split.

8. De Alva Stanwood Alexander, *A Political History of the State of New York* (New York: Henry Holt and Co., 1906–1909), 3:224–25.

to voice their opinion on equal suffrage in the referendum, claimed the Democrats, the Republicans had adopted the amendment regardless. Just as they had forced black suffrage on the South, they were now determined to make the North accept it too, despite their platform pledge in 1868 that northern states were entitled to decide for themselves whether or not they wanted blacks to vote. Such unresponsive legislators deserved defeat.[9]

The Democrats also tried to make it appear that the fate of the Fifteenth Amendment was in doubt and that New York's own ratification of it had been imperfect. The basis for this charge was the legislature's failure to request that a certified copy of its resolution of ratification be sent to Washington. When in September an official in the State Department wrote the governor requesting a copy of the resolution, one was sent. However, the *World* and other Democratic newspapers argued that the new legislature would have to reconsider the Fifteenth Amendment and that state lawmakers should be chosen with this in mind.[10] Those opposed to black suffrage should vote for the Democratic candidates.

In their platform the Democrats vigorously attacked the Fifteenth Amendment:

> *Resolved.* That the fifteenth amendment of the Federal Constitution, proposed by the radical majority in Congress in a spirit of contempt of the people and of the right of the States to regulate the elective franchise, and in utter disregard of the pledges of the party, and attempted to be forced upon the States as a condition of their restoration to civil government and to their representation in the national Legislature, is intended to place the question of suffrage in the hands of the central powers and by debasing to demoralize the representative system.[11]

The platform also condemned the new constitution in all its parts despite some initial Democratic sympathy for the judiciary article:

> *Resolved.* That the amended constitution of the State in its various schedules to be submitted to the electors does not commend itself to the favor of the Democrats of the State, either by the motives in which it was conceived, or by the manner in which it was presented, or by its intrinsic worth.[12]

9. *New York World*, Sept. 2, 22, 30, 1869; *New York Herald*, Sept. 4, 1869.

10. *New York World*, Sept. 16, 22, 1869; *Brooklyn Daily Eagle*, Sept. 20, 1869; *Utica Daily Observer*, Sept. 6, 1869.

11. *The American Annual Cyclopaedia & Register of Important Events of the Year 1869* (New York: D. Appleton & Co., 1870), p. 488.

12. Amasa J. Parker to Samuel J. Tilden, Sept. 2, 1869; William F. Allen to Tilden, Oct. 21, 1869; George F. Comstock to Tilden, Oct. 23, 1869, Samuel J. Tilden Papers,

These planks represented an effort to harmonize differences between the purists and legitimists in the Democratic ranks. Some Tammany Hall Democrats successfully challenged a more racist version contending they were too "ultra Southern," especially since, in order to carry the legislature, the party would have to win many upstate votes in areas very sensitive to the "copperhead" question. To Tammanyites, too, the worst feature of the Fifteenth Amendment was not its generosity to blacks but the opening it gave to future federal oversight of elections.[13] Samuel J. Tilden's address to the convention voiced the concerns of the purists. Stressing the suffrage issue almost exclusively, Tilden condemned efforts to force black voting on the North and asserted that the party opposed "the doctrine that any Chinaman or African has a right to come into this country and claim suffrage as a natural right, and enter into complete political partnership with us without our consent." Evoking images of interracial sex, he proclaimed, "We reject that doctrine as we would reject the doctrine that an African or a negro has a right to marry our daughter without our consent." Seeking common ground, the *World* abandoned its argument of the previous year that Democrats should avoid taking positions on suffrage. Instead it called black voting an "odious and abominable system" and explained that it had formerly advised "acquiescence" only to obtain black votes in the South.[14]

The wide variety of arguments against suffrage in 1869, in contrast to the simple and blatant appeals to racism in 1860, reflected the new range of approaches to black rights within the Democratic Party in 1869.[15] At one extreme, racism still reigned supreme. The *Brooklyn Daily Eagle* asked, "Are you willing to declare by your vote [on the property qualification] that you are exactly and precisely the equivalent of a negro, neither more nor less?" The *Schenectady Weekly Reflector* asserted that equal suffrage inevitably led to "amalgamation and miscegenation." A Steuben County paper cited a Horace Greeley statement that Union soldiers who claimed to oppose

---

New York Public Library, New York City. Quote is from *American Annual Cyclopaedia*, p. 488.

13. *New York Herald,* Sept. 25, 1869; Matthew P. Breen, *Thirty Years of New York Politics Up-To-Date* (New York: John Polhemus, 1899), p. 188; *New York Herald,* Nov. 26, 28, 1869. See also Albie Burke, "Federal Regulation of Congressional Elections in Northern Cities, 1871–94," *American Journal of Legal History,* 14 (Jan. 1970), 17–34.

14. Quotes are from *New York World,* Sept. 23, 8, 1869, respectively.

15. Lawrence Grossman, *The Democratic Party and the Negro: Northern and National Politics, 1868–92* (Urbana, Ill.: University of Illinois Press, 1976), pp. 8–20.

equal suffrage must have enlisted for the bounty and told its soldier readers that it expected them to "'tear down the flaunting lie' that you shed your heart's blood to make the jay-bird heeled black barbarians of the South your equal."[16]

In contrast, some Democrats virtually ignored black suffrage. The *Buffalo Courier* called the Fifteenth Amendment a dead issue and praised the Democratic platform because "there is no word in the resolutions which intimates that the color of a man's skin has aught to do with his political rights."[17] The *Courier* generated little enthusiasm among Democrats for its views.[18] Yet the change since 1860 was still clear. *No* Democrat then would have considered race an unsatisfactory issue.

Democratic leaders clearly expected the equal suffrage issue to still be attractive to ethnic minorities and the socially insecure. While Republicans tried to eliminate discrimination against blacks, they pointed out, they took few steps to prevent mistreatment of other groups. The Fifteenth Amendment, they insisted, could be used to hurt white people. With doubtful logic the Democrats argued, "The Congress may 'enforce this article' [the Fifteenth Amendment] by saying that no Catholic shall vote, or that no liquor drinker shall vote, or no man shall vote who was born in Europe, or who has not lived here fifty years."[19] Democrats continually mentioned the Frelinghuysen bill, which Congress had recently considered and which would have made naturalization more difficult. Samuel J. Tilden asserted that while a few Republicans were sincere in their beliefs on suffrage, "if you take one of your Republican friends aside and talk with him on the question of suffrage, in five minutes he will tell you he does not think the poor white ought to vote, and by the same logical necessity which determines the Democracy to stand by and defend and protect the suffrage of the common white man."[20]

Since dedicated Republicans could be expected to view with suspicion Democratic editorial warnings concerning the dangers of the black man, Democrats in 1869 made extensive use of "news" reports

16. *Brooklyn Daily Eagle*, Oct. 28, 1869; *Schenectady Weekly Reflector*, Oct. 21, 1869; *Steuben Farmer's Advocate* (Bath), Oct. 20, 1869.

17. *Buffalo Courier*, Sept. 21, 1869.

18. See *Albany Argus*, Sept. 10, 1869, for criticism of this position.

19. *Brooklyn Daily Eagle*, Sept. 20, 1869. See also *Rochester Daily Union & Advertiser*, Sept. 16, 1869.

20. Allen G. Sexton, "The Democratic Party in Western New York, 1865–1870" (M.A. thesis, University of Buffalo, 1951), p. 58. Quote is from *New York World*, Sept. 23, 1869.

to suggest the evils of black power and equality. The *New York World,* for example, shortly before election day ran a story under the headline of "Negro Outrages" telling of a series of black rapist attacks in Washington, D.C., on white women ranging in age from ten to seventy. The story attributed the attacks to the bestial nature of the black man who could not control his animalistic urges when freed from societal restraints. Another Democratic paper, using black dialect, told of a black jury's acquittal of a black man for the murder of a white sheriff in Virginia. The *Ithaca Democrat* recounted the alleged unwillingness of Washington blacks to let their children attend integrated schools with "mean white folk," while another paper described with disgust a bridal party, observed by a Washington reporter, consisting of a "full blooded negro and a beautiful young white girl, scarcely 18 years old."[21] Thus Democrats used the news columns to make the points they wanted made while avoiding the impression of being blatantly partisan.

Perhaps the most interesting aspect of the Democrats' treatment of the suffrage issue in 1869, given their obviously deep feelings about it and their early intentions to use it to carry the legislature, was their *failure* to capitalize on the issue in the later stages of the campaign. The Republicans seem to have been responsible for this change in emphasis. Through a quirk of fate more than deliberate intent, they chose a slate of candidates peculiarly suited to upset the Democrats' campaign strategy. Concerned about intraparty divisions over alleged corruption in the legislature, the Republicans originally nominated two men of unquestioned integrity, George W. Curtis and Thomas Hillhouse, to run for the top offices of secretary of state and comptroller. To the acute embarrassment of the party, however, both men immediately declined to run. To fill the vacancies, the state committee chose Franz Sigel, a German-born American who had been a popular, if ineffectual, Civil War general, and Horace Greeley, the editor of the *New York Tribune,* to run for secretary of state and comptroller respectively.[22] Sigel was the first nonnative American to head a Republican ticket in New York, and he represented the strongest Republican threat in years to normally Democratic German voters. This threat was underscored when the usually protemperance Republicans tabled a temperance resolution

21. *New York World,* Oct. 24, 1869; *Glens Falls Republican,* Sept. 21, 1869. Quotes are from *Ithaca Democrat,* Sept. 9, 1869, and *Glens Falls Republican,* Aug. 24, 1869.
22. Alexander, *Political History,* 3:225.

at their convention. Both the Germans and Irish came from cultures where drinking was considered normal and proper, and one of the reasons they often adhered to the Democracy was their perception of Republicans as intolerant of such behavior.

In their desire to carry the legislature, the Democrats had selected a state ticket calculated to appeal to upstate (largely native-born) voters. (Only two nominees, in fact, were from normally Democratic areas.[23]) They had designed their platform, too, to attract upstate support. The party was ill prepared, thus, to counter threats made to its traditional supporters. The Democrats had to reverse their field promptly and begin to reassure their German and Irish followers that the Republicans were indeed dedicated prohibitionists. Temperance became the central issue, and the *World* even ended the campaign reminding German Republicans that they could support the constitution if they wished and still vote Democratic to preserve their right to drink.[24]

As a consequence of this change in strategy black suffrage received less attention from the Democrats than it probably would have otherwise. Whether this change affected the referendum a great deal is debatable since the Democrats' steadfast opposition to equal suffrage was already well known. What is clear was that as in 1846 and 1860 the Democrats' use of the suffrage issue was essentially opportunistic. They attempted to utilize the issue to help their candidates, but when it appeared more important to stress another issue, they did so without hesitation.

Republicans, too, handled suffrage in ways designed to foster party unity and electoral success. In 1860 such a strategy had dictated treating black rights as a matter essentially extraneous to the party. In 1869, however, the Republican leadership was unanimous in upholding the general principle of equal suffrage. The state convention resolved "that every American citizen, whether naturalized or native, should have an equal right to the suffrage without regard to nation, race, or religion" and "that the fifteenth amendment to the Constitution of the United States, as proposed, ought to be adopted."[25] While an occasional Republican editor had opposed

23. *New York Evening Post*, Sept. 23, 1869.
24. *New York World*, Oct. 27, 1869; see also ibid., Oct. 1, 28, 1869; *New York Herald*, Oct. 28, 1869.
25. *American Annual Cyclopaedia*, p. 489. Ironically the state constitution, which the Republican convention delegates in 1868 had been so eager to save from the association with black suffrage, was *not* officially endorsed by the party—apparently because

black suffrage in 1860, none apparently did so in 1869. A few ignored the issue as much as possible, of course.

The Republicans' partisan support for equal suffrage was perfectly logical. Since the party had in effect already abandoned its ambiguous 1868 stand on black suffrage by passing the Fifteenth Amendment, it was reasonable for it to endorse it as a part of the state constitution as well. And indeed the fear that systematic opposition by the Democrats would defeat the referendum and embarrass the party spurred Republicans to greater efforts.[26]

Yet there were peculiarities to the Republican support of black suffrage. It was clearly *not* an issue on which they wished to dwell. In contrast to Samuel J. Tilden at the Democratic convention, John A. Griswold, who addressed the Republicans at their gathering, did not mention suffrage once. Instead he stressed Democratic disloyalty during the war, an issue which could be counted on to stimulate even the most blasé Republican.[27] The very wording of the suffrage planks showed Republican desires to recognize and accommodate not only the radical faction, but also conservatives who doubted the wisdom of the party's involvement with racial matters. Thus the platform's references to the suffrage of native and naturalized citizens and promises of equal voting rights regardless of *religion*, a subject not at all at issue, deliberately obfuscated the point that it was blacks who would obtain the vote.[28] Even the endorsement of the Fifteenth Amendment did not point out *what* the amendment was supposed to accomplish. Franz Sigel in campaigning among Germans tried to give the impression that the Fifteenth Amendment applied to more than racial minorities: "The XVth Amendment annihilates the right of any state to exclude any class or nation from suffrage on the grounds of birth, race or color. It is simply to prevent any State from making laws forbidding universal suffrage. . . . Why should we Germans be excluded from, or have only partly, rights at the polls, thus being less free than in despotic Europe?"[29]

Once again Republicans prompted voters to see suffrage reform

---

some Republican newspapers had in the meantime objected to some of its provisions on the canals, the legislature, and other matters. See, for example, *Rochester Daily Democrat*, Sept. 28, 1869.

26. *New York Tribune*, Oct. 23, 1869; *Oneonta Herald*, Oct. 27, 1869.

27. *New York Tribune*, Sept. 30, 1869.

28. In general, legislators restricted voting by naturalized citizens through registration and naturalization laws rather than laws limiting the suffrage on the basis of place of birth or religion.

29. *New York Tribune*, Oct. 28, 1869.

in patriotic rather than racial terms. Only southern sympathizers, they argued, could reasonably defend a discrimination that had originated under slavery. The *Tribune* appealed for prosuffrage votes from "all electors who have not forgotten Appomattox; all who remember that chattel Slavery is no longer 'the peculiar institution' of this republic." Republicans recalled the service of black soldiers. Blacks were "a part of our own citizens, who were required to serve and *did* serve, in the armies of the Union." Supporting equal suffrage was a way for voters to defend their party and its programs. By rejecting the property qualification for blacks in New York, Jefferson County Republicans were told, they would "indorse the Congressional policy of reconstruction, President Grant's administration, and the fifteenth amendment."[30]

As in 1860, some papers insisted that the real point at issue was not race but property. "While it [the property qualification] stands there, it continually says that the State of New York believes that a poor man is not as safe and intelligent a voter as a rich man."[31] And this time the Republicans had made sure that the form of the ballot with its reference to the "property qualification" made this aspect of the question obvious.

Rather than question the whole process of racial stereotyping, Republicans instead merely substituted for the Democrats' image of the brutal, mindless black a more harmless one of a passive, long-suffering Uncle Tom. As they had during the draft riots, they used news reports to arouse sympathy for the poor, persecuted Negroes. Thus a Buffalo paper told of an innocent black hanged for rape during the war, while, just before election day in 1869, Republican papers throughout the state copied a story first appearing in the *New York Tribune* which gave an account of white atrocities against innocent blacks in Georgia. The *Tribune* assured its readers that blacks were "inoffensive, peaceful, lawabiding" but contradicted this favorable image by asserting that those who were "shiftless and indolent" should not be disfranchised.[32]

The Republicans also tried to create the impression that black suffrage was inevitable and that opposition to it, therefore, was pointless. They kept track of ratifications of the Fifteenth Amendment

30. Ibid., Oct. 28, 11, 1869; *New York Daily Reformer* (Watertown), Oct. 22, 1869.
31. *Albany Evening Journal*, Nov. 1, 1869.
32. *Buffalo Express*, Aug. 26, 1869; *New York Tribune*, Oct. 30, 1869.

and predicted that it would soon be a part of the constitution.[33] (By election day nineteen of the required twenty-eight states had ratified.) Even intelligent Democrats, Greeley asserted, "know, and in conversation admit, that ours must inevitably become a land of equal rights and equal laws."[34] Black suffrage was a dying issue. The Fifteenth Amendment was the capstone of Reconstruction, and its enactment, it was promised, would take the "negro question" out of politics once and for all.[35] This was indeed a happy thought to those who had wrestled with the irksome issue for many years.

Not all Republicans, of course, catered to popular prejudice. As in 1860 there was a strong, distinct element in the party who were elated by the reform and who stressed morality and justice as the most important reasons to support it. To the *Independent* the black man was a "citizen like other citizens" and the property qualification "a dastardly affront by the strong to the weak." The *Syracuse Daily Standard* found prejudice to be "illogical" and "antiquated." The Yates County Republican convention resolved in favor of the Fifteenth Amendment as a consummation of the struggle "against those unjust and wicked prejudices which would place one class of men under the heels of another, for no better reason than the color of their skin," and the local Republican paper, the *Yates County Chronicle*, attempted to make suffrage a major issue and a reason to support the Republican ticket.[36]

In general, however, Republicans brought up black suffrage only when they had to. The Democrats' switch to the temperance issue toward the end of the campaign was a great relief. Some party journals managed to avoid mentioning the referendum entirely.[37] Republicans defended their party's actions on black voting, but, in an attempt to reach as many different types of voters as possible, they

33. *Harper's Weekly* (New York), Sept. 25, 1869; *Buffalo Express*, Oct. 19, 1869; *Lowville Journal and Republican*, Sept. 15, 1869; *St. Lawrence Republican* (Ogdensburg), Oct. 26, 1869; *Rochester Daily Democrat*, Oct. 22, 1869.

34. *New York Tribune*, Oct. 11, 1869. See also *Albany Evening Journal*, Oct. 27, 1869.

35. *New York Times* quoted in *Schenectady Evening Star*, Nov. 22, 1869; *Saratogian* (Saratoga Springs), Sept. 30, 1869; *New York World*, Oct. 21, 1869; *Harper's Weekly*, Sept. 18, 1869; *Long Islander* (Huntington), Oct. 22, 1869.

36. *Independent* (New York), Oct. 28, 1869; *Syracuse Daily Standard*, Nov. 1, 1869; *Yates County Chronicle* (Penn Yan), Sept. 30, Oct. 21, 28, 1869. (The report of the Yates convention is from the Sept. 30 issue.)

37. See, for example, *Orange County Press* (Middletown). The paper was published in an area traditionally opposed to equal suffrage.

chose a wide variety of ways to do it. And, as usual, many people's prejudices were left completely intact.

Even blacks did not wage a strong campaign against the property qualification in 1869 in sharp contrast to 1846 and 1860. The war and Reconstruction, on one hand, had stimulated black endeavors to obtain the vote, but they had also broadened black objectives and extended the geographic range of their activities. New York blacks became increasingly involved in pressuring the federal government for equal rights legislation, helping to reconstruct the South, and demanding equal rights in New York in new areas such as education. They devoted less attention exclusively to suffrage. Before the constitutional convention in 1867 blacks did assemble in convention to demand full voting rights because of their war service. Again they rejected pleas to encourage the parties to compete for the black vote in favor of strong support for the Republicans.[38]

This faith in the Republican Party (and the federal government) continued through 1869. In June a convention of blacks met theoretically to organize for a systematic canvass of the state to promote equal suffrage in the referendum. Yet the resolutions and address issued were frankly congratulatory and seemed to assume the battle was already won. The blacks thanked Congress and the Republican legislature for adopting the Fifteenth Amendment, and only in passing did they mention that blacks could not count on the success of the separate submission on suffrage. Although blacks did publish some appeals in newspapers during the campaign, their role on the whole seems to have been less than in 1860.[39]

In sum, each of the groups addressing the suffrage question in 1869 consciously used the issue to try to promote its own interests. The Democrats stressed racism (although not as much as usual) in the hope of winning conservatives' votes. The Republicans tried to play down race in favor of emphasizing the relation of the issue to the war and Reconstruction. The blacks were more open in their praise of equal rights but were less active in the campaign. New York

38. *New York Times*, June 6, 1866; *National Anti-Slavery Standard* (New York), Oct. 27, 1866; David P. Thelan and Leslie H. Fishel, Jr., "Reconstruction in the North: The *World* Looks at New York's Negroes, March 16, 1867," *New York History*, 49 (Oct. 1968), 428.

39. Ena Lunette Farley, "The Issue of Black Equality in New York State, 1865–1873" (Ph.D. diss., University of Wisconsin, 1973), p. 81; *New York Tribune*, June 4, 1869; *National Anti-Slavery Standard*, Oct. 23, 1869; *Nation* (New York), Oct. 28, 1869; Herbert Aptheker, ed., *A Documentary History of the Negro People in the United States* (New York: Citadel Press, 1951), pp. 616–17.

was certainly unprepared for any serious examination of its real racial problems, the reasons for them, or possible solutions.

As the referendum approached, racial conservatives in both parties began to predict its defeat.[40] The past history of attempts to promote black voting equality in other states encouraged such doubts. In the previous four years voters had rejected black suffrage in seven states plus the territory of Colorado. (See Table 6.1.) Support for the reform had always lagged behind that for the Republican Party, even in Minnesota and Iowa, which had adopted black voting in 1868. In a closely divided state like New York, the referendum's fate seemed doubtful. Many politicians would obviously note carefully the type of popular response to it. The future course of the parties on racial matters could easily be shaped by it.

The waiting ended on election day, when returns showed that voters had refused to remove the property qualification by a vote of 282,403 to 249,802.[41] The margin was some ten percentage points closer than in 1860, but 53.1 per cent of the electorate had still resisted the effort to expand black voting.

Two items of obvious interest to politicians were the degree of

TABLE 6.1.

Prosuffrage and Republican voting in northern referenda, 1865-1868

	Per cent prosuffrage	*Per cent Republican*
Colorado Territory 1865	10.6	40.6
Connecticut 1865	44.6	57.5
Wisconsin 1865	46.0	54.3
Minnesota 1865	45.2	55.6
Kansas 1867	34.9	70.4
Minnesota 1867	48.8	54.1
Ohio 1867	45.9	50.3
Missouri 1868	42.7	58.9
Iowa 1868	56.5	61.9
Minnesota 1868	56.8	60.8

SOURCES: *Evening Journal Almanac*, 1866-1869; *Tribune Almanac*, 1866-1869.

40. *Albany Evening Journal*, Oct. 27, 1869; *Auburn Daily Advertiser*, Oct. 26, 1869; *New York World*, Sept. 2, 1869; *Albany Argus*, Mar. 4, 1869. For a more optimistic view see *New York Tribune*, Sept. 15, 1869.

41. *Tribune Almanac for 1870*, p. 53. The vote by county is listed in Appendix B.

voter interest in the referendum and its impact on the election's outcome. Participation was quite high. The proportion of those voting
for secretary of state who also voted on equal suffrage was 82.9 per
cent, 2.6 per cent higher than the referendum participation rate in
1860 and 6.6 per cent higher than in 1846. More voted on equal
suffrage than on any other part of the constitution. Equal suffrage
received 17,814 more votes than the constitution and 75,133 more
votes than the uniform taxation provision. Of six referenda in the
previous ten years only one had had a higher rate of voter participation.[42] This high rate of participation in 1869 came despite a
rather complicated voting procedure. (There were separate ballots
and ballot boxes for each of the four constitutional submissions and,
in addition, for each category of elective officers—state officials,
judges, state legislators, etc. Depending on his place of residence, a
voter had to cast seven to ten ballots to vote on all matters to be
decided.[43]) Apparently many voters were still extremely sensitive to
the race issue, a point that politicians would have to ponder.

The Democrats swept the state. Their candidate for secretary of
state received 51.6 per cent of the vote, and the rest of the state
ticket over 52 per cent; they carried the Assembly by twenty-four
seats and the Senate by two. What was particularly significant, however, was that the suffrage issue apparently did *not* play much of a
part in their triumph. Republicans did not lose because racial conservatives balked at supporting the party's candidates. Rather, both
parties attributed the result to a peculiar pattern of turnout.[44] The
Republicans were much less successful in mobilizing the vote in
their traditional, racially liberal, upstate strongholds than in the cities, while the Democrats found it easier to mobilize their voters upstate than in their usual urban strongholds. Of course, neither party
received as many votes as in the preceding presidential canvass, but
the votes for the two parties did not drop off equally across the state.
For example, in New York County the Republican vote in 1869 was
85.1 per cent of what it had been in 1868, the Democratic vote, 70.6
per cent. In upstate Cortland County the pattern was reversed with
the Republicans mobilizing 69.2 per cent of their 1868 vote to the

42. In 1866 84.8 per cent of those voting for governor expressed an opinion on the
calling of a constitutional convention.
43. See *Watkins Express*, Nov. 11, 1869, for complaints.
44. *New York Tribune*, Nov. 5, 1869; *New York World*, Nov. 4, 6, 1869; *Fredonia Censor*,
Nov. 3, 1869; *Yates County Chronicle*, Nov. 4, 1869; *St. Lawrence Plain Dealer* (Canton),
Nov. 14, 1869.

Democrats' 77.4 per cent. These figures accord well with an explanation of the election stressing ethnocultural issues. The Republicans, by heading their ticket with a German antiprohibitionist, offended many of their usual supporters. A St. Lawrence paper, for instance, complained after the election that many Republicans had scratched Sigel's name off their ballots or refused to vote, and many upstate papers during the campaign had to labor very hard to convince their followers that the party had not betrayed them on temperance.[45] Similarly, the Democratic candidates seemed relatively less attractive to urban ethnic voters than they usually did. Analysis shows that the largest Republican losses (compared to 1868) were definitely *not* in areas that were heavily antisuffrage or in areas of weak Republican support for the suffrage amendment.[46]

This result is quite interesting because it underscores the Republicans' continued ability to keep their party from splitting on the race issue. Although they lost the election, it was not for the same reasons that equal suffrage failed. As in 1860 when Lincoln won and equal suffrage lost, Republican leaders had succeeded in keeping the race issue from determining the election's outcome. In fact, as Table 6.1 illustrates, Republicans were frequently able to carry states even when black suffrage itself went down to defeat. They could do so, however, only by playing down the question and presenting it in ways that would not alienate prejudiced portions of the party's rank and file. In the one county, Yates, where Republicans made a major issue of equal suffrage in 1869, the percentage of voters opposed to black voting *increased* over 1860, and the Republican share of the vote fell to the second lowest level of the decade.[47]

The significance of the suffrage referendum lies less in its contribution to Democratic victory than in its revelations about white reactions to black voting equality in 1869. Figure 6.1 shows the distribution of the vote in 1869. For the first time a majority of all counties (thirty-two) voted in favor of equal suffrage. Extreme opposition to suffrage virtually disappeared. In 1860 nineteen counties had been more than seventy per cent opposed to increased black

45. *St. Lawrence Plain Dealer* (Canton), Nov. 14, 1869; *Auburn Daily Advertiser,* Oct. 28, 1869; *Poughkeepsie Daily Eagle,* Oct. 29, 1869; *New York Herald,* Oct. 28, 1869; *New York Daily Reformer,* Oct. 28, 1869.

46. This conclusion is based on a .22 correlation between Republican change 1868–1869 and per cent prosuffrage in 1869 and on a −.01 correlation between the former variable and the Republican percentage in 1869 less the prosuffrage percentage.

47. The percentage favoring suffrage declined 2.3 per cent, the second highest decline in the state. Equal suffrage still passed by a large margin.

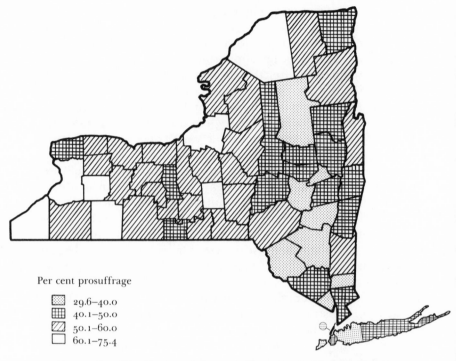

Per cent prosuffrage

29.6–40.0
40.1–50.0
50.1–60.0
60.1–75.4

FIGURE 6.1. Distribution of the prosuffrage vote, 1869 referendum.

voting; in 1869 only one was (New York at 70.4 per cent). At the other end of the scale, increases in prosuffrage voting were much less dramatic. Seven counties in 1869, compared to five in 1860, were over sixty per cent prosuffrage and the results in one of these, Erie, were misleading.[48] St. Lawrence, the banner prosuffrage county, raised its support, but only from 66.8 to 75.4 per cent. As Table 6.2 illustrates, most counties fell into the middle ranges of support for equal suffrage. The proportion of the population living in counties that were between forty and sixty per cent prosuffrage increased from 35.6 to 59.1 per cent between 1860 and 1869. Much of western New York came to endorse black voting, and strong resistance to it was pretty well limited to a wide band of counties from New York City northward.

48. There were massive abstentions in the voting on all parts of the constitution in Erie County, possibly due to the *Buffalo Courier's* (a Democratic paper which backed the constitution) failure to supply enough ballots.

TABLE 6.2.

Prosuffrage voting by counties, 1869 referendum

Per cent prosuffrage	Counties		Per cent of state population[a]	
	Number	Per cent[a]		
29.6-40.0	11	18.3 (42.4)	29.6	(58.8)
40.1-50.0	17	28.3 (27.1)	30.7	(19.8)
50.1-60.0	25	41.7 (22.0)	28.4	(15.8)
60.1-75.4	7	11.7 (8.5)	11.3	(5.6)
Total	60	100.0 (100.0)	100.0	(100.0)

[a]Comparable percentages from 1860 referendum are in parentheses.

Figure 6.2 and Table 6.3 indicate how the suffrage vote had changed between 1860 and 1869. In contrast to 1860, there were no spectacular increases in opposition to black voting despite the very real changes in the position of blacks in America that had occurred. Only five counties were more opposed to black voting in 1869 than in 1860 and none by more than 2.6 per cent. Half the counties (mostly in western and northern New York) increased their prosuffrage votes by modest amounts (up to ten per cent). Another sixteen counties, however, all but one in eastern New York, showed exceptional increases (up to 37.6 per cent) in support of equal suffrage.[49] Over half (54.5 per cent) of the state's population lived in counties whose prosuffrage vote increased more than fifteen percentage points.

A closer analysis of returns for 954 towns in fifty-one of the state's fifty-nine counties shows on what basis the electorate was apparently voting.[50] As in 1860 political loyalties were expected to affect the referendum vote. The *Albany Evening Journal* insisted that the property qualification clause "merely presented in distinct form an issue of national importance, concerning which the attitude of Republicans and Democrats alike has been most clearly determined by the various aspects of the reconstruction controversy." On the morning after the election Horace Greeley charged that Democratic votes had "upheld and perpetuated" the property qualification. *Harper's*

49. Again the large change in Erie County (32.1%) is misleading.
50. These counties are listed in Appendix C and compared to the state as a whole. The demographic data for this analysis comes from the *New York State Census for 1865.*

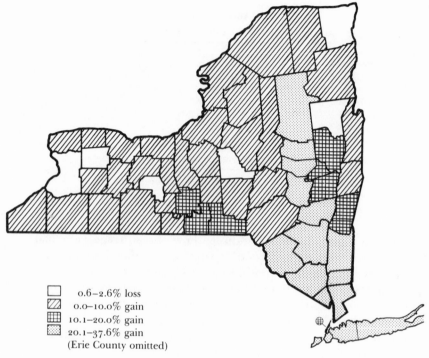

0.6–2.6% loss
0.0–10.0% gain
10.1–20.0% gain
20.1–37.6% gain
(Erie County omitted)

FIGURE 6.2. Losses and gains in prosuffrage voting, 1860–1869.

TABLE 6.3.
Losses and gains in prosuffrage voting, 1860-1869, by county

Per cent change	Counties[a]		Per cent of state population
	Number	Per cent	
Loss, 0.6-2.6	5	8.5	3.8
Gain, 0.0-5.0	16	27.1	16.9
Gain, 5.1-10.0	14	23.7	19.3
Gain, 10.1-15.0	4	6.8	5.5
Gain, 15.1-20.0	4	6.8	24.2
Gain, 20.1-25.0	4	6.8	11.7
Gain, 25.1-30.0	5	8.5	5.8
Gain, 30.1-37.6	7	11.9	12.7
Total	59	100.1	99.9

[a]Fulton and Hamilton treated as one county.

Weekly readily agreed.[51] The degree of party voting was indeed quite notable, although more than Democrats had to be blamed for the referendum's defeat. The correlation between the prosuffrage and Republican percentages in 1869 was .89, an extremely high figure. The Republican vote in 1868, which could not have been affected by the presence of the referendum, correlated with the 1869 prosuffrage vote at .83.

In 1860 there were more opponents of equal suffrage than there were Democrats, indicating some Republicans must have opposed the suffrage amendment. In 1869 Republican defections on suffrage were also present but far less noticeable. One must go to the township-level data to detect any definite Republican crossovers.[52] In 251 towns (26.3 per cent of the total towns surveyed) the number of votes cast against equal suffrage exceeded the total Democratic vote. The comparable figure in 1860 was eighty-six per cent of all towns. In only 69 towns (7.2 per cent of the total towns surveyed) did at least five per cent of all Republicans definitely vote antisuffrage, and in only thirty-two towns (3.4 per cent) did over ten per cent. There were at least some defections in the towns in all but three counties.[53] The most extensive were in Greene and Ulster Counties (where many Republicans had also opposed black voting in 1860). Again, however, Republican opposition to equal suffrage in these areas was far less widespread or uniform than in the earlier referendum. In contrast to 1860 also, there was no marked tendency for Republicans in antisuffrage areas to abstain. Almost no correlation (.16) existed between the extent voters participated in the referendum and the amount of support given to equal suffrage. In short, Republican voters were much more united in support of equal suffrage than they ever had been before. Defections were not massive or systematic. Still, the opposition of a critical minority in the closely divided state had been sufficient to prevent the removal of the property qualification once and for all.

For the first time since the realignment of the 1850s the statistics show that some Democrats definitely supported black voting. In twenty-five towns (2.6 per cent of the total towns surveyed) there

51. *Albany Evening Journal,* Nov. 3, 1869; *New York Tribune,* Nov. 3, 1869; *Harper's Weekly,* Nov. 20, 1869.
52. Statewide the number of prosuffrage votes was 78 per cent of the number of Republican votes and the antisuffrage votes, 85 per cent of the Democratic votes.
53. The three were New York, Putnam, and Seneca. Again, only minimum defection rates are being discussed.

were more persons favoring equal suffrage than there were Republican voters. Obviously, defections were not a serious problem to the Democrats. Indeed voters in seven towns may have simply been confused by the ballots and accidentally voted the wrong way.[54] As Democratic newspapers had warned before the election, voters wishing to vote *against* equal suffrage might select a ballot *against* the property qualification by mistake, especially since the ballots required to reject the other three portions of the constitution all began with the word "against."[55] To prevent such confusion, Democratic papers for weeks had published the correct ballot form to oppose the suffrage proposal, but several papers observed after the election that some individuals or whole towns had voted the wrong way.[56] Yet in the remaining towns with Democratic prosuffrage voters a minimum of one to thirty-seven Democrats apparently did vote for equal suffrage. These towns were almost all prosuffrage and widely scattered in fifteen different counties. The legitimist argument that black suffrage was no longer a proper issue for Democrats had not gone entirely unheeded. Nevertheless, Democrats' resistance to their party's position on the issue remained largely sporadic and idiosyncratic. After four years of war and five more of Reconstruction most Democrats seem to have been as convinced as ever of the merits of limiting the black vote.

The significance of party in the 1869 referendum may be further tested by examining whether important social, economic, or cultural variables had an independent influence on the vote or were merely related to it through the intermediary of party. Table 6.4 displays the simple correlations between various population subgroups and the prosuffrage and Republican votes in 1869. The correlations as a whole are somewhat lower than the corresponding coefficients in 1860. (See Table 4.3.) The prosuffrage and Republican correlations in 1869 were basically similar, but not identical, suggesting that areas dominated by particular groups did not behave exactly the same on the two matters.

Support for equal suffrage continued to come from areas of substantial New England, Welsh, Scotch, and English settlement. Ap-

54. The vote in these appears to be entirely reversed, Democrats supporting and Republicans opposing black suffrage. Probably those responsible for handing out the ballots simply became confused.

55. *Plattsburgh Republican*, Oct. 23, 1869; *Rochester Daily Union & Advertiser*, Oct. 28, 1869.

56. *Geneva Gazette*, Nov. 12, 1869; *Rochester Express* quoted in *New York Tribune*, Nov. 5, 1869; *Poughkeepsie Daily Eagle*, Nov. 4, 1869.

TABLE 6.4.

Correlation between population subgroups and prosuffrage and Republican voting, 1869[a]

Variable	Per cent Republican[b] (correlation)	Per cent prosuffrage (correlation)	Coefficient of variability
Per cent born Ireland	−.42	−.23	1.04
Per cent born Germany	−.35	−.27	0.53
Per cent born Ireland and Germany	−.51	−.33	1.05
Per cent born New England	.48	.44	1.48
Per cent Dutch Reformed of communicants	−.15	−.17	0.31
Per cent nonevangelical of communicants	−.37	−.27	0.71
Per cent black	−.20	−.20	0.56
Per cent landowners	.42	.29	3.05
Average value of dwelling per family	−.29	−.17	0.93

N = 954.
[a]Town-level data.
[b]1868.

proximately two-thirds (66 per cent) of all prosuffrage towns surveyed had a New England-born population greater than the mean for all towns. This percentage was less than in either 1846 (88 per cent) or 1860 (75 per cent), however. This persistent downward trend indicates the transformation of the suffrage cause from one dominated by Yankee reformers to one more broadly based in the Republican Party. Similarly, towns where more than ten per cent of the residents were born in Wales or England and Scotland continued to be predominantly prosuffrage. Ten of twelve of these English-Scotch towns voted in favor of equal suffrage, as did four of six Welsh ones.[57] Among all these towns, however, the suffrage vote largely paralleled the party vote.

With concern for morality again a part of the prosuffrage argument, one would also expect support for blacks to appear not only among Yankees but evangelical Protestants generally.[58] Although, again, religious data for New York do not give a complete picture of the actual religious composition of the population, one may note that areas with large proportions of definitely nonevangelical

57. The exceptions were either in rugged, wilderness areas where voter participation was extremely erratic or in towns where there were more Irish and Germans than in the prosuffrage towns.
58. For a rather mixed review of the attitudes of Baptist and Methodist leaders on black rights see Ena L. Farley, "Methodists and Baptists on the Issue of Black Equality in New York 1865 to 1868," *Journal of Negro History*, 61 (Oct. 1976), 374–92.

groups (Catholic, Dutch Reformed, Lutheran, Episcopalian, etc.) were more likely to be antisuffrage than those with smaller numbers of such communicants. (The correlation between the percentage of all communicants who were nonevangelical and the percentage voting prosuffrage was −.27.) Seventy-six per cent of the towns containing *only* nonevangelical churches were antisuffrage. Again, however, such areas also tended to be Democratic.

Americans born in Canada, as in 1860, were an ambiguous group. Of twenty-six towns where they made up ten per cent or more of the population, fifteen were prosuffrage and eleven antisuffrage. The situation continued to be complicated by the tendency of many Canadians not to seek citizenship. In Clinton, the premier Canadian town (29.1 per cent), where there were also many Irish (eighty per cent of all voters were naturalized), only 8.6 per cent of the voters approved equal suffrage. The town of Waddington in St. Lawrence County, however, with a Canadian-born population of 12.1 per cent, was almost unanimous in support of equal suffrage (99.1 per cent). Most of the prosuffrage Canadian towns were in St. Lawrence County, where access to Canada was easy and many Canadian residents failed to put down permanent roots. Still, Canadians may have been divided in their suffrage sentiments.[59]

In general, the groups that were most antisuffrage in 1860 continued in this category in 1869, but the level of their opposition declined, most notably in areas of original Dutch settlement (indicated by the presence of Dutch Reformed churches). Seventy-four per cent of the 111 towns surveyed containing Dutch Reformed communicants were antisuffrage compared to over ninety per cent in 1860. Most were in the thirty-five to fifty per cent prosuffrage range as well, higher than in 1860. Only seven per cent were less than twenty per cent prosuffrage. Of the towns where all the communicants were Dutch Reformed, all were again antisuffrage, but the least antisuffrage of these was more than forty per cent favorable to black voting. Equal suffrage was far from popular in such places, but at least an increasing minority was willing to consider it. This minority was certainly important to the Republican Party because it was primarily these areas that had shown the most hostility toward Republican involvement in racial politics.

59. On Canadians in the U.S. in this period see Theresa Bilodeau, "The French in Holyoke," *Historical Journal of Western Massachusetts,* 3 (Spr. 1974), 1–12; Joseph Carvalko III, and Robert Everett, "Statistical Analysis of Springfield's French Canadians," *Historical Journal of Western Massachusetts,* 3 (Spr. 1974), 59–63.

The Irish remained an important reference group for Republicans taking a position on black rights. The *New York Times* in 1869 insisted that racial prejudice was "bitterly and intensely fostered by the Irish element," and the *Independent* spoke with disgust of Irish Catholics who "have been rallied to the polls by inflammatory appeals whereof the burden was 'nigger.'"[60] The Irish proved their continuing dislike of the black and his Republican allies on election day. The most heavily Irish areas were the most solidly antiblack. (The correlation with the prosuffrage vote was only − .23, in part because the majority of towns had few or no Irish-born residents.) Not one of the state's eleven urban wards over thirty per cent Irish was over 31.8 per cent prosuffrage. (The average for this group was 17.5 per cent.) This opposition to equal suffrage went hand in hand with strong support for the Democratic Party. (The same eleven wards were an average of 78.5 per cent Democratic.)

The second largest immigrant group in the state, the Germans, were probably slightly less opposed to black voting than the Irish, despite the similarity of the correlation coefficients for each group with the prosuffrage vote. Indeed the *New York Times* praised Germans for their tolerance: "The only class in this city who appear to be really uninfluenced by this intolerant spirit of prejudice against the color of the negro are the Germans. They seem, as a general thing, to have no objection to let lodgings to them, they willingly employ them and pay them fair wages."[61] Surely, however, it was not the usual German immigrant that had lodgings to let or a job to offer. The *Tribune* felt, on the other hand, that while Germans were innately sympathetic to equal rights they might oppose them regardless. There were many Germans, it noted,

> who usually vote the Democratic ticket, and they, as a body, are favorable to Impartial Suffrage. They may be dragooned into voting otherwise; but, if they do it, such a vote will be the dictate of their partisan affiliation, not of their unbiased judgment. Left to themselves, nine-tenths of our German-born citizens would vote to accord every native of the soil all the rights they claim for themselves.[62]

The Republican statements indicate a strong desire to win some German voters, a strategy the party was already following with its nomination of Sigel and tabling of temperance at the convention. The referendum returns, however, revealed heavily German areas

60. *New York Times*, Mar. 2, 1869; *Independent*, Nov. 25, 1869.
61. *New York Times*, Mar. 2, 1869.
62. *New York Tribune*, Sept. 3, 1869.

to be about as antisuffrage as they had been in 1860 and 1846. The low participation rate by Buffalo and Erie County voters left the behavior of one important German area unclear. Still, eighty-two per cent of the remaining towns and wards over fifteen per cent German-born were antisuffrage, including those that were almost entirely German. (See Table 6.5.) There was enough prosuffrage strength in some of these towns (Syracuse's second ward, for example) to indicate that probably there was some German support for equal suffrage, but this was a distinctly minority sentiment.[63] It is also apparent that not even all Republicans in German areas were prosuffrage (that is, if one goes by the 1869 vote, which was unusually Republican due to Sigel's candidacy). A third of the thirty-four towns over fifteen per cent German had at least some Republican voters definitely voting antisuffrage. The *Times* vision of color-blind Germans had been largely illusory. Most Germans remained loyal both to the Democratic party and to its posture on black rights.

Areas inhabited by native-born groups other than the Yankees and Dutch were generally hostile to black voting. Towns where many New Jerseyites had settled were almost exclusively antisuffrage, although not to the extent they had been in 1860. (Those where over ten per cent of the population had originated in New Jersey were only an average 38.2 per cent prosuffrage.) Towns which have been impressionistically labeled Palatine or Old British fall into the same category.[64] However, the towns of western New York along the Pennsylvania border where many Pennsylvanians had settled continued to be about as prosuffrage as the state as a whole. Towns with more than ten per cent of their population born in this state averaged 53.4 per cent prosuffrage. In a few areas, such as Chemung County, there was an unusual amount of resistance to black voting; however, the divisions within the group seemed to parallel party divisions.

In general, the more traditional, staid eastern part of the state, that area that had had centuries to settle into its racial patterns, was more conservative than the western and northern regions. This older area also contained most of New York's black population, but once again the physical presence of blacks was not the most decisive factor influencing the referendum. Blacks had declined to 1.2 per

63. As in 1860 German divisions may have been along religious lines with more evangelical Protestant Germans favoring the Republicans.
64. The classification follows Lee Benson, *The Concept of Jacksonian Democracy: New York as a Test Case* (Princeton: Princeton University Press, 1961).

TABLE 6.5.

Republican and prosuffrage voting of most heavily German towns and wards, 1869

Town or ward	Per cent German-born	Per cent voters natu-ralized	Per cent Republican in 1868	Per cent Republican in 1869	Per cent pro-suffrage
Syracuse Ward 2	44.7	90.1	46.1	51.3	46.2
West Seneca, Erie	36.7	78.4	42.2	32.2	26.9
New York Ward 10	34.2	69.5	26.3	44.5	31.7
Wheatfield, Niagara	34.7	67.3	36.0	43.9	43.9
Rochester Ward 13	33.6	81.6	57.6	66.0	45.2
New York Ward 17[a]	30.6	75.0	25.9	44.7	32.7
New York Ward 11	30.2	72.1	19.4	32.2	29.7

[a]Large Irish population also.

cent of the total population of New York by 1870. The town of Harrison in Westchester County, which had the largest proportion of blacks in the sample (12.7 per cent), was only 33.3 per cent prosuffrage. And all but one town over six per cent black was also antisuffrage. However, there were only fourteen such towns. The overwhelming majority (75 per cent) of the towns that were antisuffrage had almost no blacks (less than two per cent). As had been characteristic of New York since its first suffrage referendum, racial bias was not dependent only upon the actual presence of blacks.

As in 1860, one reason given by commentators for the willingness to discriminate against blacks was their supposed competition with white workers for jobs. The Democrats had played on this fear for years, and actual conflicts between black and white workers had occurred in several cities during the decade.[65] Equal suffrage certainly did not do well in these cities. Indeed antisuffrage sentiment was greatest in areas where individual landholding was least. (The correlation between per cent of the population owning land and per cent prosuffrage was .29.) This correlation implies that areas dominated by the urban proletariat and high tenancy regions (primarily the large estates of eastern New York) were somewhat more anti-black than the rest of the state. One may ask further, however, whether economically depressed areas in general were opposed to

65. Williston Lofton, "Northern Labor and the Negro during the Civil War," *Journal of Negro History*, 34 (July 1949), 261–62, 272; Albon P. Man, Jr., "Labor Competition and the New York Draft Riots of 1863," *Journal of Negro History*, 36 (Oct. 1951), 375–405.

political equality for blacks. The answer seems to be no. Places with a high average value of dwelling per family tended to be more opposed to black voting than poorer areas. Of the ten most prosuffrage towns in the state only one had an average home value greater than that for the state as a whole.[66]

The independent influence on the prosuffrage vote of all these factors may be weighed in a stepwise multiple regression. Table 6.6 summarizes the results of such a regression.[67] The two variables listed added one per cent or more to explained variance. It is apparent that practically *all* of the explainable variation in the prosuffrage vote could be attributed to the single variable, party. Most other characteristics were subsumed under one of the parties. The only other factor having an independent influence was the percentage of the population born in Ireland and Germany, and this surprisingly was *positively* related to the prosuffrage vote indicating relatively more support for suffrage in such areas. This unusual result was related to the higher proportionate vote for Republicans (and hence for equal suffrage) in immigrant areas in 1869. Since the *1868* Republican vote appeared in the regression, the prosuffrage strength in Irish/German areas in 1869 appeared unusually large.[68] If one uses the 1869 Republican figures in the regression, *only* per cent Republican appears significant. One may conclude that by 1869 most voters were increasngly ignoring all other influences to vote along party lines on the suffrage question. There were, of course, innumerable deviations from a strict partisan vote, but these were not systematic in nature. They reflected apparently random resistance to party cues on the issue. Partisans could persuade most voters to cast their ballots according to the parties' wishes, but never all of them.

Figure 6.3 shows the differences between prosuffrage and Republican voting across New York State. The most significant deviations from a straight party vote occurred in the southeastern counties, the

66. The correlation was quite low, −.17. It remains low even controlling for level of urbanization.

67. The variables entered were per cent Republican 1868, per cent born in New England, per cent born in Ireland and Germany, per cent nonevangelical of communicants, value of dwelling per family, and area of pre-1790 settlement. See Appendix E for a further methodological discussion.

68. It might also be noted that Tammany had softened its opposition to black suffrage as a state measure due to a greater fear of the federal enforcement provision of the Fifteenth Amendment and its possible impact on New York City elections. See *New York Herald,* Nov. 26–28, 1869.

TABLE 6.6.

Variables explaining votes for equal suffrage,
1869 (partial regression coefficients)[a]

Variable	Beta
Per cent Republican, 1868	.90
Per cent born Ireland and Germany	.14

Fraction of explained variance, 70.9%.
N = 954.
[a]Town-level data.

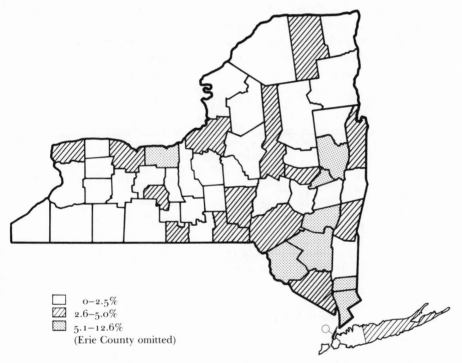

0–2.5%
2.6–5.0%
5.1–12.6%
(Erie County omitted)

FIGURE 6.3. Percentages by which Republican votes exceeded prosuffrage votes, 1869 referendum.

ones most opposed to equal suffrage in 1846 and 1860, but not all such counties showed a significant difference. Black suffrage may still have been fairly unpopular among Republicans in this region, but the party organization was effective in some portions of it in marshalling support for the referendum.[69]

The distinctly particularistic nature of Republican defections on equal suffrage may be noted in a slightly different way as well. Table 6.7 shows the simple correlations between various social and demographic variables and the percentage difference between the Republican and prosuffrage votes in 1869. Again one sees that there was little pattern to the differences except for the −.56 correlation with per cent prosuffrage, a relationship to be anticipated since the larger the prosuffrage vote, the less likely for the Republican vote to exceed it by a substantial amount.

While in 1860 weak Republican areas showed high abstention on or opposition to black suffrage, in 1869 many Republicans in such areas were apparently supporting equal suffrage for the first time.

TABLE 6.7.

Correlation between differences between prosuffrage
and Republican percentages and population
characteristics, 1869[a]

Variable	Correlation
Per cent prosuffrage	−.56
Per cent Republican 1869	−.01
Per cent born Ireland	−.14
Per cent born Germany	−.03
Per cent born Ireland and Germany	−.11
Per cent born New England	−.04
Per cent Dutch Reformed of communicants	.05
Per cent nonevangelical of communicants	.04
Per cent black	.08
Per cent landowners	.09
Average value of dwelling per family	−.08

N = 954.

[a]Town-level data. Dependent variable was calculated by subtracting prosuffrage percentage from Republican percentage in 1869.

69. An examination of the residuals from a regression using per cent Republican to estimate the prosuffrage vote showed no particular pattern among the largest residual cases.

Some towns still had Republican dissenters, of course, but to persuade even some of the most prejudiced members of the party to vote for equal rights was no mean achievement.

One can more precisely judge the types of changes taking place since 1860 by observing the 805 towns in forty-four counties for which returns are available for both referenda.[70] Three-quarters of these towns increased their equal suffrage totals over the nine years, the rest declining. Large gains were far more common than large losses. Seventy-four towns increased their prosuffrage vote by thirty per cent or more while of the 205 towns that became more opposed to equal suffrage, only fifty-five changed by ten per cent or more and only four by thirty per cent or more. About half the counties surveyed, primarily ones that had decisively rejected black voting in 1860, contained most of the seventy-four towns with large gains. In fact, despite the large increases, most were still antisuffrage in 1869. The dismissal of black rights was simply less automatic and universal. On the other side, the towns with growing opposition to black suffrage were not in areas that in the past had shown the greatest suspicion of racial change. Rather they were most common in areas that had supported black rights in both 1860 and 1869. Such areas may possibly have felt that the battle was already won and that extensive exertions in behalf of equal suffrage were no longer needed.

Despite the many changes, there was general continuity between the two referenda, which correlated at .68. There was some departure from a simple linear relationship between them, however, since the heavily antisuffrage towns of 1860 made much larger advances in support of equal suffrage by 1869 than did towns that had already been prosuffrage in the earlier year.

The population characteristics of the towns participating in both referenda may be examined further in Table 6.8.[71] Substantial growth in support for the black man was most likely to occur in areas that were the least prosuffrage in 1860, which had had a relatively poor turnout on the suffrage question in 1860 (due to Republican abstentions), and which had had an unusually low prosuffrage vote in 1860 given their Republican strength. Prosuffrage support was unlikely to increase much in areas dominated by groups (such as Yankees) that were already favorable to the reform in 1860. In

---

70. The counties are listed and examined in Appendix C.

71. Prosuffrage change was measured by subtracting the percentage for equal suffrage in 1860 from that in 1869. Republican change was similarly calculated.

TABLE 6.8.

Correlation between change in prosuffrage votes, 1860-1869, and
population characteristics

Variable	Correlation	Coefficient of variability
Per cent Republican 1860	−.33	4.54
Per cent Republican 1868	−.21	4.20
Change per cent Republicans 1860 to 1869	.37	0.63
Per cent prosuffrage 1860	−.66	2.02
Suffrage turnout 1860	−.53	7.25
Republican 1860 minus prosuffrage 1860	.75	1.25
Per cent born Ireland	.18	1.03
Per cent born Germany	.09	0.55
Per cent born Ireland and Germany	.17	1.06
Per cent born New England	−.35	1.54
Per cent black	.29	0.58
Per cent Dutch Reformed of communicants	.28	0.31
Per cent nonevangelical of communicants	.20	0.68
Per cent landowners	−.26	2.98
Average value of dwelling per family	.26	0.96

N = 805.

these areas the Republican vote and suffrage vote were already
much alike in 1860 and there was relatively little change over the
decade. Areas that lost in Republican voting power between 1860
and 1869 (owing to population shifts primarily or in some cases actual rejection of the Republican creed) also tended to become more
opposed to black voting. The increasing significance of party cues
could not be clearer.

The results of a multiple regression (Table 6.9) show those variables having an independent influence on prosuffrage change.[72]
The most important factor associated with change was the extent to
which the suffrage vote and party vote had diverged in 1860. (The
1860 residuals represent the difference between the actual prosuffrage votes of towns and their expected vote estimated from their
Republican strength. These estimates were based on the least
squares regression of Republican per cent on per cent prosuffrage
in 1860.) Thus areas that were becoming more prosuffrage tended

72. The variables entered were 1860 residuals, change per cent Republican 1860–
1869, per cent born in New England, per cent born in Ireland and Germany, per cent
black, per cent American Party for governor in 1858, and area of pre-1790 settlement. Variables listed in the table added at least one per cent to explained variance.

TABLE 6.9.

Variables explaining equal suffrage
voting shifts, 1860-1869
(partial regression coefficients)

Variable	Beta
1860 residuals	.72
Change per cent Republican, 1860-1869	.44
Per cent born New England	−.11

Fraction of explained variance, 73.2%.
N = 805.

to be those that had been unusually antisuffrage in 1860, had experienced Republican gains over the decade, and had relatively few persons of New England origin.

By insisting that voters see the suffrage question in partisan terms, the Republicans had convinced those who had abstained on the suffrage question in 1860 and whose involvement with the Republican Party was more likely to have been in spite of, rather than because of, its racial policies, to vote in favor of equal rights. Between 1846 and 1860 prosuffrage sentiment had increased among the groups that had been more sympathetic to the cause in 1846. Between 1860 and 1869, however, support for equal suffrage grew in areas where it had been almost universally reviled in both 1846 and 1860. In the years between 1846 and 1869 the typical prosuffrage town had changed from one of recent New England origin with an orientation towards reform (1846), to one that was Republican but also Yankee, solidly white, and not involved with the American Party (1860), to one that was purely and simply Republican (1869).

The responsibility of the Republican Party nationally for black suffrage in the South was absolutely crucial to the result in New York. Pressured by suffrage activists, convinced that the party could not avoid the issue and would be hurt by its continual airing, Republicans struggled to resolve their dilemma by securing the enactment of equal voting rights for blacks. The party put substantial pressure on even its conservative members to recognize the necessity for black suffrage. Republicans did not ignore partisan needs, as both the timing of the referendum and the rhetoric it elicited demonstrated. But Republicans did manage to get out the vote in areas that had resisted equal rights in the past. Indeed, if they had put as much effort into stressing the need for a large turnout in normally prosuffrage areas, the referendum might have done even better. As it was, Republicans in New York gave more consistent support to black voting rights than their fellow partisans in any other northern state. (The holding of the referendum after the party's endorsement of the Fifteenth Amendment, of course, encouraged this result.) The failure of the referendum obscures the very real contribution Republican voters made. A few defections in conjunction with the general close division between the state's parties spelled the referendum's defeat.

Republicans did not obtain support for equal suffrage without cost both to the cause and to their party, however. Greater Republican unity on black suffrage was in part the result of an overall decline in Republican strength. In 1860 the Republicans had won 53.7 per cent of the vote, in 1869 only 48.4 per cent. Even with this narrower base, Republicans still had to make important concessions to prejudiced voters. When not avoiding the issue entirely, they had played upon their supporters' attitudes toward the war, the Democrats, and the Irish among others to try to get equal suffrage passed. They had been aided by a ballot that was confusing to some and a cumbersome voting procedure. In essence, Republicans persuaded many people to vote in favor of equal suffrage, but not out of a regard for blacks or an understanding of the problems they faced. The party's short-term interests were served. It remained united, vigorous, and competitive. The Democrats' victory was narrow and not really attributable to defections on the race issue. But Republicans had failed to build a base from which to extend the struggle against discrimination. Republicans could survive the race issue, but not really profit from it. Many were inevitably eager to be free of its complications and embarrassments.

Still the passage of the Fifteenth Amendment, if not the defeat of the suffrage referendum, was a minor milestone in the history of New York. Although the triumphant Democrats tried to withdraw New York's ratification of the Fifteenth Amendment, the Grant administration refused to permit them to do so and declared the amendment ratified on March 30, 1870.[73] The next Republican legislature (1872) rescinded the resolutions by which the Democrats

73. New York State Senate, *Journal*, 93rd Sess., 1870, pp. 6, 7, 30, 32; New York State Assembly, *Journal*, 93rd Sess., 1870, p. 43. In the Assembly one Democrat, Jay A. Pease of Lewis County, voted against the measure as a lost cause. For the debates see the *Albany Argus* and *Albany Evening Journal*, Jan. 5–7, 1870.

had attempted to revoke the ratification of the Fifteenth Amendment.[74] Once black suffrage was in fact realized, resistance to it waned, even when the black population in the state began to increase again in the latter part of the century.[75] Other forms of discrimination continued unabated,[76] but white New Yorkers eventually came to accept from force of habit what they had stubbornly resisted for so long—equal suffrage with black men.

74. *Laws of the State of New York,* 95th Sess., 1872, p. 2189. Apparently unaware of the 1872 rescission and responding to the political needs of a new age, the New York legislature of 1970 also overrode the resolutions. *New York Times,* Mar. 31, 1970, p. 26.

75. There was a small amount of resistance when the amendment first went into effect. See Ena L. Farley, "The Denial of Black Equality under the States Rights Dictum: New York, 1865 to 1873," *Afro-Americans in New York Life and History,* 1 (Jan. 1977), 16–17.

76. Civil Rights Acts passed in 1874 and 1881 were easily circumvented. Gilbert T. Stephenson, *Race Distinctions in American Law* (New York: D. Appleton and Co., 1910), p. 115; Leslie H. Fishel, Jr., "The North and the Negro, 1865–1900: A Study in Race Discrimination" (Ph.D. diss., Harvard University, 1953), 1:298–99. Farley, "Issue of Black Equality," demonstrates that the social and economic condition of New York blacks changed very little during this period.

Race and Party Politics

The passage of the Fifteenth Amendment ultimately resolved the struggle for equal suffrage in New York. By 1870 adult male blacks could vote in all elections by federal, not state, action. But the political battles in New York that culminated in full black suffrage have even greater significance than the extension of the franchise to blacks, important as that was. They are crucial for understanding political and social divisions on race in New York and by extension in the North, the role of the nineteenth century political party in social change, and the nature of "reconstruction" in the North.

The suffrage struggle in New York passed through three stages. In the first, which encompassed the period of the 1846 referendum, opposition to equal suffrage was overwhelming. What little support there was for it was largely along cultural lines. Groups that traditionally believed in the need for each man to develop unhindered his own talents and virtues spearheaded the drive to abolish the property qualification. (For the next quarter century this belief was to remain the *central* rationale for suffrage reform.) Thus areas inhabited by Yankees, political abolitionists, and temperance men opposed the property qualification most fiercely. Interestingly, an analysis of voter reactions to black suffrage in Michigan in 1850 shows a similar pattern of cultural divisions.[1]

1. Ronald P. Formisano, "The Edge of Caste: Colored Suffrage in Michigan 1827–1861," *Michigan History*, 56 (Spring 1972), 33–34.

The relation of these cultural divisions to existing political divisions was complex. There was a tendency for more Whigs to favor equal rights and more Democrats to oppose them, based in part on the Whigs' image as a party favorable to the promotion of "moral right" and the Democrats' image as a party opposed to the imposition of cultural values (such as racial equality) upon others.[2] But neither party was united. Parties directed much of their political maneuvering in this stage to trying to strengthen the two-party system by drawing back into it those dedicated abolitionists who put principle above political expediency and supported the highly disruptive Liberty Party. Black suffrage was a useful issue to attract the attention of Liberty men and show them the very real difficulties of securing the enactment of equal suffrage.

By 1860 sentiment on black suffrage in New York had reached a transitional stage. Political parties played a much larger role in the suffrage struggle, although cultural factors remained important. The realignment of the 1850s was apparently the key event in generating change. It brought a greater correspondence between cultural orientations and political affiliations as Yankees, the principal group whose egalitarian values rejected the notion of discrimination based solely on race, moved into the Republican Party in droves. That party articulated a world view in which an aggressive Slave Power, supported by masses of alien Catholics herded to the polls on election day by their Democratic overlords, was threatening America with a reign of tyranny and corruption and attempting to debase and degrade democratic values. The Republicans attracted those who saw Republican policies as likely to create a purer, more moral America. With their strength in racially conservative eastern New York diminished, Republican leaders could take stronger stands on black suffrage. But not all their supporters saw the connection between the Slave Power and New York's property qualification. The party remained divided on equal suffrage.

The Democracy during this transitional period also underwent changes. Threatened with the loss of its traditional partisan edge both in New York and in the nation, it sought new ways to keep northerners and southerners, native-born Americans and immi-

2. For an excellent description of the philosophies and images of the two parties in 1844 see Lee Benson, *The Concept of Jacksonian Democracy: New York as a Test Case* (Princeton: Princeton University Press, 1961), chapter 11.

grants, happy in the same political organization. Democrats sought to avoid confrontation by adhering to a very strict constitutionalism that severely limited the government's ability to interfere with any group's special concerns. Most Democrats could also unite emotionally in their rejection of a biracial society. The arousal of racial fears became a common technique in Democratic campaigning.

Opposition to equal suffrage among the voters continued to be massive, although less than it had been at the time of the 1846 referendum. The suffrage vote in 1860 was more partisan, but Republicans who were not culturally predisposed to favor equal suffrage (i.e., were not Yankees, early supporters of the Republican Party, or from formerly nonslaveholding regions) tended to abstain or oppose black rights. Nevertheless, this tendency to abstain was significant, for it showed the unwillingness of some Republicans at least to identify with the Democrats' position on the issue.

The Civil War and its aftermath were fundamental in bringing black suffrage as an issue to the fore and shaping the suffrage struggle in its final stage. The Civil War intensified partisan divisions on racial issues such as emancipation and the use of black troops. Reconstruction further focused attention on the black man and the role he was to play in politics. More and more Republicans were made to see that for the party of patriotism, union, and decency to triumph, changes would have to be made in the black man's status in America. Gradually the party assumed responsibility for reorganizing southern governments with the help of black voters. As the Republicans recognized *as a party* the validity of black suffrage, the issue assumed a dominant position in the partisan debate, a place it was to hold until the adoption of the Fifteenth Amendment conveniently removed it from the political arena.

The 1860s, a period of change in the black man's legal position, was an ideal time for Democrats to fan the flames of prejudice which had always burned in America. But so completely had Republicans succeeded in identifying the Democrats' party with "treason most foul," that there were surprisingly few Republican defections over the issue. The referendum of 1869 showed almost a totally partisan reaction to the suffrage question. It was in this "political" phase that equal suffrage won its greatest support—46.9 per cent of the vote, only 1.5 per cent less than the Republican Party received in the same election. A systematic analysis of the Iowa referendum in 1868 also showed party to have been the major factor in the voting. In Iowa, however, a 5.4 per cent differential separated the party and suffrage votes.[3]

The important role played by partisanship and political parties in the changing reactions to equal suffrage is particularly impressive. Two aspects of this role may be distinguished, one having to do with the incorporating of racial attitudes into party images and the other with the process of bringing together diverse elements within the party. First, parties—especially after the realignment of the 1850s—identified the already existing racial tensions in New York and responded to them in party rhetoric. Thus general tensions in the society were channeled into differences between the parties. In the process much stereotyping and oversimplification took place. The two groups who seemed to symbolize party differences most clearly and whose position on the black man also seemed quite clear-cut were the Irish in the Democratic Party and the Yankees in the Republican Party. The presumed racial proclivities of these two groups became part of the partisan images of the political organizations to which they adhered.

To Democrats the archetypical Republican was the Yankee Puritan—grim, fanatical, moralistic, and self-righteous—a person who tried to force his peculiar, impractical notions upon others. To Republicans the stereotypic Democrat was the Irishman—alien, ignorant, vicious, and degraded.[4] Both images were highly (and deliberately) exaggerated, indeed caricatures. Few Republicans were in fact meddlesome fanatics or Democrats drunken Irish toughs. But such stereotypes served to simplify New York's complex political world, made it easier for persons to arrive at a party identification by giving them something clear-cut to fear in the opposition, and allowed people to see how a political issue like black suffrage fit into the general political scheme of things. One can see how the simplifying process worked in the comments of diarist George Templeton

3. Robert R. Dykstra, "Iowa: 'Bright Radical Star,'" in James C. Mohr, ed., *Radical Republicans in the North: State Politics during Reconstruction* (Baltimore: Johns Hopkins University Press, 1976), 167–93. A number of the other essays in this volume touch on the suffrage question, although only Dykstra's essay attempts a systematic analysis of voter opinion.

4. Interestingly, Leigh Dana Johnsen, "Equal Rights and the 'Heathen "Chinee"': Black Activism in San Francisco, 1865–1875," *Western Historical Quarterly*, 11 (Jan. 1980), 61, 67, indicates that in California the Chinese replaced the Irish as a negative reference group. In Colorado it apparently was the Mexicans. See Eugene H. Berwanger, "Reconstruction on the Frontier: The Equal Rights Struggle in Colorado, 1865–1867," *Pacific Historical Review*, 44 (Aug. 1975), 315.

Strong on the reactions in New York City to the Democrats' gains in Pennsylvania and Ohio in 1867: "There is joy among the *canaille* of Manhattan tonight. Its 'Dutch' lager-bier saloons and Celtic whiskey-mills lift up their heads, for their Republican 'Puritan' excise law and Sunday law enemies are smitten, at least for a season; and the chances of their discomfiture in New York next month is doubled. 'Hurrah for ould Oireland, and down with thim d—— Yankees and Naygurs!'"[5] This type of reaction is a reminder that important as race was, it was far from the only tension in nineteenth century American life. People could react just as strongly (perhaps more so, given the relatively small number of blacks in New York) to ethnic groups such as the Irish, Germans, and Yankees.

One might wonder why the same groups did not support or oppose the Irish and the blacks, both in a sense "aliens" in the eyes of native whites. Of course, one can find many individuals who were prejudiced against or sympathetic to both; yet in general this was not the case. While there is no definitive answer, one possible explanation is that the Irish were often seen as victims of their own vice while blacks appeared to be oppressed by external forces such as discriminatory laws. Removal of such laws would give the black a chance to prove himself, an opportunity which the Irish already had, but seemed unwilling to use.[6] Party needs were important too. The Irish were a valuable negative reference group for Republicans. The Democrats, though, were too dependent on immigrant voters to reject them outright as they did the blacks. Democrats who did object strongly to the party's reliance on immigrant voters generally left the party during the 1850s.

Parties did more, however, than merely channel conflicts between important groups. They also seem to have exerted an independent influence on the suffrage vote through their partisan activities. Political parties in the mid-nineteenth century were powerful institutions. They won unswerving loyalty from nearly all their adherents. They also had great control over the elective process, providing the ballots at the polls. This control helped foster a partisan vote once parties became committed on the suffrage issue. Thus the Republicans in 1869 could not be content with organizing only the "puri-

5. Allan Nevins and Milton Halsey Thomas, eds., *The Diary of George Templeton Strong* (New York: Macmillan Co., 1952), 4:152.
6. An interesting analysis of the liberal view of minorities may be found in Wilbert H. Ahern, "Laissez Faire vs. Equal Rights: Liberal Republicans and Limits to Reconstruction," *Phylon*, 60 (Mar. 1979), 52–65.

tans" behind equal suffrage. They had to broaden their appeal to include groups less inclined to be problack. Thus they argued that suffrage was linked with the war ("it [the adoption of equal suffrage] will put the constitution in harmony with reconstruction in the South"[7]) and with the well-being of the Republican Party. The strategy was effective to some degree, for although equal suffrage was defeated in 1869, support for it increased, and that increase was almost entirely among *Republicans* and in areas where suffrage had *not* been popular in 1860.

The Democrats, too, tried to influence their supporters to act together with respect to suffrage. Suffrage was never as difficult an issue for the Democratic Party as it was for the Republicans; still, the Democrats had to try to recognize the positions of both the purists and legitimists and to let neither have an unqualified triumph within the party. They watched over and controlled the use of the race issue as carefully as the Republicans.

Historians have pondered how the Republicans managed to stay in power in the 1860s when much of the North seemed hostile to legislation changing the status of the black man.[8] The answer seems to lie not only in strong partisan loyalties but also in the political stratagems used by party leaders. Republicans persistently parried the Democrats' arguments on the race question by reassuring their supporters that they contemplated no drastic changes in race relations, by stressing the expediency of their reforms, and by ridiculing the Democrats for their exaggerations on the race issue. They also hammered away at the Democrats, in traditional partisan fashion, for being prosouthern and sympathetic to the Confederacy. As a result, the Republican Party never lost in an election the support of all those who questioned its racial policies. In short, the Republicans made a poor target, and their evasive tactics usually stymied the Democrats.

Historians have long had difficulty characterizing the Republican position on black suffrage. It is possible to argue either that most leaders really wanted the reform but occasionally were forced to cite reasons of expediency (i.e., it would keep the South in check, would help Republicans, etc.) in order to overcome the objections of prejudiced whites or to say that suffrage itself would never have been

---

7. *New York Daily Reformer* (Watertown), Oct. 22, 1869.

8. Larry Kincaid, "Victims of Circumstance: An Interpretation of Changing Attitudes toward Republican Policy Makers and Reconstruction," *Journal of American History*, 57 (June 1970), 63, 66.

seriously considered *except* for those expedient reasons. Perhaps one could best characterize the Republican Party as a complex organism divided on the question of suffrage both at the leadership and grass-roots levels. Yet this division was never acceptable, for the party required and sought harmony in its operations. In the early years party leaders tried to simply dissociate the suffrage issue from the party itself. Later when the course of Reconstruction made such dissociation impossible, the party tried to manufacture unity by making appeals that would move the most prejudiced as well as the least prejudiced of its supporters. The important thing was unity.

The party did have its ideologues on behalf of equal rights, but most of them showed astute political consciousness as well. With the demise of the Liberty Party, the concept of placing adherence to principle above *every* other consideration had lost almost all its supporters. Even blacks, who certainly had the most at stake, usually accepted the political realities as defined by the major parties. Their campaign techniques and rhetoric often bore a great similarity to those used by the Republican Party. Despite some dissent, blacks normally endorsed that party as a practical, if not ideal, vehicle for achieving their goals. Rather than cling to principle to the point of dividing the party, suffrage advocates compromised at key points. They gave up on including an endorsement of black suffrage in the party platform in 1865, supported the constitutional convention bill in 1867, even after black suffrage was removed, and agreed to submitting black suffrage to the voters separately from the rest of the constitution in 1868.

On the other side, conservatives on the race question—those who did not feel morally committed to the issue or overly concerned about its fate—also showed a political consciousness and willingness to compromise. Separatist movements such as the proposed National Union Party in 1866 made little headway among them. Most legislative votes on the general *principle* of black suffrage were unanimous. In fact, the Republican Party in New York probably experienced fewer problems from factionalism and third parties in the 1860s than in any other decade of the nineteenth century.[9] Both

9. Most of this period was stable, but the 1860s were the most stable years. See Lee Benson, Joel H. Silbey, and Phyllis F. Field, "Toward a Theory of Stability and Change in American Voting Patterns: New York State, 1792–1970," in Joel H. Silbey, Allan G. Bogue, and William H. Flanigan, eds., *The History of American Electoral Behavior* (Princeton: Princeton University Press, 1978), pp. 92–94.

elements in the party were able to unite "for the good of the party." Because of these efforts to maintain unity, it is difficult to assess precisely which element was dominant in the party. The presumption, however, must be on the side of the racial liberals if only because of the significant support for the reform even before the Civil War.

It is important to understand the nature and limits of the political parties' power over the suffrage issue, however. Several historians have argued that had Republicans tried harder—stressed the issue of suffrage more and campaigned harder for it among their supporters—black suffrage might have been adopted in more states.[10] Arguments based on "if only . . ." are difficult to refute. Still, judging from New York, it is doubtful that stronger advocacy would have significantly improved the chances of the reform. Parties were powerful because they accommodated the views of a wide range of people. Had they been doctrinaire on controversial topics, the kind of blind devotion accorded them would have been far more difficult, perhaps impossible, to achieve. Voters would not accept just *anything* party leaders demanded of them. Thus in 1869 some Republicans refused to turn out for the German "wet," Sigel, just as in 1865 Democrats had rejected a state ticket featuring former Republicans.

By blurring the significance of equal suffrage, Republicans encouraged voters to support it who might not otherwise have done so. Strong advocacy of the reform promised merely to alienate people. Certainly the emphasis on equal suffrage in Yates County in 1869, for example, helped neither that cause (which received less support than in 1860) nor the Republican candidates.

While politicians tried to influence the conduct of their constituents and to maintain party unity, the rank and file also affected the behavior of their leaders. The actions of party elites—their explanations and arguments on the suffrage question and the various forms of suffrage proposals—become both logical and predictable when seen in the context of the nature and extent of political divisions on the topic. The Democrats' racism in 1860, for instance, can be seen as an attempt to stress the agreement between northern and southern Democrats on the race issue and to exploit Republican weaknesses. The Republicans in 1860 largely steered clear of black

10. See Edgar A. Toppin, "Negro Emancipation in Historic Retrospect: Ohio, the Negro Suffrage Issue in Postbellum Ohio Politics," *Journal of Human Relations*, 11 (Winter 1963), 232–46, and Michael J. McManus, "Wisconsin Republicans and Negro Suffrage: Attitudes and Behavior, 1857," *Civil War History*, 25 (Mar. 1979), 54.

suffrage to prevent a possible split. In the aftermath of the 1867 election, the Republicans agreed to separate submission of equal suffrage to the voters, apart from the constitution. In 1869 the party appealed to Germans by creating an image of the Fifteenth Amendment as one that would protect the rights of the foreign born. The amendment itself was an admission of the need to resolve the suffrage issue, but it was also an indication of the party's sense that the states could not institute the reform themselves.

The translation of equal suffrage into a partisan issue in the middle of the nineteenth century had important implications. Once it was established that the black rights question might affect whether a party won or lost an election, politicians could never view the issue without taking this important fact into consideration. Political calculations inevitably affected how the race issue was presented to the voters. Years before, Gerrit Smith had warned against any approach to the suffrage question which hinged upon political expediency rather than moral principle. As he had predicted, political pragmatists, putting party needs first, were as apt to back off from as to back black rights in times of danger. In 1867 Horace Greeley opposed allowing blacks to vote for convention delegates because "it would enable the Copperheads to raise the mad-dog cry of 'Nigger! nigger!' and so galvanize their corpse of a party into a hideous semblance of vitality."[11] Defeating Democrats came to be the main concern, not black rights per se.

Because of the kinds of appeals made, the type of commitment the Republican rank and file made to equal suffrage is open to question. Republican voters had learned more about the wrongs of traitorous copperheads than about the wrongs of racial prejudice and discrimination. Most of them came to support black voting, but the rejection of other forms of discrimination was not automatic. Thus blacks enjoyed few substantive changes in their status in many other areas. They were still aliens and outcasts when it came to attending the public schools, obtaining jobs, and using most public facilities. Most whites had never come to terms with their own prejudices. As in the period following the abolition of slavery in the North, the status of the black was merely redefined, not markedly changed. The Republican Party of this period, viewed as a whole, seemed not to have dispelled prejudice so much as to have organized support against a particular form of discrimination without necessarily

11. *New York Tribune*, Feb. 8, 1867.

trying to reduce prejudice.[12] Such limitations were inherent in the nature of America's political system. Small changes could be made; major, substantive ones were too disruptive and could not. The politics of race was grounded in this basic truth.

Thus the racial changes in the Civil War era tended to be limited and shallowly based. Even *with* the backing of the Republican Party only a minority of the public favored equal suffrage in New York in 1869, only a few months before the Fifteenth Amendment was incorporated in the U.S. Constitution. The North, like the South, seems to have found this aspect of "Reconstruction" difficult to accept. In this context of limited support for black suffrage in the North, it becomes easier to understand why the collapse of the Reconstruction governments in the South was not resisted more firmly. A reform that remained suspect from a political standpoint was always vulnerable.

To underplay the suffrage struggle, however, would be as great a mistake as to attribute too much to it. Certainly the broadening of popular support for equal suffrage for *whatever* reasons helped to remove the stigma attached to the advocacy of black rights and make it a more acceptable activity. And, as noted in the previous chapter, New Yorkers accepted black voters in practice and learned to live without the property qualification. New York no longer made an obvious distinction between black and white citizens, certainly an important first step if the state were ever to take on the responsibility of bringing about true racial equality.

The conflict over equal suffrage highlights certain characteristics of American society in the mid-nineteenth century. The lack of cultural homogeneity brought about by the massive shifts in America's growing population became the fundamental social concern. This concern arose neither from nor about a *single* group; blacks were not the only victims of discrimination. Rather, there was a whole network of group conflicts—between Catholic immigrants and the native born, Catholic and non-Catholic immigrants, evangelical and nonevangelical whites, blacks and immigrants, natives and blacks, etc. Each group felt its own identity in some way threatened by the presence of "outsiders." Thus America in this period was a nation of prejudice, discrimination, and group hostilities that involved far more than the blacks.

12. Lee Benson has suggested the need to study how political parties have served to foster and dispel prejudice. See Benson, *Concept*, p. 319n.

This conflict was not entirely random, however. Instead, the political parties in some sense managed it. They articulated in a general way the social fears of their constituent elements and used these fears as a kind of cement to bind the party together at the grass-roots level. The partisan images created over many campaigns gave voters something with which to identify (and often something to fear in the opposition). The Democrats, as the party of "limited government," appealed to those who felt themselves threatened by governmental interference with their social customs (blue laws, liquor laws, language laws, etc.). The Republicans, on the other hand, appealed precisely to those who wished to see a greater homogeneity of values achieved *through* laws. Yet as broad coalitions of many groups, parties could rarely be as positive and direct in their social statements as some of their followers might wish. What might appeal strongly to one group might offend another. Thus the Republicans, despite their "puritan" strain, for a long time avoided a forthright defense of black suffrage. They even hedged on temperance in 1869. Nor did the Democrats openly endorse Sunday drinking; instead, they insisted that the matter should be left to individual conscience, not the government, to decide. Thus the parties, while they articulated the conflict, also tended to moderate it, and to control it, in the interest of maintaining the greatest possible intraparty harmony.

This reluctance to assume extreme positions was eminently successful in achieving the objective of party unity and perhaps even in reducing the amount of violent intergroup conflict in America. People could take some satisfaction simply in the triumph of their party and not feel compelled to defend their special interests in other, more socially disruptive ways. Yet the reluctance of parties to take "radical" positions on issues also limited the possibilities for real social change in America. Parties avoided fundamental problems. Black suffrage and liquor legislation, for instance, were essentially peripheral, if highly symbolic, issues. The triumph or failure of either cause would not be earthshaking in its consequences to either party. Thus in 1870 the battle for black suffrage could be won, but the battle for black equality was never really fought.

Appendix A

Scalogram of Black Suffrage Votes
at the 1846 Constitutional Convention

Scale type	Name: County	Party	Vote 1	2	3	4
0	Archer: Wayne	Whig	+	+	+	+
0	Ayrault: Livingston	Whig	+	+	+	+
0	Bruce: Madison	Whig	+	+	+	+
0	Burr: Delaware	Whig	+	+	*	+
0	Candee: Oneida	Whig	+	+	+	+
0	Crocker: Cattaraugus	Whig	+	+	+	+
0	Dana: Madison	Whig	+	+	+	+
0	Dodd: Washington	Whig	+	+	+	+
0	Dorlon: Greene	Whig	+	+	*	*
0	Hotchkiss: Warren	Dem	+	+	+	+
0	Miller: Cortland	Whig	+	+	o	+
0	Parish: Lewis	Whig	+	+	+	+
0	Patterson: Chautauqua	Whig	+	+	+	+
0	Penniman: Orleans	Whig	+	+	+	+
0	Rhoades: Onondaga	Whig	+	+	+	+
0	Shaver: Albany	Whig	+	+	+	+
0	Simmons: Essex	Whig	+	+	+	+
0	E. Spencer: Yates	Whig	+	+	*	+
0	W. Spencer: Livingston	Whig	+	+	+	+
0	Stanton: Albany	Dem	+	+	*	+
0	Strong: Monroe	Whig	+	+	+	+
0	Taggart: Genesee	Whig	+	+	+	+
0	Waterbury: Delaware	Dem	+	+	+	+
0	Young: Wyoming	Whig	+	+	o	+
1	F. Backus: Monroe	Whig	−	+	+	+

Scale type	Name: County	Party	Vote 1	2	3	4
1	H. Backus: Monroe	Whig	−	+	+	+
1	Baker: Washington	Whig	−	+	+	+
1	Hawley: Cattaraugus	Whig	o	+	+	+
1	Kirkland: Oneida	Whig	−	+	+	+
1	McNeil: Jefferson	Dem	−	+	+	*
1	Marvin: Chautauqua	Whig	−	+	+	+
1	Richmond: Genesee	Whig	o	+	+	+
1	Tallmadge: Dutchess	Whig	−	+	+	+
1	Van Schoonhoven: Rensselaer	Whig	−	+	+	o
1	Warren: Rensselaer	Whig	−	+	+	+
1	Worden: Ontario	Whig	−	+	+	+
2	Bull: Erie	Whig	−	−	+	+
2	Danforth: Jefferson	Dem	−	−	+	*
2	Graham: Ulster	Whig	−	−	o	+
2	Greene: Jefferson	Dem	o	−	+	+
2	Hoffman: Herkimer	Dem	−	−	+	+
2	Hutchinson: Fulton & Hamilton	Dem	o	−	+	+
2	Loomis: Herkimer	Dem	−	−	+	o
2	Maxwell: Chemung	Dem	−	−	+	+
2	Nicholas: Ontario	Whig	−	−	+	+
2	Stow: Erie	Whig	−	−	+	+
2	Willard: Albany	Dem	−	−	+	o
3	Allen: New York	Dem	−	−	−	+
3	Bergen: Kings	Dem	−	−	−	+
3	Bowdish: Montgomery	Dem	−	−	−	+
3	D. Campbell: Schenectady	Dem	−	−	−	o
3	Cook: Saratoga	Whig	−	−	−	+
3	Harrison: Richmond	Whig	−	−	−	+
3	Kemble: Putnam	Dem	o	−	−	+
3	Kernan: Steuben	Dem	−	−	−	+
3	Kingsley: Onondaga	Dem	−	−	−	+
3	Munro: Onondaga	Dem	−	−	−	+
3	Nellis: Montgomery	Dem	−	−	−	+
3	Porter: Saratoga	Whig	−	−	−	+
3	Ruggles: Dutchess	Dem	−	o	−	+
3	St. John: Otsego	Dem	−	−	−	+
3	Shaw: Cayuga	Dem	−	−	−	o
3	Taft: Wayne	Dem	−	−	−	o
3	Tuthill: Orange	Dem	−	−	−	+
3	Wright: Erie	Whig	−	−	−	+
4	Brown: Orange	Dem	o	−	−	−
4	Brundage: Steuben	Dem	−	−	−	−
4	Clark: Oswego	Dem	o	−	−	−
4	Conely: New York	Dem	−	−	−	−
4	Cornell: New York	Dem	*	−	−	−

Scale type	Name: County	Party	Vote 1	2	3	4
4	Cuddeback: Orange	Dem	–	–	–	–
4	Dubois: Dutchess	Dem	–	–	–	–
4	Hunt: New York	Dem	–	–	–	–
4	A. Huntington: Suffolk	Dem	–	–	–	–
4	Jones: New York	Dem	o	–	–	–
4	Kennedy: New York	Dem	–	–	–	–
4	Mann: New York	Dem	o	–	–	–
4	Morris: New York	Dem	–	–	–	–
4	Nicoll: New York	Dem	–	–	–	–
4	O'Conor: New York	Dem	–	–	–	–
4	Perkins: St. Lawrence	Dem	–	–	–	–
4	Riker: Queens	Dem	–	–	–	–
4	Russell: St. Lawrence	Dem	–	–	o	–
4	Sanford: St. Lawrence	Dem	–	–	–	–
4	Sheldon: Cayuga	Dem	–	–	–	–
4	Stephens: New York	Dem	o	–	–	–
4	Swackhamer: Kings	Dem	–	–	–	–
4	J. Taylor: Tioga	Dem	–	–	–	–
4	Tilden: New York	Dem	o	–	–	–
4	Townshend: New York	Dem	–	–	–	–
4	Tracy: Chenango	Dem	–	–	–	–
4	Wood: Rockland	Dem	–	–	–	–
4	Yawger: Cayuga	Dem	–	–	–	–
4	Youngs: Tompkins	Dem	–	–	–	–

Coefficient of reproducibility = .97.

Five Democrats were absent on all roll calls (Bouck of Sullivan, Chatfield and Nelson of Otsego, Gardiner of Niagara, and Hunter of Westchester), as were three Whigs (Gebbard of Schoharie, Harris of Albany, and Jordan of Columbia).

+, favorable to suffrage; –, unfavorable to suffrage; o, absent; *, inconsistent response (explained below).

The four votes (in scale order) were:

Vote 1—Motion to remove the property qualification (at end of session). Defeated 29–75.

Vote 2—Motion to remove word white from voter qualifications. Defeated 37–63.

Vote 3—Motion to reduce property qualification to $100. Defeated 42–50.

Vote 4—Motion to keep $250 property qualification for blacks. Passed 62–32.

Delegates absent on two or more roll calls

		Vote			
Name: County	Party	1	2	3	4
Brayton: Oneida	Whig	+	o	o	o
Flanders: Franklin	Dem	+	o	o	o
E. Huntington: Oneida	Whig	+	o	o	+
Stetson: Clinton	Dem	+	o	o	o
Bascom: Seneca	Whig	o	+	o	o
Hart: Oswego	Dem	o	o	+	+
Wright: Sullivan	Whig	o	o	+	+
R. Campbell: Steuben	Dem	o	−	o	+
Ward: Westchester	Dem	o	o	o	+
Angel: Allegany	Dem	−	−	o	o
Cambrelling: Suffolk	Dem	−	o	o	o
Chamberlain: Allegany	Dem	−	o	o	o
Clyde: Columbia	Whig	−	−	o	o
Forsythe: Ulster	Whig	−	o	o	o
Hyde: Broome	Dem	−	o	o	o
McNitt: Niagara	Dem	−	−	o	o
Murphy: Kings	Dem	−	o	o	o
Powers: Greene	Dem	−	−	o	o
Salisbury: Erie	Whig	−	o	o	o
Sears: Tompkins	Dem	−	o	o	o
Shepard: New York	Dem	−	o	o	o
Smith: Chenango	Dem	−	o	o	o
W. Taylor: Onondaga	Dem	−	−	o	o
Vache: New York	Dem	−	o	o	o
White: New York	Dem	−	o	o	o
Witback: Rensselaer	Dem	−	o	o	o

Absences and "inconsistent" responses (favoring an extreme measure but opposing a less extreme one, e.g., voting to let all blacks vote but then rejecting the property qualification so that no blacks would be able to vote) create classification problems in a Guttman scale. Individuals missing two or more roll calls were excluded from the scale and are listed separately above. Single absences that left it unclear in which scale type a man belonged have been resolved by choosing the one nearest to the median for the entire group. Similarly, delegates responding inconsistently were placed in the category where those inconsistencies were minimized. Most of these delegates were troubled by the proposal to reduce the property qualification to $100. Some initially opposed *any* property qualification but later changed their minds when reminded that blacks

would be distressed to lose the few rights they then had. See William
G. Bishop and William H. Attree, *Report of the Debates and Proceedings
of the Convention for the Revision of the Constitution of the State of New
York, 1846* (Albany: Evening Atlas, 1846), pp. 1034, 1036.

Appendix B

Per Cent Voting Prosuffrage, by Counties, 1846, 1860, and 1869

County	*1846*	*1860*	*Change 1846–60*	*1869*	*Change 1860–69*
Albany	25.6	34.5	8.9	44.9	10.4
Allegany	35.1	61.5	26.4	65.3	3.8
Broome	21.1	44.3	23.1	56.2	11.9
Cattaraugus	53.7	56.5	2.8	57.9	1.4
Cayuga	23.6	57.3	33.7	59.6	2.3
Chautauqua	40.1	57.9	17.8	65.2	7.3
Chemung	24.5	33.7	9.2	42.4	8.7
Chenango	25.5	46.9	21.4	52.4	5.5
Clinton	72.8	47.1	− 25.7	44.5	− 2.6
Columbia	11.2	25.0	13.8	43.8	18.8
Cortland	52.5	60.6	8.1	62.0	1.4
Delaware	33.3	44.7	11.4	50.7	6.0
Dutchess	11.6	21.9	10.3	50.4	28.5
Erie	28.2	31.3	3.1	63.4	32.1
Essex	70.8	57.8	− 13.0	58.0	0.2
Franklin	58.8	52.3	− 6.5	54.9	2.6
Fulton/Hamilton	15.1	24.7	9.6	47.1	22.4
Genesee	43.6	59.7	16.1	59.1	− 0.6
Greene	5.3	10.8	5.5	33.9	23.1
Herkimer	31.4	48.0	16.6	49.5	1.5
Jefferson	38.1	48.4	10.3	54.0	5.6
Kings	20.3	19.1	− 1.2	41.8	22.7
Lewis	42.5	42.7	0.2	51.5	8.8
Livingston	27.2	49.0	21.8	56.3	7.3

County	1846	1860	Change 1846–60	1869	Change 1860–69
Madison	53.1	62.2	9.0	59.9	−2.3
Monroe	47.0	42.2	−4.8	51.6	9.4
Montgomery	13.4	10.6	−2.8	43.7	33.1
New York	14.6	13.9	−0.7	29.6	15.7
Niagara	27.8	37.8	10.0	47.8	10.0
Oneida	39.4	46.6	7.2	51.7	5.1
Onondaga	39.3	52.8	13.5	55.4	2.6
Ontario	36.5	51.4	14.9	56.9	5.5
Orange	6.9	10.2	3.3	47.8	37.6
Orleans	37.1	53.8	16.7	58.8	5.0
Oswego	57.8	57.3	−0.5	61.6	4.3
Otsego	22.4	44.0	21.6	48.1	4.1
Putnam	2.3	7.0	4.7	32.9	25.9
Queens	2.1	7.7	5.6	38.5	30.8
Rensselaer	38.6	40.0	1.4	47.4	7.4
Richmond	4.5	5.4	0.9	38.9	33.5
Rockland	3.6	2.4	−1.2	35.5	33.1
St. Lawrence	34.7	66.8	32.1	75.4	8.6
Saratoga	14.6	27.5	12.9	43.8	16.3
Schenectady	16.0	19.9	3.9	36.0	16.1
Schoharie	7.2	18.0	10.8	38.7	20.7
Schuyler	24.1	48.3	24.2	53.0	4.7
Seneca	21.5	35.4	13.9	44.1	8.7
Steuben	19.1	47.8	28.6	52.6	4.8
Suffolk	7.9	19.0	11.1	45.9	26.9
Sullivan	8.4	10.7	2.3	38.6	27.9
Tioga	26.7	43.6	16.9	55.4	11.8
Tompkins	26.2	48.7	22.5	58.9	10.2
Ulster	4.4	13.1	8.7	39.4	26.3
Warren	56.3	48.0	−8.3	47.1	−0.9
Washington	60.0	56.2	−3.8	56.9	0.7
Wayne	30.9	50.2	19.3	50.2	0.0
Westchester	4.1	11.3	7.2	42.7	31.4
Wyoming	57.7	58.2	0.5	61.8	3.6
Yates	35.4	60.7	25.3	58.4	−2.3

Appendix C

The Township Data

New York State election officials preserved only the county returns from the three equal suffrage referenda. The township returns upon which much of the analysis of the referenda is based had to be recovered from various county sources (see Appendix D). Not all returns could be located. Thus the township sample is based on availability and must be carefully scrutinized. Tables A.1 to A.3 compare the counties for which township data were available to the state as a whole in order to alert readers to any possible biases in these counties. In general the "township counties" closely resembled the state as a whole. The most noticeable difference was that the township returns in 1846 were somewhat more heavily from the eastern, older area of New York, but even so the discrepancy was not very great.

The thirty-five counties for which township returns were located in 1846 were: Albany, Broome, Cattaraugus, Cayuga, Chemung, Chenango, Clinton, Cortland, Delaware, Dutchess, Greene, Herkimer, Lewis, Madison, Monroe, New York, Oneida, Ontario, Orange, Oswego, Queens, Rensselaer, Saratoga, Schenectady, Schoharie, Schuyler, Seneca, Steuben, Suffolk, Tompkins, Ulster, Warren, Westchester, Wyoming, and Yates. Table A.1 compares characteristics of these counties to the state as a whole.

In 1860 township returns were found for forty-nine counties: Albany, Allegany, Broome, Cattaraugus, Cayuga, Chautauqua, Che-

TABLE A.3.

Characteristics of "township counties" in 1869 and combined 1860 and 1869, and of whole state

Characteristic	Township counties 1869	Township counties 1860 and 1869	Whole state
Per cent prosuffrage 1869	47.2	46.7	46.9
Per cent Republican[a] 1869	49.0	48.6	48.4
Per cent born New England	4.3	4.1	4.3
Per cent born Ireland	11.0	11.4	11.6
Per cent born Germany[b]	6.4	6.8	6.5
Per cent born England, Scotland, Wales	3.1	3.1	3.3
Per cent born Canada[c]	1.8	1.6	1.7
Per cent born New Jersey	0.9	0.9	1.0
Per cent born Pennsylvania	1.0	1.0	1.0
Per cent black	1.0	1.1	1.2
Per cent Dutch Reformed communicants	4.2	4.2	4.7
Per cent population in area settled pre-1790	51.1	52.1	55.9
Average value of dwelling per family	$1,345	$1,396	$1,390
Per cent landowners	10.1	9.9	9.8

[a]Voting for secretary of state.
[b]Includes Prussia.
[c]Includes Newfoundland, Nova Scotia, and Prince Edward Island.
SOURCES: *Evening Journal Almanac,* 1870; *Census of the State of New York for 1865* (Albany, 1867).

Appendix D

Sources of Township Returns

Albany
1846: *Albany Argus*, Nov. 21, 1846.
1860: *Albany Argus*, Dec. 18, 1860.
1869: *Albany Argus*, Nov. 29, 1869.

Allegany
1860: *Genesee Valley Free Press* (Wellsville), Nov. 22, 1860.
1869: *Angelica Reporter*, Dec. 15, 1869.

Broome
1846: *Broome Republican* (Binghamton), Nov. 18, 1846.
1860: Broome County Board of Supervisors, *Proceedings*, 1860.
1869: Broome County Board of Supervisors, *Proceedings*, 1869.

Cattaraugus
1846: *Cattaraugus Republican* (Ellicottville), Nov. 16, 1846.
1860: *Olean Times*, Nov. 24, 1860.
1869: *Cattaraugus Republican*, Nov. 18, 1869.

Cayuga
1846: *Auburn Journal & Advertiser*, Nov. 18, 1846.
1860: *Auburn Daily Advertiser*, Nov. 16, 1860.
1869: *Auburn Daily Advertiser*, Nov. 12, 1869.

Chautauqua
1860: *Mayville Sentinel*, Nov. 28, 1860.
1869: Chautauqua County Board of Supervisors, *Proceedings*, 1869.

Chemung
1846: *Elmira Gazette*, Nov. 12, 1846.

1860: *Elmira Weekly Advertiser,* Nov. 24, 1860.
1869: *Elmira Daily Advertiser,* Nov. 13, 1869.
Chenango
1846: *Chenango Telegraph* (Norwich), Nov. 18, 1846.
1860: *Chenango Telegraph,* Nov. 21, 1860.
1869: *Chenango Telegraph,* Nov. 17, 1869.
Clinton
1846: *Plattsburgh Republican,* Nov. 14, 1846.
1860: *Plattsburgh Republican,* Nov. 24, 1860.
1869: *Plattsburgh Republican,* Nov. 13, 1869.
Columbia
1860: Columbia County Board of Supervisors, *Proceedings,* 1860.
1869: Columbia County Board of Supervisors, *Proceedings,* 1869.
Cortland
1846: John Langley Stanley, "Majority Tyranny in Tocqueville's America: The Failure of Negro Suffrage in New York State in 1846" (Ph.D. diss., Cornell University, 1966), p. 192.
1860: *Cortland Republican Banner,* Dec. 5, 1860.
1869: *Cortland County Democrat,* Nov. 19, 1869.
Delaware
1846: *Delaware Gazette* (Delhi), Nov. 18, 1846.
1860: *Delaware Gazette,* Nov. 21, 1860.
1869: *Delaware Gazette,* Dec. 15, 1869.
Dutchess
1846: *Poughkeepsie Journal & Eagle,* Nov. 14, 1846.
1860: *Poughkeepsie Eagle,* Nov. 24, 1860.
Erie
1860: *Buffalo Express,* Nov. 27, 1860.
1869: *Buffalo Express,* Nov. 30, 1869.
Essex
1860: *Elizabethtown Post,* Nov. 23, 1860.
1869: *Elizabethtown Post,* Nov. 18, 1869.
Fulton
1869: Fulton County Board of Supervisors, *Proceedings.* 1869.
Genesee
1860: *Republican Advocate* (Batavia), Nov. 27, 1860.
1869: *The Spirit of the Times* (Batavia), Nov. 13, 1869.
Greene
1846: *Catskill Democrat,* Nov. 13, 1846.
1869: *Catskill Recorder and Democrat,* Nov. 19, 1869.
Herkimer
1846: *Mohawk Courier* (Little Falls), Nov. 19, 1846.

1860: Herkimer County Board of Supervisors, *Proceedings,* 1860.
1869: Herkimer County Board of Supervisors, *Proceedings,* 1869.

Jefferson

1860: *New York Reformer* (Watertown), Nov. 22, 1860.
1869: Jefferson County Board of Supervisors, *Proceedings,* 1869.

Lewis

1846: *Lewis County Republican* (Lowville), Nov. 18, 1846.
1860: *Lowville Journal & Republican,* Nov. 28, 1860.
1869: *Lowville Journal & Republican,* Nov. 17, 1869.

Livingston

1860: *Livingston Republican* (Geneseo), Nov. 22, 1860.
1869: *Livingston Republican,* Nov. 18, 1869.

Madison

1846: *Madison Democrat* (Chittenango), Nov. 18, 1846.
1860: *Oneida Sachem,* Nov. 22, 1860.
1869: *Oneida Dispatch,* Nov. 19, 1869.

Monroe

1846: *Rochester Daily American,* Nov. 21, 1846.
1860: *Rochester Union and Advertiser,* Nov. 21, 1860.
1869: Monroe County Board of Supervisors, *Proceedings,* 1869.

Montgomery

1860: *Montgomery Republican* (Fultonville), Nov. 27, 1860.
1869: *Montgomery County Republican,* Nov. 16, 1869.

New York

1846: *New York Tribune,* Nov. 7, 1846.
1860: *New York Tribune,* Nov. 16, 1860 (incomplete).
1869: *New York Tribune,* Dec. 1, 1869.

Niagara

1860: *Niagara Falls Gazette,* Nov. 28, 1860.
1869: Niagara County Board of Supervisors, *Proceedings,* 1869.

Oneida

1846: *The Roman Citizen,* Nov. 24, 1846.
1860: *The Roman Citizen,* Nov. 28, 1860.
1869: *Utica Morning Herald,* Nov. 15, 1869.

Onondaga

1860: Onondaga County Board of Supervisors, *Proceedings,* 1860.
1869: Onondaga County Board of Supervisors, *Proceedings,* 1869.

Ontario

1846: *Ontario Repository* (Canandaigua), Nov. 17, 1846.

Orange

1846: *Newburgh Telegraph,* Nov. 19, 1846.
1860: *Middletown Mercury,* Nov. 23, 1860.

1869: Orange County Board of Supervisors, *Proceedings,* 1869.

Orleans

1869: Orleans County Board of Supervisors, *Proceedings,* 1869.

Oswego

1846: *Oswego Palladium,* Nov. 17, 1846.

1860: Oswego County Board of Supervisors, *Proceedings,* 1860.

1869: Oswego County Board of Supervisors, *Proceedings,* 1869.

Otsego

1860: *Freeman's Journal* (Cooperstown), Nov. 23, 1860.

1869: *Oneonta Herald,* Nov. 17, 1869.

Putnam

1869: *Putnam County Courier* (Carmel), Nov. 13, 1869.

Queens

1846: Stanley, "Majority Tyranny," p. 179.

1860: *Long Island Democrat* (Jamaica), Nov. 20, 1860.

Rensselaer

1846: *Troy Daily Whig,* Nov. 13, 1846.

1860: *Troy Daily Budget,* Dec. 5, 1860.

1869: Rensselaer County Board of Supervisors, *Proceedings,* 1869.

Richmond

1860: *Richmond County Gazette* (Staten Island), Nov. 7, 1860.

Rockland

1860: *Rockland County Messenger* (Haverstraw), Nov. 15, 1860.

1869: *Rockland County Messenger,* Nov. 11, 1869.

St. Lawrence

1869: St. Lawrence County Board of Supervisors, *Proceedings,* 1869.

Saratoga

1846: Saratoga County Commissioner of Elections Office.

1860: Saratoga County Commissioner of Elections Office.

1869: *Saratogian* (Saratoga Springs), Nov. 11, 1869.

Schenectady

1846: *The Schenectady Cabinet,* Nov. 17, 1846.

1860: *Schenectady Democrat and Reflector,* Nov. 22, 1860.

Schoharie

1846: *Schoharie Republican,* Nov. 24, 1846.

1860: *The Schoharie Patriot,* Nov. 29, 1860.

1869: *Schoharie Republican,* Nov. 18, 1869.

Schuyler

1846: Recreated from Tompkins, Steuben, and Chemung returns (see Appendix E).

1860: *Havana Journal,* Nov. 24, 1860.

1869: *Watkins Express,* Nov. 11, 1869.

Seneca
1846: Seneca County Election Commissioners Office.
1860: Seneca County Election Commissioners Office.
1869: Seneca County Election Commissioners Office.
Steuben
1846: *Steuben Courier* (Bath), date unknown.
1860: *Steuben Farmer's Advocate* (Bath), Nov. 21, 1860.
1869: *Corning Journal*, Nov. 25, 1869.
Suffolk
1846: *Sag Harbor Corrector*, Nov. 21, 1846.
1860: *Sag Harbor Express*, Nov. 22, 1860.
1869: *The Long Islander* (Huntington), Dec. 3, 1869.
Sullivan
1869: Sullivan County Board of Supervisors, *Proceedings*, 1869.
Tioga
1860: *The Owego Times*, Nov. 22, 1860.
1869: *Owego Gazette*, Nov. 18, 1869.
Tompkins
1846: *Ithaca Journal & General Advertiser*, Nov. 18, 1846.
1860: *Ithaca Journal*, Nov. 14, 1860.
1869: *Ithaca Democrat*, Nov. 18, 1869.
Ulster
1846: Provided by John Langley Stanley, source unknown.
1860: *Kingston Democratic Journal*, Nov. 21, 1860.
1869: *Kingston Journal*, Nov. 17, 1869.
Warren
1846: *Glens Falls Republican*, Nov. 24, 1846.
1869: *Glens Falls Republican*, Nov. 16, 1869.
Washington
1860: *Salem Press*, Nov. 27, 1860.
1869: *Washington County Post* (Cambridge), Nov. 19, 1869.
Wayne
1860: *Wayne Democratic Press* (Lyons), Nov. 28, 1860.
1869: *Clyde Times*, Dec. 2, 1869.
Westchester
1846: *Westchester Herald* (White Plains), Nov. 17, 1846.
1860: Westchester County Board of Supervisors, *Proceedings*, 1860.
1869: Westchester County Board of Supervisors, *Proceedings*, 1869.
Wyoming
1846: *Western New Yorker* (Warsaw), Nov. 18, 1846.
1860: *Wyoming County Mirror* (Warsaw), Nov. 28, 1860.

Yates

1846: *Yates County Whig* (Penn Yan), Nov. 24, 1846.
1860: *Yates County Chronicle* (Penn Yan), Nov. 22, 1860.
1869: *Yates County Chronicle,* Nov. 25, 1869.

I am indebted to the Steuben County historian, Greene County historian, Orleans County historian, and John Langley Stanley for locating or providing canvasses.

Appendix E

Data Analysis

The analysis of voting returns from as early as the 1840s presents a number of problems for the researcher. One difficulty involves shifts in town and ward boundaries. When data from different years have been correlated, it has been necessary to combine those areas whose borders changed in the interim. It was also deemed appropriate to exclude from correlation analysis any town at least half of whose voters failed to participate in a suffrage referendum. Thus in 1846, 5 of 525 towns were omitted; in 1860, 8 of 892; and in 1869, 44 of 954.

The electoral analysis in Chapter 3 was based on county-level returns because full township returns were unavailable before 1858. Schuyler County was created in 1854 from parts of three other counties. For analyses before that date the votes of the townships that eventually made up Schuyler have been combined to create a "dummy" county for the purposes of the correlation. Electoral reports often combined the returns of the relatively unpopulated Hamilton County with its neighbor Fulton, and so they were treated as one county throughout. A total of fifty-nine counties, therefore, were used in the voting analysis. Returns used were always those for the highest state office except in 1859 when the two top offices were used because the American Party in that year supported the Democratic candidate for secretary of state but the Republican nominee for comptroller.

Measuring the strength of religious denominations was quite difficult. The 1845 state census simply listed the churches of each denomination in a town. Two variables were derived from this information. One gave the proportion of all churches belonging to a particular denomination (possibly biased if some churches accommodated more than others); the other compared the number of churches of a denomination to the size of the town's population. Both variables correlated highly but still gave only a very general view of the actual religious makeup of towns. Subsequent state censuses in 1855 and 1865 gave more precise information on the number of communicants a church had, its usual attendance, etc. However, individual churches provided this information and undoubtedly used different definitions for these terms. The matter is further complicated by possible church attendance across township or ward lines.

It was also difficult to establish which churches were evangelical and which nonevangelical since many denominations (such as the Presbyterians) were divided. Descriptions in county histories were sometimes helpful, but such information was not generally available for all locales. Therefore a variable was created that encompassed only denominations that appeared definitely to be nonevangelical (Catholics, Dutch Reformed, Episcopalians, Calvinist Methodists, and Old School Baptists) and this variable was used in the analysis. Given the difficulties, the data on religion can only suggest trends, rather than measure them precisely.

The state censuses were the usual sources for demographic data even though two referenda, 1860 and 1869, were nearer the dates of federal censuses. Only the state censuses, however, gave detailed information on townships. Although towns could and did change in a four or five year period, their *relative* position with respect to other towns was less likely to change drastically. Towns that had many Irishmen in 1855, for example, would usually also be among the leaders in that category in 1860 as well.

Voting returns may be analyzed in several ways. With simple correlation coefficients one can measure the extent to which the presence or absence of some population characteristic varied with the prosuffrage percentages across a state. The closer the coefficient is to one, the stronger the relationship; the sign of the coefficient indicates whether the two variables are moving in the same or opposing directions. A positive correlation means the two variables increase or decrease together, a negative correlation that one increases while the other decreases. The square of the correlation coefficient (r^2) indicates the proportion of the variation in the dependent variable that can be "explained" by the independent variable. Several caveats are associated with the use of correlations. Correlation does not necessarily mean causation. Because two variables correlate well or poorly at the township level, it does not follow that the same relationship holds between individuals in those towns. Outliers (extreme cases) and nonlinear relationships may bias correlations, and they necessitate the checking of scatterplots before the validity of a correlation can be established.

Since some characteristics were present in only a limited number of towns (German population, for instance), it is also fruitful at times to study separately those towns most heavily populated by a particular group. However, groups who live together may also tend to reinforce each other's outlooks, whereas members of a group living isolated from other members of the group may be somewhat more likely to hold contrary opinions. It was certainly most common, however, for a minority to cluster together and to form institutions (such as churches) which brought its members together and reinforced their common backgrounds and values.

Multiple regression helps to measure the independent contribution of a variety of variables in explaining a dependent variable, such as the support for equal suffrage. Independent variables must be selected carefully for a regression equation because a high correlation between any of them would result in an infinite number of possible solutions for the regression equation and thus cause the results to be misleading. The criteria used for the selection of variables were a correlation of at least .3 with the dependent variable but no more than .7 with any other independent variable.

Historians have increasingly turned to ecological regression to estimate, using ecological data, how individuals voted. Using this method, one can estimate the actual percentage of Democrats and Republicans who voted for equal suffrage, opposed it, or abstained. This method has not been employed because it was felt that the statistical assumptions on which it is based (especially that the affected groups divided the same way in all the townships or differed only randomly in how they divided) were not met in New York in the voting on the suffrage referenda. For instance, in 1860 it is clear that Republicans in the eastern part of the state were much more likely to abstain than were those in the west.

BIBLIOGRAPHY OF
PRIMARY SOURCES

A. MANUSCRIPTS

Albany. New York State Library:
Edwin D. Morgan papers, Horatio Seymour papers, and John V. S. L. Pruyn journals (microfilm).
Ithaca. Cornell University Library:
Francis Kernan papers and Andrew D. White papers.
New York City. New York Historical Society:
Horatio Seymour papers.
New York City. New York Public Library:
Horace Greeley papers and Samuel J. Tilden papers.
Rochester. University of Rochester Library:
Thurlow Weed papers and William Henry Seward papers.
Syracuse. George Arents Research Library at Syracuse University:
Gerrit Smith papers.
Washington. Library of Congress:
Salmon P. Chase papers, James P. Doolittle papers, William P. Fessenden papers, Andrew Johnson papers (microfilm), Manton M. Marble papers, and Gideon Welles papers.

B. NEWSPAPERS (ARRANGED BY COUNTY)

Albany	*Albany Argus*, 1845–1870
	Albany Evening Journal, 1845–1870
Allegany	*Angelica Reporter*, 1869
	Genesee Valley Free Press (Wellsville), 1860
Cattaraugus	*Cattaraugus Republican* (Ellicottville), 1846
	Cattaraugus Republican (Little Valley), 1869
	Olean Times, 1860
Cayuga	*Auburn Daily Advertiser*, 1846, 1860, 1869
	Auburn Daily Union, 1860
	Auburn Journal and Advertiser, 1846

Chautauqua   *Fredonia Censor,* 1860
              Jamestown Journal, 1846, 1860, 1869
              Mayville Sentinel, 1860
Chemung   *Elmira Advertiser,* 1860, 1869
              Elmira Gazette, 1846
Chenango   *Chenango American* (Greene), 1860, 1869
              Chenango Telegraph (Norwich), 1846, 1860, 1869
Clinton   *Plattsburgh Republican,* 1846, 1860, 1869
Cortland   *Cortland County Democrat,* 1869
              Cortland Democrat, 1846
              Cortland Republican Banner, 1860
Delaware   *Delaware Gazette* (Delhi), 1846, 1860, 1869
Dutchess   *Poughkeepsie Eagle,* 1860, 1869
              Poughkeepsie Journal and Eagle, 1846
Erie   *Buffalo Courier,* 1860, 1867–1870
              Buffalo Courier and Pilot, 1846
              Buffalo Demokrat, 1869
Essex   *Elizabethtown Post,* 1860, 1869
Franklin   *Malone Palladium,* 1860, 1869
Genesee   *Republican Advocate* (Batavia), 1860
              Spirit of the Times (Batavia), 1846, 1869
Herkimer   *Herkimer County Journal* (Little Falls), 1860
Jefferson   *New York Reformer* (Watertown), 1860, 1869
Kings   *Brooklyn City News,* 1860
              Brooklyn Eagle, 1846, 1860, 1869
              Brooklyn Evening Star, 1846, 1860
              Brooklyn Standard, 1860
Lewis   *Lowville Journal & Republican,* 1860, 1869
Livingston   *Dansville Advertiser,* 1860, 1869
              Livingston Democrat (Dansville), 1860
              Livingston Republican (Geneseo), 1860, 1869
Madison   *Madison Democrat* (Chittenango), 1846
              Madison Observer (Morrisville), 1846, 1860, 1869
              Oneida Dispatch, 1869
              Oneida Sachem, 1860
Monroe   *Douglass' Monthly,* 1859–1860
              Frederick Douglass' Paper, 1855
              Rochester Daily Advertiser, 1846
              Rochester Daily American, 1846
              Rochester Democrat, 1846
              Rochester Union and Advertiser, 1860, 1869
Montgomery   *Montgomery County Republican* (Fultonville), 1860, 1869
New York   *The Day Book,* 1860
              Harper's Weekly, 1865–1870
              The Independent, 1865, 1867, 1869

	The Nation, 1865–1870
	National Anti-Slavery Standard, 1858–1861, 1867–1869
	New York Evening Post, 1860, 1867, 1869
	New York Herald, 1846, 1855–1869
	New York Morning Express, 1860
	New York Times, 1855–1870
	New York Tribune, 1845–1870
	New York World, 1860–1870
	Radical Abolitionist, 1855–1858
	Weekly Anglo-African, 1859–1860
Niagara	*Niagara Falls Gazette,* 1860, 1869
Oneida	*Roman Citizen,* 1846, 1860
	Utica Daily Gazette, 1846
	Utica Daily Observer, 1869
	Utica Morning Herald, 1860, 1869
Onondaga	*Skaneateles Democrat,* 1846
	Syracuse Daily Standard, 1860, 1869
Ontario	*Geneva Courier,* 1860
	Geneva Gazette, 1869
	Ontario County Times (Canandaigua), 1860, 1869
Orange	*Middletown Mercury,* 1860
	Newburgh Daily News, 1860
	Newburgh Telegraph, 1846, 1860
Oswego	*Oswego Palladium,* 1846
Otsego	*Freeman's Journal* (Cooperstown), 1860
	Oneonta Herald, 1860, 1869
Putnam	*Putnam County Courier* (Carmel), 1869
Queens	*Flushing Journal,* 1869
	Long Island Democrat (Jamaica), 1860, 1869
	Long Island Times (Flushing), 1869
	Queens County Sentinel (Hempstead), 1869
Rensselaer	*Troy Daily Budget,* 1860
	Troy Daily Whig, 1846
Richmond	*Richmond County Gazette* (Staten Island), 1860, 1869
Rockland	*Rockland County Messenger* (Haverstraw), 1860, 1869
St. Lawrence	*St. Lawrence Plain Dealer* (Canton), 1869
	St. Lawrence Republican (Ogdensburg), 1846, 1860, 1869
Saratoga	*Saratogian* (Saratoga Springs), 1869
Schenectady	*Schenectady Daily Union,* 1869
	Schenectady Democrat and Reflector, 1860
	Schenectady Evening Star, 1869
	Schenectady Reflector, 1869
Schoharie	*Schoharie Patriot,* 1860
	Schoharie Republican, 1846, 1869
	Schoharie Union, 1869

Schuyler   *Havana Journal*, 1860
              Watkins Express, 1869
Seneca   *Ovid Bee*, 1860, 1869
Steuben   *Corning Journal*, 1860, 1869
              Steuben Courier (Bath), 1846
              Steuben Farmer's Advocate (Bath), 1860, 1869
Suffolk   *The Long Islander* (Huntington), 1846, 1860, 1869
              Sag Harbor Corrector, 1846
              Sag Harbor Express, 1860
              Suffolk Herald (Patchogue), 1860
              Suffolk Union (Riverhead), 1860
              Suffolk Weekly Times (Greenport), 1860
Tioga   *Owego Gazette*, 1869
              Owego Times, 1860
Tompkins   *American Citizen* (Ithaca), 1860
              Ithaca Daily Chronicle, 1846
              Ithaca Democrat, 1869
              Ithaca Journal, 1846, 1860, 1869
              Trumansburg Free Press, 1869
Ulster   *Kingston Journal*, 1860, 1869
Warren   *Glens Falls Republican*, 1860, 1869
Washington   *Salem Press*, 1860, 1869
              Washington County Post (Cambridge), 1869
Wayne   *Clyde Times*, 1869
              Lyons Republican, 1869
              Newark Courier, 1869
              Palmyra Courier-Journal, 1869
              Wayne Democratic Press (Lyons), 1860
Westchester   *Peekskill Republican*, 1846
              Yonkers Statesman, 1869
Wyoming   *Silver Lake Sun* (Perry), 1869
              Western New Yorker (Warsaw), 1846, 1869
              Wyoming County Mirror (Warsaw), 1860
Yates   *Yates County Chronicle* (Penn Yan), 1860, 1869
              Yates County Whig (Penn Yan), 1846.

C. PRINTED SOURCE COLLECTIONS AND OFFICIAL DOCUMENTS

The American Annual Cyclopaedia and Register of Important Events of the Year 1861 [and succeeding years to 1869]. New York: D. Appleton & Co., 1862–1870.
Census of the State of New York for 1845. Albany: Carroll and Cook, 1846.
Census of the State of New York for 1855. Albany: C. Van Benthuysen, 1857.
Census of the State of New York for 1865. Albany: Charles Van Benthuysen & Son, 1867.
Census of the State of New York for 1875. Albany: Weed, Parsons & Co., 1877.

Debates and Proceedings in the New York State Convention for the Revision of the Constitution. Reported by S. Croswell and R. Sutton. New York: Albany Argus, 1846.

Documents of the Convention of the State of New York, 1867–68. 5 vols. Albany: Weed, Parsons & Co., 1868.

Evening Journal Almanac (Albany), 1859–1870.

Foner, Philip S. And Walker, George W., eds. *Proceedings of the Black State Conventions, 1840–1865.* Philadelphia: Temple University Press, 1979-. One volume to date.

Journal of the Convention of the State of New York. Albany: Weed, Parsons & Co., 1868.

McPherson, Edward. *The Political History of the United States of America during the Period of Reconstruction.* 2nd ed. Washington, D.C.: Solomons & Chapman, 1871.

Manual for the Use of the Legislature of the State of New York, 1854 [and succeeding years through 1872]. Albany: Weed, Parsons & Co., 1854–1872.

New York (County) Supervisers Board. *Documents.* 1870.

New York State Assembly. *Documents.* 60th–93rd Sess. 1837–1870.

New York State Assembly, *Journal.* 60th–93rd Sess. 1837–1870.

New York State Senate. *Documents.* 60th–93rd Sess. 1837–1870.

New York State Senate. *Journal.* 60th–93rd Sess. 1837–1870.

Population Schedules of the Seventh Census of the United States: New York (microfilm).

Population of the United States in 1860. Washington, D.C.: Government Printing Office, 1864.

Porter, Kirk H. and Johnson, Donald B. *National Party Platforms, 1840–1964.* Urbana: University of Illinois Press, 1966.

Proceedings and Debates of the Constitutional Convention of the State of New York. Reported by Edward F. Underhill. 5 vols. Albany: Weed, Parsons & Co., 1868.

Report of the Debates and Proceedings of the Convention for the Revision of the Constitution of the State of New York, 1846. Reported by William G. Bishop and William H. Attree. Albany: Evening Atlas, 1846.

Reports of the Proceedings and Debates of the Convention of 1821. Reported by Nathaniel H. Carter and William L. Stone. Albany: E. And E. Hosford, 1821.

Revision Documents of the Constitutional Convention of the State of New York, 1867–68. Albany: Weed, Parsons & Co., 1868.

The Seventh Census of the United States: 1850. Washington, D.C.: R. Armstrong, 1853.

The Statistics of the Population of the United States 9th census, [1870] Washington, D.C.: Government Printing Office, 1872.

Tribune Almanac, 1844–1870. (Earlier volumes titled *Whig Almanac*).

D. DIARIES, LETTERS, RECOLLECTIONS

Abdy, E. S. *Journal of a Residence and Tour in the United States of North America, from April, 1833, to October, 1834.* 3 vols. London: John Murray, 1835.

Baker, George E., ed. *The Works of William H. Seward.* 5 vols. Boston: Houghton, Mifflin and Co., 1884.

Beale, Howard K., ed. *Diary of Gideon Welles.* 3 vols. New York: W. W. Norton & Co., 1960.

Belmont, August. *Letters, Speeches and Addresses of August Belmont.* New York: Privately printed, 1890.

Bigelow, John, ed. *Letters and Literary Memorials of Samuel J. Tilden.* 2 vols. New York: Harper & Bros., 1908.

———. *The Writings and Speeches of Samuel J. Tilden.* 2 vols. New York: Harper & Bros., 1885.

Breen, Matthew P. *Thirty Years of New York Politics Up-to-Date.* New York: John Polhemus, 1899.

Chase, Salmon P. "Diary and Correspondence of Salmon P. Chase," *Annual Report of the American Historical Association 1902.* Washington: Government Printing Office, 1903.

Clemenceau, Georges E. B. *American Reconstruction, 1865–1870.* Translated by Margaret MacVeagh. New York: Lincoln MacVeagh, 1928.

Dix, Morgan, compiler. *Memoirs of John Adams Dix.* 2 vols. New York: Harper & Bros., 1883.

Donald, David, ed. *Inside Lincoln's Cabinet: The Civil War Diaries of Salmon P. Chase.* New York: Longmans, Green and Co., 1954.

Greeley, Horace. *Recollections of a Busy Life.* New York: J. B. Ford & Co., 1868.

Hamilton, Thomas. *Men and Manners in America.* 2 vols. 2nd ed. Philadelphia: Carey, Lea & Blanchard, 1833.

Hammond, Harold Earl, ed. *Diary of a Union Lady, 1861–1865.* New York: Funk & Wagnalls Co., 1962.

Moore, John Bassett, ed. *The Works of James Buchanan.* 12 vols. Philadelphia: J. B. Lippincott Co., 1908–1911.

Nevins, Allan and Thomas, Milton Halsey, eds. *The Diary of George Templeton Strong.* 4 vols. New York: Macmillan Co., 1952.

Tocqueville, Alexis de. *Democracy in America.* 2 vols. The Henry Reeves translation as revised by Francis Bowen and Phillips Bradley. New York: Vintage Books, 1954.

White, Andrew Dickson. *Autobiography.* 2 vols. New York: Century Co., 1905.

E. PAMPHLETS, BROADSIDES, CIRCULARS

"Abolition Philanthropy!" Political broadside, [1864].

Black, Hon. Jeremiah S. *The Doctrines of the Democratic and Abolition Parties Contrasted . . . Speech of Hon. Jeremiah S. Black, at the Hall of the Keystone Club in Philadelphia, October 24, 1864.* Philadelphia: Philadelphia Age Office, 1864.

Church, Sanford E. *Speech by Hon. Sanford E. Church, at Batavia, October 13, 1863.* n.p., [1863].

Davis, Thomas T. *Speech of Hon. Thomas T. Davis, of New York, on Equality of Rights.* Washington: Congressional Globe Office, 1866.

Dickinson, Daniel S. *The Duty of Loyal Men. Speech of Daniel S. Dickinson, at the Union Meeting in New York, Oct. 9, 1862.* n.p., [1862].

Franklin [pseudonym]. *An Examination of Mr. Bradish's Answer to the Interrogations Presented to Him by a Committee of the State Anti-Slavery Society, October 1, 1838.* Albany: Hoffman & White, 1838.

Freidel, Frank, ed. *Union Pamphlets of the Civil War,* 1861–1865. 2 vols. Cambridge, Mass.: Belknap Press of Harvard University Press, 1967.

Garrison, William Lloyd. *An Address, Delivered Before the Free People of Color in Philadelphia, New-York, and Other Cities during the Month of June, 1831.* 3rd ed. Boston: Stephen Foster, 1831.

"Miscegenation Indorsed by the Republican Party," [New York?], [1864].

Nell, William C. *Property Qualification or No Property Qualification.* New York, 1860.

O'Rielly, Henry. *First Organization of Colored Troops in the State of New York, to Aid in Suppressing the Slaveholders' Rebellion.* New York: Baker & Godwin, 1864.

Porter, John K. *Speech of John K. Porter at the Union Ratification Meeting Held at Glens Falls October 21.* Albany: Weed, Parsons & Co., 1862.

Republican Congressional Committee. *Emancipation! Enfranchisement! Reconstruction! Legislative Record of the Republican Party during and since the War.* Washington, D.C.: Union Republican Congressional Committee, 1868.

"Rollo," S. A. [Pseud.] *The New Pantheon or the Age of Black.* New York, 1860.

Seymour, Horatio and Tilden, Samuel J. *Speeches of Ex-Gov. Horatio Seymour & Hon. Samuel J. Tilden, before the Democratic State Convention at Albany, March 11, 1868.* [New York]: [The World], [1868].

Smith, Gerrit. *Gerrit Smith on Suffrage. His Speech in the Capitol, Albany, February 28th 1856.* n.p., [1856].

———. "Gerrit Smith's Reply to Colored Citizens of Albany." Open letter. n.p., 1846.

———. "To Frederick Douglass." Open letter dated Peterboro, July 13, 1860.

———. "To the Voters of the State of New York." Open letter dated Peterboro, October 10, 1846.

Stearns, George Luther, compiler. *Equality of all Men before the Law Claimed and Defended.* Boston: Geo. C. Rand & Avery, 1865.

Sumner, Charles. *Powers of Congress to Prohibit Inequality, Caste, and Oligarchy of the Skin.* Washington, D.C.: F. & J. Rives & Geo. A. Bailey, 1869.

———. *The Republican Party; Its Origin, Necessity, and Permanence. Speech of Hon. Charles Sumner, Before the Young Men's Republican Union of New-York, July 11th, 1860.* New York, 1860.

Van Evrie, J. H. *White Supremacy and Negro Subordination.* New York: Van Evrie, Horton & Co., 1867.

White, Andrew Dickson. *The Constitutional Convention. Delegates at Large . . . Remarks of Hon. Andrew D. White, of Onondaga in the Senate.* Albany: Weed, Parsons and Co., 1867.

Williams, Stephen K. *Speech of Hon. S. K. Williams, of 25th District, on the Resolutions in regard to National Affairs.* Albany: Weed, Parsons & Co., 1866.

Wright, T. S., et al. *An Address to the Three Thousand Colored Citizens of New-York Who Are the Owners of One Hundred and Twenty Thousand Acres of Land, in the State of New-York Given to Them by Gerrit Smith, Esq. of Peterboro, September 1, 1846.* New York, n.p., 1846.

INDEX

Abolition movement, 23, 24, 34, 39, 41, 45–46, 66, 126. *See also* Emancipation of slaves; Liberty Party

Albany Argus: on black suffrage 1860, 116, 118, 138; on black suffrage 1867, 175, 188; on 1868 election, 179; on proposed suffrage amendment 1857, 104–108; on Republican abstentions 1860, 131

Albany (city), 45, 74, 76

Albany County, 45

Albany Evening Journal: attacks on property qualifications, 104, 121; on black suffrage 1846, 49; on black suffrage 1857–1860, 107, 109, 139; on black suffrage 1867, 164, 165; in 1862 election, 151; on Reconstruction and suffrage, 182, 203

American Anti-Slavery Society, 24

American Party, 81, 86, 87; suffrage views of legislators, 99, 100; suffrage views of supporters, 89, 128–130, 141, 144. *See also* Nativism

American Revolution, 20, 26, 59

Anti-abolition sentiment, 39, 49, 60–61, 153–154

Anti-Masonic movement, 21

Anti-Mormon movement, 21

Anti-rent movement, 44, 78

Assembly, actions on black rights: to 1846, 26, 48; 1847–1855, 85–87, 91;

Assembly, action on black rights *(continued)* 1856–1860, 99, 100; 1861–1869, 156, 165–167, 183, 188–189

Barnburners, 44, 83

Bell, John, 115

Benson, Lee, 8, 69, 70

Black laws, 27–29, 159

Black soldier issue, 157–159

Black suffrage: arguments against, 1846, 60–61, 71; arguments against, 1860, 116–119; arguments against, 1869, 191–193; arguments for, 1846, 58–60, 77; arguments for, 1860, 119–123; arguments for, 1869, 194–197; in northern states, 6, 28–29, 160, 173, 175, 187, 199; in the South, 164, 172, 174, 180, 182

Blacks in New York: campaigns for equal rights to 1846, 38, 45, 48, 59–60, 66; campaigns for equal rights 1847–1860, 86, 90, 93–97, 107, 110, 124–126; campaigns for equal rights 1861–1869, 160, 198, 226; impact of presence on suffrage voting, 66–67, 77, 138–139, 141, 210–211; partisan stereotyping of, 58, 60, 116–117, 122, 151, 157, 193, 196; political role of, 35, 37, 46, 49, 60, 94–97, 116,

The Politics of Race in New York

Designed by G. T. Whipple, Jr.
Composed by Graphic Composition, Inc.
in 10 point Baskerville, 2 points leaded,
with display lines in Baskerville.
Printed offset by Thomson-Shore, Inc.
on Warren's Number 66 text, 50 pound basis.
Bound by John H. Dekker & Sons, Inc.
in Holliston book cloth
and stamped in Kurz-Hastings foil.

Library of Congress Cataloging in Publication Data

FIELD, PHYLLIS F.
    The politics of race in New York.

    Bibliography: p.
    Includes index.
    1. Afro-Americans—New York (State)—Politics and
suffrage. 2. New York (State)—Politics and government
—1775–1865. 3. New York (State)—Politics and
government—1865–1950. 4. New York (State)—Race
relations. 5. Voting—New York (State)—History—19th
century. I. Title.
E185.93.N56F54   323.1′196073′0747   81–70717
ISBN 0–8014–1408–3   AACR2